Youth Justice Handbook

The collection of readings in this Handbook has been chosen to examine critically the various theories underpinning practice within the field of youth justice. The approach is to offer material that will benefit youth justice professionals and undergraduates, and also be of interest to related professionals and the wider public.

Opinions expressed in the Handbook are not necessarily those of The Open University.

Details of Open University courses can be obtained from the Student Registration and Enquiry Service, The Open University, PO Box 197, Milton Keynes MK7 6BJ, United Kingdom: tel. +44 (0) 845 300 6090, e-mail **general-enquiries@open.ac.uk**.

Alternatively, you may wish to visit The Open University website at **http://www.open.ac.uk**, where you can learn more about the wide range of courses and packs offered at all levels by The Open University.

Youth Justice Handbook
Theory, Policy and Practice

Edited by

Wayne Taylor, Rod Earle and Richard Hester

WILLAN
PUBLISHING

The Open
University

Published by

Willan Publishing
Culmcott House
Mill Street, Uffculme
Cullompton, Devon
EX15 3AT, UK
Tel: +44(0)1884 840337
Fax: +44(0)1884 840251
e-mail: info@willanpublishing.co.uk
Website: www.willanpublishing.co.uk

In association with
The Open University, Walton Hall, Milton Keynes, MK7 6AA, United Kingdom
www.open.ac.uk

Published simultaneously in the USA and Canada by

Willan Publishing
c/o ISBS, 920 NE 58th Ave, Suite 300,
Portland, Oregon 97213-3786, USA
Tel: +001(0)503 287 3093
Fax: +001(0)503 280 8832
e-mail: info@isbs.com
Website: www.isbs.com

First Published in 2010

Paperback
ISBN-13: 978-1-84392-716-7
Hardback
ISBN-13: 978-1-84392-717-4

British Library Cataloguing-in-Publication Data
A catalogue record for this book is available from the British Library

Project management by Deer Park Productions, Tavistock, Devon
Typeset by TW Typesetting, Plymouth, Devon
Printed and bound by T J International Ltd, Trecerus Industrial Estate, Padstow, Cornwall

Contents

List of abbreviations

APIS	Assessment Planning Interventions and Supervision
ASBO	anti-social behaviour order
BASW	British Association of Social Workers
CCCS	Centre for Contemporary Cultural Studies
CCW	Care Council for Wales
CHIPS	ChildLine in Partnership with Schools
CPT	Committee for the Prevention of Torture
CRAE	Children's Rights Alliance for England
CRC	Convention on the Rights of the Child
CRE	Commission for Racial Equality
CSM	community sanctions and measures
DCFS	Department for Children, Families and Schools
DfES	Department for Education and Skills
DTO	detention and training order/drug treatment order
ECHR	European Convention on Human Rights
ERA	experience followed by reflection followed by informed action
ESRC	Economic and Social Research Council
FGC	family group conferencing
GSCC	General Social Care Council
HMIP	Her Majesty's Inspectorate of Prisons
HMP	Her Majesty's prison
HMYOI	Her Majesty's young offender institution
LEA	local education authority
NEET	not economically active
NISCC	Northern Ireland Social Care Council
NSPCC	National Society for the Prevention of Cruelty to Children
OECD	Organization for Economic Co-operation and Development

PTSD	post-traumatic stress disorder
RFPP	risk factor prevention paradigm
RISE	reintegrative shaming experiments
RJ	restorative justice
RNR	risk, need and responsivity
SAJJ	South Australia Juvenile Justice
SCH	secure care home
SSSC	Scottish Social Services Council
STC	secure training centre
STO	secure training order
UNCRC	United Nations Convention on the Rights of the Child
UNICEF	United Nations International Children's Emergency Fund
WAG	Welsh Assembly Government
YIP	youth inclusion programme
YISP	youth inclusion and support panel
YJB	Youth Justice Board
YJS	youth justice system
YOI	young offender institution
YOP	youth offender panel
YOT	young offender team

Acknowledgements

The ideas featured in this publication were first discussed at a colloquium organized by The Open University and held at Blenheim Palace on 3 October 2007. Many of those who attended this event subsequently agreed to contribute to this volume, while others helped to identify its key themes and focus through their contributions to the debate on the day. As such, acknowledgements are due to all who participated. These were:

Jane Aldgate, Stephen Case, David Coulter, Rod Earle, Helen Evans, Mary Geaney, Barry Goldson, Kevin Haines, Peta Halls, Richard Hester, Carol Johnson, Diane Johnson, Dusty Kennedy, Les Lawrence, Bill Lockhart, Rod Morgan, John Muncie, Mike Nellis, Jo Phoenix, Jeremy Roche, Anna Souhami, Wendy Stainton Rogers, Martin Stephenson, Nigel Stone, Wayne Taylor, Sue Wade, Colin Webster and Bill Whyte.

Particular thanks are due to Carol Johnson both for her role in making the colloquium happen and for the expertise and experience she brings to the management of the various components of the youth justice programme. In this she is ably assisted by her colleague, Ann-Marie Doody, who shares the ability to be calm, collected and even gracious at times of crisis.

The authors would also like to thank Gill Gowans and Mick Jones for their support and guidance and Sarah Shelley for the arduous task of preparing and styling the various manuscripts. Finally, we would like to acknowledge the support of Brian Willan and colleagues from Willan Publishing in supporting this book's passage into print.

The way things are geared here
The way it's all framed
The names are named
And now they're all naming names
They're putting on human faces
Say 'There is no alternative'
v Carved in stone
And I want nothing
It's what I'm trained to believe in
But I can still dream of things
That have never been
But someday will be

('TINA', from *Journey to the End of the Night*,
The Mekons, Label Music, 2000)

When you and Adam talk, I hear you say 'Why?' Always 'Why?' You see things; and you say 'Why?' But I dream things that never were; and I say 'Why not?'

(The Serpent, *Back to Methuselah*,
George Bernard Shaw, 1918, Etc Publishing)

List of contributors

Mo Barratt, Associate Lecturer, Faculty of Health and Social Care, The Open University.

Monica Barry, Senior Research Fellow, Glasgow School of Social Work, University of Strathclyde.

Rob Canton, Professor of Community and Criminal Justice, Faculty of Health and Life Sciences, De Montfort University.

Stephen Case, Lecturer in Criminology, Centre for Criminal Justice and Criminology, Swansea University.

Kelvin Doherty, Assistant Director, Youth Justice Agency, Northern Ireland.

Rod Earle, Lecturer, Faculty of Health and Social Care, The Open University.

Barry Goldson, Professor of Criminology and Social Policy, School of Sociology and Social Policy, University of Liverpool.

Kevin Haines, Reader in Criminology and Director of the Centre for Criminal Justice and Criminology, Centre for Criminal Justice and Criminology, Swansea University.

Richard Hester, Senior Lecturer in Youth Justice Practice, Faculty of Health and Social Care, The Open University.

Jean Hine, Reader in Criminology, Faculty of Health and Life Sciences, De Montfort University.

Amanda Holt, Senior Lecturer in Criminal Psychology, Institute of Criminal Justice Studies, University of Portsmouth.

Mary Jane Kehily, Senior Lecturer, Faculty of Education and Language Studies, The Open University.

Helen Mahaffey, Systemic Psychotherapist and Independent Consultant in Restorative Approaches with Children and Young People, Families and Communities.

Rod Morgan, Professor of Criminal Justice, University of Bristol.

John Muncie, Professor of Criminology, Faculty of Social Sciences, The Open University.

Carrie-Anne Myers, Lecturer in Criminology, Department of Sociology, City University, London.

Lindsay O'Dell, Lecturer, Faculty of Health and Social Care, The Open University.

Jo Phoenix, Reader, School of Applied Social Sciences, University of Durham.

Wendy Stainton Rogers, Professor of Health Psychology, Faculty of Health and Social Care, The Open University.

Wayne Taylor, Lecturer, Faculty of Health and Social Care, The Open University.

Rachel Thomson, Professor of Social Research, Faculty of Health and Social Care, The Open University.

Bill Whyte, Professor of Social Work Studies in Criminal and Youth Justice and Director, Criminal Justice Social Work Development Centre for Scotland, University of Edinburgh.

Joe Yates, Principal Lecturer and subject leader in Criminology, Liverpool John Moores University.

Introduction: a handbook of youth justice?

Wayne Taylor

What knowledge and skills do you need to practise effectively as a professional within the youth justice system? This was the central question posed to a range of senior academics, policy advisers, youth justice managers and practitioners, and representatives of several criminal justice voluntary agencies at a colloquium held at Blenheim Palace in October 2007. The colloquium was organized by The Open University, to help inform the curriculum for the Foundation Degree in Youth Justice. An associated aim was to provide a forum for discussing how best to further the debate about what one contributor dubbed the 'overarching knowledge' required for practising effectively and ethically in youth justice.

The notion of 'overarching' knowledge distinguishes it from the 'unpinning' skills and practical expertise also necessary for professional competency. But what exactly does this 'overarching' knowledge consist of? Does it involve the acquisition of 'facts'? Or an ability to question them? Does it involve the commitment to a particular theory and, if so, which one? What should youth justice workers *know*? For the contributors to the colloquium, a good understanding of the following five areas was seen as essential for the development of a fully rounded, 'reflective' criminal justice practitioner.

Knowledge of context and comparative studies

Reflecting perhaps the Bob Marley dictum to 'know where you're coming from', the contributors to the colloquium felt strongly that those currently working in a criminal justice setting with children and young people should be able to place this work in a wider set of contexts. Hence, a reasonable knowledge of the history of youth justice in the UK – including a detailed understanding of the rise and fall of different ways of working – was required. So, too, was an understanding about how things are done differently *now* in other jurisdictions (both within and outside the UK). Together, these contexts – temporal and geographical – were seen as essential tools for shining a light on current practice, identifying its relative merits and deficits. More generally, such knowledge was also seen as necessary to provide anchorage for practitioners who must carry out their work in an environment that is sometimes made hostile as a result of seemingly irrational responses to youth crime by politicians and (some members of) the public.

Interpreting and applying data and research

The modern world of youth justice is framed within a body of research that is sometimes presented as a set of instructions for 'what works' with children and young people who get into trouble with the law. Without doubt, much of this research is highly valuable as an aide to informed practice. However, as a corpus of knowledge, it is not without its limitations – although these are not routinely acknowledged. Critics have several concerns about the 'what works' canon. The methodological discipline, in its design and the dissemination of some influential research projects, has been found to be sloppy. More fundamentally, there has been disquiet about the 'positivist' assumptions informing the research, including – as you will discover in the first part of the book – assumptions about childhood development and its relationship to offending.

So how does the hard-pressed practitioner, faced almost daily with new research and a seemingly never-ending supply of facts and figures, 'findings', evaluations and recommendations, sort the wheat from the chaff? For the contributors to the colloquium some understanding of research methodology, and a willingness to use this to approach the 'facts' with a healthy degree of scepticism, was a prerequisite of effective practice.

Working relationships

The youth offending team (YOT) has, of course, been an experiment in partnership. Leaving aside whether this experiment has been a success or not, it is logical that this should have been the case. Offending by young people will never be the preserve of one agency. As long as it is treated as a criminal act it will be subject to the involvement of criminal justice agencies, such as the police and the courts. As long as the welfare of children and young people remains a priority, it will attract a range of other interventions from the 'helping' professions. To practise effectively, the practitioner must know the purpose and function of the various other agencies and organizations they work alongside. However, to achieve 'overarching' knowledge in this area, the practitioner must also be aware of the potential differences in outlook of other professionals and have strategies for accommodating these in their ways of working. This involves a consideration of such issues as engagement, brokerage and interagency/partnership working.

The concept of 'relationships' is, of course, central to the work undertaken with children and young people. Understanding the process of relationship building and the factors that might impede this was regarded as paramount in engaging with young people (and seen as neglected by mainstream researchers in recent years). This also involves issues around 'brokerage', in the sense that the practitioner acts as an *advocate* for their client, negotiating with a variety of agencies and facilitating services. For the contributors, the objective behind considering 'relationships' in this wider sense was to go beyond the limited idea of the 'case manager' to allow practitioners and others to explore the possibilities of a user-informed, multi-agency intervention which prioritizes effectiveness and promotes social justice.

Ologies and *Isms*

This was the name given by contributors to the colloquium to cover the range of relevant disciplines – and the various theoretical and political factions within them – of which the practitioner should have knowledge. In some respects, identifying these was relatively easy. Participants in this discussion agreed that some familiarity with the ontological and epistemological under-pinnings of knowledge in the area of criminal justice would be necessary, including a critical appraisal of the status of this knowledge itself, how it is discovered and how it is tested. Clearly, academic disciplines, such as criminology, sociology and psychology, are relevant to the field. At a theoretical level, the academics in each of these disciplines can be further categorized in terms of their ideological persuasions, their proximity to or distance from the policy-making arena, their 'conservative' or 'critical' attitude to the paradigms of their subject, etc. Practitioners should be aware of these distinctions.

There are also 'forces' operating on practice that are equally influential but more elusive. This is what the colloquium meant by 'isms' – not only the 'grand narratives' of modernism, such as socialism and liberalism, but also the purportedly more 'neutral' techniques, such as 'managerialism' and ways of thinking, such as 'actuarialism', that have major consequences for the way practitioners organize and go about their work. Again, for the contributors, an understanding of all these issues was a requirement of professional practice.

Values, ethics and rights

The final area identified by the contributors was again to do with context, although the primary concern here was that the practitioner should examine their work with young people closely and self-critically, reflecting on the value base informing this. The world of youth justice is a fast-moving one in which workers are faced with practice dilemmas on a near-daily basis. How should they respond to these and what are the ethical considerations underscoring the evidence they use to guide their actions? Here international law can be a useful measure of what is considered acceptable treatment, but what if this contradicts the manner in which your agency works? There are also examples of other jurisdictions that differ in their approach to key concepts such as criminality, culpability and punishment. In comparing and considering such differences, the practitioner must go beyond notions of 'effectiveness' (in the limited sense of efficiency) and bring their moral values to bear. Being able to think, to express yourself cogently and to engage in discussion with others about such matters is perhaps the most important aspect of professional practice. It is also essential – as one contributor to the colloquium suggested – in helping practitioners to develop the ability to question and image actively a better system: to follow Shaw and the Mekons in 'dreaming of things that have never been and asking, why not?'

In addition to the contributions made at Blenheim Palace, the colloquium was also informed by a written paper presented by Peta Halls of the National Youth Agency. This was based on the views of members of the UK Youth Parliament and five focus-group interviews with 94 young people living in Corby, Northamptonshire, undertaken in September 2007. This paper was particularly instructive in raising issues around the diverse needs of young people and in identifying themes for effective engagement.

Structure

It is beyond the scope of this Handbook to do justice to the level of discussion that took place at the colloquium. As a single volume it also has no ambition to encompass the full range of themes and issues suggested as appropriate for a foundation degree. However, it is influenced by a statement of purpose agreed at the colloquium that included the following objectives:

- The youth justice system should be explained in terms of its historical development and geographical variations, with a strong comparative element comparing different ideas, policies and practice.

- It should include a detailed understanding of international rights and comparative practice (including the UN Convention on the Rights of the Child and innovative practice in Europe and the USA).

- Practitioners should be aware of the political contexts of their work, including the impact of forces, such as managerialism, on youth justice practice.

- It should encourage critical thinking and self-reflective practice, providing the skills for practitioners to evaluate their own practice.

- It should not fight shy of controversy and the ethical dilemmas of practice.

- It should address issues of equality and diversity.

- Practitioners (and others) should be encouraged to develop a sophisticated understanding of such tools as risk assessment, reflecting on their theoretical underpinnings.

- It should impart a good understanding of theoretical work around child development, including those of critical developmental psychology.

- It should emphasize the importance of relationships in promoting desistence.

- It should examine issues of resilience and encourage the adoption of a holistic approach that draws on young people's strengths as well as responding to their weaknesses.

This is an exacting list and represents a considerable challenge. Nevertheless, these objectives were at the forefront of the editors' minds when the various contributions to this volume were commissioned. The extent to which these objectives are met, of course, owes everything to the quality of the contributions themselves. Here we were extremely fortunate. The contributors to this volume include several leading academics in the fields of criminology and psychology, who have been pivotal in debates that have changed our way of thinking about crime and youth. There are also contributions from those with experience of policy-making at the highest levels, as well as from senior practitioners whose job it is to implement these policies. The mix of authors also reflects the cross-disciplinary nature of the volume, which seeks to provide insights into practice from a variety of perspectives.

The Handbook is divided into five parts, with short introductions to each describing the various chapters and analysing their connectedness. The five parts are structured in such a way as to allow exploration of the conceptual and thematic issues described above. Taken together, the five parts provide an overview of the theory, policy and practice of youth justice that will hopefully be of use to practitioners, as well as students, academics and those members of the public with an interest in the way we respond to young people who commit crime. The themes of each part are as follows.

Part I: contexts of childhood and youth

The Handbook begins with an extended chapter that examines the structural factors impacting on young people and looks at the way the youth justice system can perpetuate social injustice through its propensity to 'police the poor'. This provocative start marks our commitment to the objective of taking equality seriously and purposefully frames the subsequent contributions within a discussion that does not neglect the 'Cinderella' issue of social class and its continuing influence over the variable life chances of young people.

This theme is picked up in the other chapters of Part I by examining the various ways the experience of childhood, as well as theoretical models around 'development', are subject to different understandings on the basis of class. This can be seen in the bifurcated attitude, by both the public and professionals, to behaviours that are often tolerated in affluent settings but increasingly 'problematized' when committed by more socially disadvantaged young people. The neglect of class can also be seen in the assumptions informing some models of invention that emphasize 'individual' factors but downplay the influence of environment.

Part II: research, knowledge and evidence in youth justice

The ideas introduced in Part I are explored in Part II in relation to the body of research evidence informing current practice. The part contains a critique of the current risk-factor paradigm within its own terms of reference, as well as strident calls for a new model for research that acknowledges the inequalities within the system and works to identify and correct these. One important aspect of this remedial work relates directly to practice – the inclusion of the 'voices' of children and young people as part of a more responsive approach to interventions (a theme taken up by several of the contributors).

Of course, as several of the contributors make clear, initiatives in criminal justice are not always well informed by a body of convincing evidence. This can be the case when policies are introduced through political expediency – often in the face of negative evaluations. In highlighting the ideological and political underpinnings of some 'evidence', it is hoped that the contents of this part will fulfil the objective of encouraging a more critically aware and reflective understanding of the way practice is as it is. We feel this is essential to the project described by one contributor as 'conceptualizing a youth justice with integrity'.

Part III: policy, possibilities and penal realities in youth justice

Arguments that the current youth justice system operates with integrity are seriously damaged by evidence about the use of incarceration. This part offers a cool analysis of the current conditions in the secure estate as well as qualitative evidence regarding its impact on those imprisoned there. Unsurprisingly, the analysis of who is most likely to face imprisonment indicates that the experience of structural disadvantage – reflected in the statistical overrepresentation of working-class, black and other minority ethnic groups – is a key factor.

Part IV: reflective practice

Part IV returns to the issue of practice to consider the key principles of a model of intervention based around work on 'desistance'. This is a positive development that involves a number of features that continue the 'narrative' of the volume as a whole. For example, the use of an 'integrative' approach to evidence acknowledges the deficiencies of an approach framed solely within the psychology of the individual. An emphasis on desistance also involves a positive, future-orientated approach that avoids the moral censure and emphasis on punishment of some models of rehabilitation. Again, incorporating the 'voices' of children is integral to this method, as its relational base requires the consent and active participation of the young person.

Part V: widening contexts

Speculations regarding the future are notoriously hazardous, particularly in a rapidly changing field such as youth justice. Sometimes, however, they are difficult to resist. They are also integral to the necessary task of imaging better ways to work. In this, the final part, the aim is to provide the reader with the tools to make such speculations. It does this by returning to the notion of contexts provided by the colloquium. The part contains examples of innovative practice from within the UK (including the possible 'dragonization' of youth justice in Wales) and some thoughtful accounts of the way in which international legislation around the rights of the child might influence policy in the future taking it in a direction commensurate with the values expressed throughout this volume.

Deciding to call it a 'Handbook' involved some interesting discussions. Did it profess to provide a manual to follow when completing each of the manifold tasks that make up criminal justice work with children and young people? No. Was it an 'how to' guide? Not really. By 'Handbook' what we had in mind was a friendly companion with which to consider some – although inevitably not all – of the most pressing issues for practitioners in youth justice today. We have endeavoured to follow the spirit and wishes of the colloquium held at Blenheim and feel that, in the pages to follow, you will find much of interest and, hopefully, much of value.

Part I

Contexts of Childhood and Youth

Introduction

Wayne Taylor

This book begins with an extended chapter looking at children and young people who get into trouble and at the way their subsequent treatment by the criminal justice system is influenced by ideas. Ideas of what 'youth' means and ideas about what constitutes a 'crime'. This first chapter also looks at how the process of criminalization is mediated by 'structural factors', including social class, race and a range of disadvantages that come with poverty. In essence, this chapter tells the story of how and why some children and young people are much more likely to be the subject of criminal justice interventions than others. This is a neglected story that is told less often nowadays than it should be. Its position as the opening chapter in this collection is one small attempt to reverse this neglect.

The discussion here is wide and far-ranging, encompassing a review of historical representations of class and crime, an account of the contemporary experiences of social and economic exclusion that continue to blight the life chances of the poor, and an analysis of how the disadvantaged are over-represented within the present-day youth justice system. Joe Yates argues that recognition of these neglected issues should shape our approach to theory as well as motivating our practice, so that it is effective in redressing these disadvantages. These challenges are taken up with gusto by the rest of the contributors to this volume.

Poverty has a nefarious and insidious impact on its victims. It also increases the prospects of their involvement in the criminal justice system (as either offenders or victims or, more often than not, both). For Yates, this reflects an essential feature of contemporary policy – that the individual suffering poverty, rather than the poverty itself, is seen as the primary problem. This focus on the individual rather than the 'wider issues' has a curious further consequence: it identifies the subject of the intervention as somehow 'different' from 'us', less capable, inferior, a problem to be addressed (or at least managed). This notion of 'them' and 'us' has a moral dimension that seems to generate a *bifurcated* understanding involving 'them' and 'us' which is linked to the provision of services (e.g. the 'deserving' versus the 'undeserving'), as well as class and ethnic-based fears of the dangerous 'other'. A further crucial feature identified by Yates is the politicization of youth justice since the early 1990s, which has resulted in attitudes to youth offending (and to youth more generally) hardening and has also led to a new punitiveness in the treatment of youth crime and anti-social behaviour.

Rachel Thomson picks up the themes raised by Yates, drawing on sociological and youth studies frameworks to explore the way the markers of 'adulthood' – both subjectively experienced and culturally defined – have been subject to change in recent years. Like others in this volume, she argues that structural factors have impacted on the process of 'transition', making this an increasingly fragmented and individualized experience. This has changed the experience of growing up, prolonging childhood (for some), accelerating the arrival of adulthood (for others) and fragmenting the previously shared experience of transition for the majority. This has had implications for practice as young people adopt a variety of strategies (including crime) to gain status and recognition.

Thomson's chapter draws on empirical data from the Inventing Adulthoods study (a ten-year research project in which the author played a central role) to delineate the changing processes of transitions in relation to education, work, leisure, consumption and the nature of relationships within the domestic sphere. In each case it is clear that the choices open to young people are mediated by structural factors, such as gender, locality, ethnicity and class. Significantly for practitioners, Thomson notes the ways in which risk-taking is a normal and natural response to the challenges of transitions (rather than an indicator of problems requiring intervention). She also argues that practitioners, by recognizing and encouraging young people's achievements, enhance their feelings of competence, confidence and self-efficacy and, in so doing, assist them to develop a prosocial image of their adult selves which will help divert them from criminal and anti-social behaviour.

In the following chapter, Lindsay O'Dell picks up on this account to provide a critical dissection of the moral and ideological assumptions behind the notion of 'development' and its implicit insistence on the idea of a 'normal' trajectory to growing up. Interestingly, the author draws on ideas from critical developmental psychology which neatly complement those from sociology and youth studies used by Thomson. This gives a stimulating glimpse of what might represent an emerging cross-disciplinary counter-discourse to dominant ideas around childhood and youth.

O'Dell is deeply sceptical about stage-based models of development with their attendant assumptions of 'normalcy' and 'naturalness'. She takes the reader on a guided tour of the recent history of developmental psychology, illustrating the way that ideas about childhood and youth are socially and culturally constructed (a key theme of this book) and reflect a preoccupation

2

with individual pathology. For her, a key feature of the notion of development is an adult-centred paradigm that inevitably fosters a top-down approach to policy-making, in which the 'voices' of children and young people are rarely heard. This failure of responsiveness to the views and needs of young people is a theme that runs throughout the contributions to this volume.

The idea of 'abnormal' development – and its use to categorize children and young people (and determine the nature of interventions) – is clearly relevant to practitioners working in and around youth justice. For O'Dell the prescriptive nature of stage-based models makes them oppressive, setting up hurdles to jump at specified times and defining difference as 'failure'. It also involves a number of specific dangers, including a propensity towards early intervention (to 'nip problems in the bud') which risk labelling and, in a youth justice setting, criminal stigmatization. More generally, what O'Dell outlines is a system of *thinking* about children and young people that is inherently exclusionary and where the pressure is to operate in relation to a *binary*, with young people as either winners or losers, either good or bad, and where, in her words, the ability to negotiate the 'the boundary between victimhood and culpability is a tricky one'.

For O'Dell, then, stage-based models contain assumptions that ill-serve the reflective practitioner. Instead, she poses a way of conceptualizing growing up as a process of creative risk-taking involving a multiplicity of possible routes to adulthood, each with sufficient room to accommodate the 'differences' seen as sources of problems in more traditional accounts. This fits well with the ideas around 'desistance' and relationship-based interventions considered in later sections of this volume.

In her chapter, Mary Jane Kehily examines the consumption practices of young people and considers the societal responses this can provoke, including 'moral panic' and overly zealous policy-making. Drawing on sociological and cultural studies scholarship, the author ponders the ambivalence at the heart of cultural representations of youthful 'excess' in which, on the one hand, young people are criticized for their hedonistic pursuit of pleasures while, on the other, they are portrayed as the hapless victims of a new and aggressive consumerism.

Developing the concept of 'transitions', the author looks at the way the social construction of the 'teenager' is picked up by the globalized youth/leisure industries to expropriate the meanings young people generate – repackaging and re-selling them back to them at a profit. Kehily, however, is not satisfied with the notion of a hegemony of seller over buyer suggested by the early writings of the Frankfurt school (or the Jam's suggestion that 'the public wants what the public gets'). Rather, she is concerned to trace the ways in which young people are able to use consumption purposefully and creatively to respond to the challenges of nascent adulthood.

So are young people the dupes of snake-oil salesmen or calculating risk-takers, using cultural artefacts and commodities to gain social status and recognition and enjoying themselves along the way? Interestingly, the answer to this appears to be that 'it depends'. Looking at the issues of sexual behaviour, drug use and popular music, the author emphasizes that a young person's ability to manage the opportunities and challenges of each of these realms will vary in relation to the environmental and structural factors discussed by Yates, Thomson and the other authors in this section.

In the final chapter of this section, Carrie-Anne Myers picks up the theme of normalization and reflects on the power of words within the field of abuse. For her, the time and energy spent defining childhood and youth in terms of the threats they pose or the problems they engender can be ironically counterposed to the *lack* of emphasis on growing up as a period of potential victimhood.

Acknowledging the significant and growing literature in relation to child physical and sexual abuse, neglect and emotional abuse in both domestic and institutional settings, Myers nevertheless identifies a key area that remains relatively undeveloped, that of teenage bullying. Here she looks at the way processes of normalization seem encoded into the term itself, with many seeing 'bullying' as a minor matter requiring a more circumspect and limited official response than that prompted by the emotionally more arresting term 'abuse'. Looking at bullying and the policy response to this in the education system, the author provides evidence – both statistical and compellingly personal – indicating that bullying is depressingly pervasive and potentially devastating for victims. Again, she is able to outline the way that factors such as gender have some impact on the way this problem is experienced, although the reality seems more nuanced than the view that boys are more prone to physical violence. Instead, Myers provides a vision of the school as a site of potential physical and psychological violence that young people must negotiate on a daily basis. This can be especially distressing during the already emotionally charged period of adolescence. This is important for practitioners because it reminds them that the 'presenting' problem may mask deeper ones. For Myers this is clearly the case in relation both to truancy and exclusion, where bullying is often an underlying cause. It may also be relevant to other problems, such as drug misuse.

By arguing forcefully that we should see bullying as a serious manifestation of abuse, Myers raises the ante for professionals, whose responsibility it is to protect the vulnerable – even when these are the 'unloved' (and sometimes stubbornly unlovable) young people who populate the youth justice system. Significantly for this discussion, Myers operates from an holistic theoretical model that looks at children and young people 'in the round' and not primarily through a social policy lens that emphasizes the problems they face (or constitute) for the professional. This is a theme that will be picked up by subsequent writers looking at the full gamut of issues salient to the health and wellbeing of children and young people.

Structural disadvantage: youth, class, crime and poverty

Joe Yates

Introduction

This chapter sets out to explore critically some of the issues relating to youth, crime, class and poverty. In doing this it first explores some of the historical continuities in the representation of class and crime. It then moves on to consider the contemporary context, critically exploring the impact that structural disadvantage has in shaping the lived realities of marginalized, working-class young people and their experiences of growing up and getting by in the economic hinterlands of twenty-first century Britain. It argues that young people's experiences of crime, whether as perpetrators, victims or both, needs to be considered in relation to structural disadvantage and marginalized young people's acute experiences of poverty, inequality and exclusion. The chapter concludes by arguing that these important structural issues should not only be considered in relation to conventional mainstream criminological conceptualizations of crime, as defined by the state, but also in relation to broader issues of social harm which impact negatively on the lives of marginalized young people.

Class, disadvantage and poverty

The Social Exclusion Unit in 2004 identified that 'The social class a child is born into and their parents' level of education and health are still major determinants of their life chances' (2004: 10). And, 'As formed and reproduced by the division of labour, class continues to be the primary factor in accounting for inequalities in health and morbidity, education, income, housing, diet, consumption, and so on. As such it also pervades – albeit largely unseen – huge swathes of policy-making discourses and academic discourses'. However, while class 'remains the primary determinant of social life', Law and Mooney argue it has become the 'social condition that dare not speak its name' (2006: 523). Poverty and class-based inequality impact on people in a range of complex and inter-related ways (Scraton and Haydon 2002). It impacts on mortality, physical health, mental health, education, work and the risk of becoming involved in the criminal justice system as either a victim or a perpetrator of crime. It penetrates deeply into the lives of those who suffer it; as Davies argues, 'poverty inflicts real damage on those who live with it . . . poverty is not neutral, not just a passive background against which people live out their lives. It is "aggressive, destructive"' (1998: 146). While poverty and inequality impact on people of all ages, they have a particularly deleterious effect on the lives of children (Davies 1998; Griggs and Walker 2008). Indeed, in twenty-first century British society it is class and disadvantage and the poverty associated with it which place children 'at risk' in a range of domains.

In discussions about poverty, as Davidson and Erskine argue, 'too often, attention is directed at people who are poor rather than poverty itself' and 'this focus tends to remove attention from the processes which cause poverty' (1992: 12). In this way the public issues of poverty and structural disadvantage, and how they negatively impact on the life chances of those they effect, are presented as the 'personal troubles' (Mills 1959: 8) of 'problem populations' (Mooney 2009) – 'them' as opposed to 'us' (Young 2007) – with no attempt to contextualize them in relation to the social relations that produce them. Young argues that in this process the poor are othered, 'seen as disconnected from us, they are not part of our economic circuit: they are an object to be pitied, helped, avoided, studied . . . The poor are perceived as a residuum, a superfluity' (2007: 5–6). They are also discriminated against in a variety of ways which set them out ideologically as 'inferior' and of 'lesser value'. As Killeen argues this represents 'povertyism' and is 'a phenomenon akin to racism or sexism' (2008: 1) – a class-based form of discrimination which is often unacknowledged (Killeen 2008: 1).

In late modernity the risks associated with class-based inequality are presented as being located primarily in the domain of the individual. In this context these risks have become 'individualized' and social problems associated with poverty presented as 'individual shortcomings rather than as a result of social processes' (France 2000: 317). As part of this process populations suffering from poverty are defined not in relation to their position within unequal social structures but rather in relation to their 'morality' (Murray 1990). Thus, in the words of C. Wright Mills, the analysis tends to 'slip past structure to focus on isolated situations' (1967: 534) and there is little recognition that 'poverty is based in class and other social relations' (Killeen 2008: 4). In short the discussion does not consider poverty and disadvantage as reflecting broader structural class-based inequalities in society but rather as individualized issues or decontextualized risk factors – the fault of the individual, the result of poor choices. As Kemshall argues, 'In the "risk society" individuals are framed as shapers of their own worlds making decisions according to calculations of risk and opportunity (Petersen 1996: 47), but facing blame and punishment if they get their choices wrong' (Kemshall 2008: 22).

Class, crime and youth: historical contexts

Emsley (2007: 134) argues that 'One of the most significant contributions of historical research to the study of crime is the extent to which it shows continuities in the apprehension or development of problems'. For our purposes here we will explore, albeit in a limited may, some of the important continuities in relation to class, crime and youth. We can trace continuities in how class and disadvantage have occupied a central, if often unspoken (Law and Mooney 2006), position in narratives around crime and disorder. British society has a long and well documented history of 'respectable fears' regarding youth and crime (Pearson 1983). Throughout recent history these 'respectable fears', whether related to perceived (Pitts 2000) or actual increases in children and young people's involvement in crime (Pitts 2008), have been presented as evidence 'of the disintegration of social order' and 'as a sign that the "British way of life" is coming apart at the seams' (Hall *et al.* 1978: vii). Thus, 'historically youth – or more accurately the "threat of youth" – has served as a cipher for much wider hopes and fears about social order, progress and social change' (Jamieson and Yates 2009). There are well rehearsed and important arguments regarding the 'profound historical amnesia' and 'perpetual novelty' (Pearson 1983) which characterize hegemonic discourses around youth and crime. For example Pearson, in his work, has identified how popular and governmental discourses around crime hark back to a mythical and imaginary 'golden age' of prewar Britain (Pearson 1983) where young people, on the whole, knew how to behave, and youth crime did not represent a major social issue. However, it is apparent from a historical analysis that these discourses and the 'imagined communities' (Anderson 1983) conjured up by these 'jeremiads of national decline' (Pearson 1983: 45) are dislocated from any meaningful historical context and 'fail to stand up to sustained historical scrutiny' (Muncie 2004: 51).

In relation to continuities, first, it is apparent from historical analysis of the perennial concerns around youth and crime that class plays an important role. Therefore, while crime is committed by all occupational groups, the working classes have historically been singled out, by governments (and indeed criminology), as the most criminal group in society. So while Box argues that 'most serious crimes ... can be located in power, not weakness, in privilege not disadvantage, in wealth not poverty' (1983: 3), it is the working classes, the poor and the powerless, who are focused on as the most criminal and are the targets of the criminal justice system.

Secondly, in hegemonic discourses there is continuity in the extent to which the causes of working-class criminality have been identified not in the material conditions of poverty but rather in the 'immorality' of the poor – whether this

7

be the 'indigence' of the residual 'undeserving' poor of the 1800s (Colqhoun 1806: 7–8 cited in Reiner 2007: 345),[1] the fecklessness of the poor in the early 1900s or the morally 'other' risk-prone underclass of the late twentieth and early twenty-first centuries (Murray 1990). So here there is continuity in the extent to which crime is identified as being caused by not poverty *per se*, but by the 'otherness' of a certain type of 'undeserving' poor people presented as separate from 'us' 'spatially, socially and morally' (Young 2007: 6).

Thirdly, continuities can be identified in the extent to which working-class young people have been represented in a particularly negative and discriminatory manner in narratives and discourses around crime. While young people in general are poorly regarded in Britain (Hewlett 1993), as Cohen argues, it is those labelled as 'working class yobs' who are 'the most enduring of suitable enemies' (2002: viii). It is these young people who are singled out as the target for demonizing discourses and punitive state interventions. Historically, young people identified as posing a 'risk' have invariably been lower-class youth, the children of poor 'others', whether the 'undeserving poor of the nineteenth century' (Pearson 1983) or the 'feral' child of the 'underclass' in the late twentieth century (Murray 1990).

Within these processes the 'other' is defined by 'dominant hegemonic discourses [which] articulate difference as pejoratively relative to white, middle-class norms' (Bottrell 2002: 3) (see, for example, the work of Hadley (1990) who notes how, in the mid-nineteenth century, terms such as 'savages', 'guttersnipes' and 'street arabs' were commonly used to describe young people who were perceived as presenting a threat to 'orderly society'). This is similar to the demonizing language, such as 'yobs', 'hoodies' 'thugs' and 'chavs', used in the current context. This demonizing and 'classist' language (Mooney 2009) is in stark contrast to the language used to describe their middle-class counterparts (Cockburn 2000).

Fourthly, there is continuity in the way certain groups of young people have been singled out as of particular concern, and as the targets for particularly 'hostile' treatment (Haines and Drakeford 1998: 2) on racial lines (Hall *et al.* 1978; Goldson and Chigwada-Bailey 1999) – see, for example, Macilwee's (2006) historical account of the demonization of the 'criminal' Irish in Liverpool in the 1800s, Hall *et al.* (1978) and their analysis of the criminalization of black youth in the 1970s and more recent work on the demonization of young Muslims (Poynting *et al.* 2004: 3). There are also clear continuities in the extent to which black and minority ethnic young people have been singled out for the harshest treatment by the criminal justice system and evidence that this discriminatory treatment remains a feature of the criminal justice system (House of Commons Home Affairs Committee 2007).

However, while continuity is evident change is also apparent. Pitts observes that while 'detrimental representations of lower-class youth are perpetually recycled by government and the media', this 'is not to argue that every manifestation of youth crime, violence and disorder has the same origin, meaning or impact' (2008: 32).

Thus, while there are clearly continuities in the representation of the 'criminality' of working-class youth, we must not lose sight of the fact that these emerge from specific social, economic and historical contexts, and these contexts not only shape how criminality is represented and how the state responds to it (Jamieson and Yates 2009) but also how it manifests itself (see Hall *et al.* 2008; Pitts 2008). Thus context matters – young people growing up in post industrial Britain clearly 'face new risks and opportunities' (Furlong and Cartmel 1997: 8) as well as challenges which were 'only glimpsed by previous generations' (Wood and Hine 2009: 4). These risks are associated with the specific socioeconomic and cultural context of neoliberal Britain. For example, the structural changes to the economy, as a result of globalization and neoliberalism, have served to elongate adolescence. In the 'post-industrial cities of modern day Britain' (see Hall *et al.* 2008) adolescence has become protracted for most and hopelessly fractured for a many.

Culturally too, neoliberalism and neo-monetarist economics have heralded significant changes. While the proliferation of the mass media, with its 'speed and immediacy, its technological advances and its global reach' has transformed our existence (Young 2007: 2) the mass media have also played a significant role in fostering what Young refers to as 'heightened individualism in an era of mass consumerisms' (2007: 2) and a 'new culture of narcissism' (Hall *et al.* 2008).

In addition, youth crime has become highly politicized in the late twentieth century (Goldson 2005) and attitudes towards young people and particularly working-class children and young people have become more hardened (Hewlett 1993), their communities demonized (McCauley 2006; Yates 2006), their rights circumscribed (Goldson 2005) and new and ever more intrusive forms of social control applied to them (Jamieson and Yates 2009). Similarly, the material position of working-class young people has deteriorated, with many young people suffering 'sustained exposure to acute social and economic disadvantage' contexts which history tells us 'spawns forms of crime that have catastrophic effects upon the vulnerable populations amongst whom and against whom they are perpetrated' (Pitts 2008: 33). It is to this current context that we now turn in more detail.

The contemporary context

When New Labour came to power in 1997 relative poverty and inequality in the UK were at levels unprecedented in postwar Britain. This increase was the result of Thatcherite neo-monetarist economics which rejected the 'Butskellite' neo-Keynesian economics of the postwar settlement in favour of the unfettered market economy. This had signalled a radical economic and cultural shift as the market became dominant.

Hall *et al.* (2008) argue that there is a clear connection between the radical economic changes which occurred during this period and 'the acute marginalization that followed in its wake' (2008: 21). These economic policies left Britain a much more deeply divided and unequal society which, in turn, led to a deterioration in the economic and material condition of children and youth (Haines and Drakeford 1998) – for example, in 1979 one in eight children lived in poverty after 18 years of Thatcherite neo-monetarist economic policy. By 1997 this had spiralled to one in four. Income inequality had also widened sharply, with Bynner (2002) identifying a decline in the relative incomes of young people during the period, and many indicators of deprivation were deteriorating or high in international terms (Hills and Stewart 2005). Thus, as Haines and Drakeford argued, during this period, the fortunate became 'more powerful' and the excluded 'suffered more acute economic conditions and a sustained assault on their social rights' (1998: 1): some would argue socially harmful developments in their own right (Dorling 2005).[2]

On coming to power, the first New Labour administration made a high-profile commitment to tackle the issue of child poverty within a generation. Thus, they pledged, child poverty would be halved by 2010 and totally eradicated by 2020. This was significant in that it clearly distinguished New Labour's child poverty policies from those of the previous Conservative administration. Indeed, this seemed to identify that New Labour was taking the social problems of the mid-1990s, and in particular the issue of child poverty, seriously (Hills and Stewart 2005). In line with this 'new' pledge to end child poverty New Labour set out a number of policy strategies to achieve this aim. These included the introduction of tax benefits for the working poor and the introduction of Sure Start schemes to raise the aspirations and achievement of children living in poverty (see Grover forthcoming for a fuller discussion). The Social Exclusion Unit identified that these developments were part of a 'joined up' approach much broader in its focus than just poverty, which focused on 'the link between problems such as, for example, unemployment, poor skills, high crime, poor housing and family background' (Social Exclusion Unit 2001).

Giddens (2007) has argued that it will take more time for the inroads New Labour have made to become apparent. However, despite making some inroads, Jamieson (forthcoming) argues that three successive New Labour administrations have failed to have any significant impact on those most in need and there are examples where some vulnerable groups, such as asylum seekers, have been further excluded by New Labour policies (Hills and Stewart 2005).

This situation is borne out by a number of international measures which identify that, despite its rhetoric, New Labour has a particularly poor record on child poverty. In 2000 a 'report card' issued by UNICEF (2007), on child wellbeing after ten years of New Labour, ranked the UK bottom out of 21 OECD countries in relation to child wellbeing and identified that Britain has one of the worst rates of child poverty in the westernized world. The review, which the report was based on, ranked countries on six dimensions of wellbeing. These were material wellbeing, health and safety, educational wellbeing, family and peer relationships, behaviours and risks, and subjective wellbeing. The report identified that there were 3.9 million children living in poverty in Britain, representing more children living in poverty, as a percentage of its population, than any other industrialized country included in the review.

Poverty and structural inequality, along with the discrimination (Killeen 2008) and humiliation (Bauman and Tester 2001) associated with them, have a hugely detrimental effect on working-class communities and the children and young people who reside in them. Davies, in his journalistic account of life in Britain's 'Dark heart', describes how poverty impacted on a community in Leeds:

> The ways in which poverty has wounded this community are infinitely subtle. It has bruised the minds and the bodies of those who live with it, spoiling their health, undermining their self respect, spreading hopelessness and sadness, loneliness and anxiety, provoking frustration and anger and crime and alcoholism and drug abuse, corroding all the fibre of daily life. (1998: 114)

Children and young people, as relatively powerless individuals in these communities, are particularly vulnerable to the deleterious effects of poverty. In relation to health, young people and children who grow up in poverty are more likely to suffer debilitating health problems and higher rates of mortality than their more wealthy counterparts. The Advocacy Committee of the Royal College of Paediatrics and Health in 2007 identified that 'Income and social status gradients are found in an extensive range of health outcomes including low birth weight, developmental delay, obesity, mental health, injuries, teenage pregnancy, acute respiratory infection, poor linear growth and overall rates of disability' (2007: 4) – inequalities which the Royal College Advocacy Committee argue are 'pervasive and cumulative ... affecting children from before birth, through childhood and adolescence and into adult life' (2007: 5).

It is also apparent that the relationship between poverty and poor health is 'bidirectional' in that 'poverty contributes to ill-health and ill-health contributes to poverty' (Griggs and Walker 2008: 4). Similarly, there is a level of co-morbidity in relation to poverty and disabling conditions with disabled children more likely to be living in poverty (Grover 2008). It is also clear that children from black and minority ethnic backgrounds are far more likely to be living in poverty and suffering the debilitating conditions associated with it (see Grover 2008).

Divisions based on poverty and inequality are entrenched in 'geographies of despair' (Lister 1990) and 'exclusion' (Ruggiero 2000: 1) where acute deprivation characterizes local circumstances and shapes life chances (MacDonald and Marsh 2005). As Byrne argues, if 'cultures of poverty' do exist, 'spatial concentration is a key element in their generation' (Byrne 2005: 115), where 'very different types of social experience (are) predicated on distinctive areas of residence' (2005: 115–16). Harvey (2008) identifies the roots of this in the inequalties inherent in neo-liberal capitalism. He argues: 'we increasingly live in divided and conflict prone areas. In the past three decades, the neo-liberal turn has restored class power to rich elites . . . the results are indelibly etched on the spatial forms of our cities' (2008: 32). These spatial forms in our cities set aside 'throw away places' (Campbell 1993) where we find the communities which disporportionatley suffer the deleterious effects of neo-liberal capitalism.

Hall *et al.* detail the deterioration of once 'socially ordered working-class communities' which, as a result of neo-monetarist economics and rampant individualsim, 'began to degenerate into turbulant and deeply problematic locales often typified by high levels of violent crime, and a range of other social ills' (2008: 28). It is often in these communities experiencing such extreme poverty and economic hardship (in effect representing a state of 'permanent recession' – Hall *et al.* 2008: 22) that criminality, what has become termed 'anti-social behaviour' (see Yates 2009 for a discussion) and, as we shall see, later broader issues of social harm have the most debilitating effect. However, Young (2007) argues that while the 'poor are not as firmly corralled as some make out' and 'while urban geographers of all political persuasions would like more of a clear cut cartography . . . in reality the contours of late modernity always blur, fudge and cross over' (2007: 26). Thus these communities are not hermetically sealed; they are open to the cultural messages of consumerism and can be found physically buffered up next to enclaves of wealth.

Many of these working-class communities suffered enormously due to the decline of the manufacturing base and subsequent structural unemployment in the post-industrial cities of late twentieth and early twenty-first century Britain (Byrne 2005; Young 2007; Hall *et al.* 2008; or see McCauley 2006 or Yates 2006 for ethnographic accounts). As Kemshall argues, 'Life for young people in contemporary society is both challenging and uncertain' and the life course of individual young people is no longer 'mapped out and predictable' (2008: 21). It is working-class young people residing in 'pockets of acute marginalisation' that have developed in 'locales of permanent recession' (Hall *et al.* 2008: 22) who experience the most protracted and fractured transitions into adulthood. Byrne (2005) cites the work of McKnight (2002) which illustrates how 'negative trajectories' have become more reinforced in the 'post industrial period' (Byrne 2005: 105). Similarly, in his ethnographic account, McCauley identifies that there is an identifiable difference between the clear transitions experienced by young people during the postwar boom period and young people 'living in communities ravaged by deindustrialization' where, he argues, the transition from school to work is hopelessly fractured (2006: 22). Thus, as White and Cuneen argue, 'Many young people in "modern" and "advanced" industrialised societies are not simply marginal to the labour markets, they are literally excluded from it – by virtue of family history, structural restrictions on education and job choices, geographical location, racial and ethnic segregation, stigmatized individual and community reputation' (2006: 19–20).

For young people residing in these marginalized communities, crime can serve both instrumental and expressive functions. As such it can serve as a resource in the negotiation of what Young refers to as the 'two stigmas which the poor confront' (2007: 51). First, he identifies 'relative deprivation' (poverty and exclusion from the major labour markets) (2007: 51). Exclusion from the labour market leads to circumstances which well established criminological theories identify limit young people's opportunities to achieve the material goals set out for them in a legitimate manner (see Merton 1957). As Young argues, the problem with such communities is 'not so much the process of . . . being simply excluded but rather one which was all too strongly included in the culture but, then, systematically excluded from its realisation' (2007: 25). Thus, as Scraton and Haydon argue, 'young people's "offensive" or "offending" acts may be ways of coping with, or reacting to, their experiences of social injustice rather than pathological symptoms of a deficient personality or a dysfunctional family' (2002: 325). The second dilemma Young identifies is 'misregonition' (lower status and lack of respect) (2007: 51). In this sense crime can serve as an expressive function. Thus, crime has a 'transgressive edge' and can offer the 'buzz' of excitement and as such can be 'seductive' (Katz 1988) as well as engendering 'respect' and status.

Criminal justice

Cavadino and Dignan (2007) argue that, while 'the regular official series of criminal and penal statistics do not provide data on social class or occupation, it is clear that the penal system's subjects are overwhelmingly working class, and that unskilled and unemployed people are particularly over represented in the penal population' (2007: 345). This is borne out by data from the Social Exclusion Unit report (2002) which identified that, of the prison population in Britain prior to imprisonment, 72 per cent were in receipt of benefits (13.7 per cent of the general population); 4.7 per cent were homeless (0.001 per cent of the general population) and 67 per cent were unemployed (5 per cent of the general population). As Grover argues, the 'criminal justice agencies basically manage poor people' (2008: 3).

In the youth justice system the evidence sets out a similar state of affairs. We know, for example, that children from poor backgrounds are more likely than their middle-class counterparts to get caught up in the criminal justice system. Specifically in relation to youth justice, Goldson argues that 'The research evidence is unequivocal. It is children and young people from the most disadvantaged families and the poorest communities who provide the bulk of the business for the youth justice system' (2001: 78). The Social Exclusion Unit report in 2002 provides similar evidence, identifying that juveniles serving custodial sentences have experienced a range of social exclusion factors, which may have contributed to their offending behaviour. These include low educational attainment; disrupted family backgrounds; coming from a black or minority ethnic background; behavioural and mental health problems; and problems of alcohol and/or drug misuse (Social Exclusion Unit 2002: 156).

Research, on a national and local level, identifies that young people caught up in the criminal justice system are often vulnerable in a range of other ways too. As Goldson argues 'the "young offender" could just as readily be conceptualised as the "child in need" if child welfare assessments and provisions of the Children's Act 1989 were applied' (2001: 78). The work of Gwyneth Boswell (1995) on children who had committed 'grave' crimes identified that many had suffered bereavement and loss or had experienced significant trauma in their short lives. This reflects Dimon *et al.*'s (2001: 345) assertion that 'Children in prison constitute one of the most socially and psychologically deprived and needy youth populations in society'. A study by the Youth Justice Trust, which surveyed the case files of 1,027 children and young people under the supervision of youth offending teams (YOTs), identified that more than 90 per cent had 'significant experience of loss or rejection, usually losing contact with a parent because of family breakdown, bereavement, or the onset of mental illness or physical disability for a parent' (Youth Justice Trust 2003: 28). The Youth Justice Trust research clearly indicated that that such experiences are more common in the lives of children in trouble. It also identified that these young people's experiences of grief, loss and rejection were rarely acknowledged (2003: 18).

Similarly, a local study by Goldson on 'heavy-end offenders' in Merseyside (1998) identified that they:

> suffered complex, multiple and interlocking patterns of disadvantage. Social services involvement; fractured and impoverished families; neighbourhoods beset with multiple forms of deprivation; disrupted, incomplete, unhappy and relatively unproductive school careers; unemployment, boredom and poverty; and health related problems invariably connected to alcohol and drug misuse comprised the social landscapes and lived realities for the young people. (2001: 77)

In relation to family disruption and experience of abuse, Lader *et al.* (2000) identified that 42 per cent of male remand prisoners had been in care. The same survey found that about 20 per cent of female and about 25 per cent of male prisoners reported having suffered violence at home, while 30 per cent of female and 5 per cent of male prisoners reported sexual abuse. The work of Singleton *et al.* (1998) also illustrates that young people caught up in the criminal justice system have a higher level of mental health problems than other sections of the youth population (Youth Justice Trust 2003).

However, it also apparent that young people with *diagnosable* mental health problems and specific learning disabilities are disproportionately being caught up in the criminal justice system and, as the nets of control widen, these young people are increasingly being caught in them (Yates and Fyson 2007; Yates 2009). For example, research by the British Institute for Brain Injured Children

(2005) into anti-social behaviour orders (ASBOs) identified very high levels of children with a diagnosable learning disability or mental health problems who had received ASBOs. Worryingly, such control measures are presented as a way for troubled young people to access much needed support (Casey 2004), reflecting the criminalization of social policy with respect to youth. In terms of general health there are similar concerns. The survey by the Youth Justice Trust (2003) identified that the health of children and young people under supervision by the YOTs surveyed was not 'generally good'. They identified characteristics including 'poor nutrition; low levels of immunisations; poor take-up of appointments to see GPs; particularly low levels of health education awareness and examples of prematurely restricted growth or chronic health conditions where the children involved have never sought assistance' (2003: 26) – findings reflected in a range of other studies (see Griggs and Walker 2008 for a discussion).

Education is identified in governmental discourses as the route to address some of the inequalities which impact on young people's lives. However, this serves to reproduce class divisions (see Willis 1977). While there is evidence that poor children are disadvantaged educationally (Griggs and Walker 2008), it is also evident that once again the child population caught up in the criminal justice system fares particularly poorly. Research by ECOTEC indicated that nearly half of the young people in custody had literacy and numeracy levels below those of the average 11-year-old (ECOTEC 2001a cited in Social Exclusion Unit 2002).

In addition, the Social Exclusion Unit 2002 report conducted a survey of children in custody in a secure training centre and found 88 per cent functioning below their chronological age in relation to literacy skills and 90 per cent functioning below their chronological age in relation to mathematical ability. The study also identified that 87 per cent had missed 'significant periods' of school and 41 per cent had been excluded from school. The research by the Youth Justice Trust presents similar findings in their cohort of young people supervised in the community. This identified that 32 per cent of the schoolchildren under the supervision of the YOTs had special educational needs; over 60 per cent of these had been statemented and 38 per cent were described as having 'behaviour problems'. This led the researchers to argue that:

> the key predictor that children and young people will be arrested for a criminal offence is 'low achievement at school'. Low achievement is defined primarily as a feeling on the part of the child that they have somehow 'failed' or that they are a 'failure'. This factor alone increases the likelihood of arrest by 90 per cent when compared to the norm. (Youth Justice Trust 2003: 22)

However, this study did not consider class or any co-morbidity between poverty and educational disadvantage or involvement with the YOT. The study did note that the majority of the young people past school leaving age under YOT supervision in the study were unemployed (Youth Justice Trust 2003).

While the young people caught up in the criminal justice system as perpetrators are disproportionately drawn from working-class backgrounds with biographies replete with examples of their vulnerability, it is also apparent that the victims of crime are also drawn from the same group. Those growing up in deprived areas also have a much greater chance of being a victim of crime. Hirsch (2008) identifies a strong association between having experienced crime as a victim and becoming an offender. Most children raised in poverty do not become involved in crime, but there are higher victim and fear of crime rates in disadvantaged areas (Griggs and Walker 2008: 5).

Once exposed to crime it is apparent that children are more likely to experience emotional and behavioural difficulties as a direct result of this exposure (HM Treasury 2008 cited in Griggs and Walker 2008). However, in policy discourses the victims as a term is employed as a symbolic device to rationalize calls for more punishment. The manner in which it is mobilized implies a clear demarcation between the victims, on one hand, and the perpetrators of crime on the other. However, it is apparent that children residing in the poorest areas and those disproportionately caught up in the criminal justice system are drawn from the same group.

The state focuses on the crimes of the poor (Tombs and Whyte 2003) and in particular on the crimes of marginalized young people who represent the paradigmatic target of the criminal justice system (Hillyard *et al.* 2004). Indeed, as Muncie argues: 'As the criminal law is in the main directed against forms of behaviour associated with the young, the working-class and the poor, we should not be surprised to find out that, officially, it is these groups that are ''found'' to be the most criminal' (1999: 38).

However, offending is not simply the preserve of the poor. As Tombs and Whyte argue: 'Crimes committed by states and corporations have far greater economic, physical and social costs than those associated with the ''conventional'' criminals who continue to represent the fixation of contemporary criminal justice systems . . . yet this pressing aspect of social reality is generally ignored' (2003: 3). Indeed, as Pitts and Bateman argue, corporate crime 'dwarfs the proceeds of youth crime and victimizes far more people indirectly' (2005: 17). In relation to the victims of this form of crime, it is apparent that corporate crime disproportionately impacts on the relatively vulnerable (Tombs and Williams 2008: 175). As Young observes, the poor have a 'markedly unfavourable predicament as victims of corporate, white collar and state crime' (2007: 48). However, despite evidence regarding the widespread nature of victimization as a result of corporate crime (see Tombs and Williams 2008 for a discussion), the victims of corporate crime are neglected – sidelined in criminal justice policy and practices and in criminological discourses (Tombs and Williams 2008). It is also apparent that the more vulnerable poor victims of corporate crimes and harms are less likely to receive justice (Spalek and King

2007). Indeed, often these acts are often not even not defined as criminal (Hillyard and Tombs 2005).

One of the problems here lies in the extent to which criminal justice and criminology have been wedded to narrow state definitions of crime. This, Hillyard and Tombs argue, gives 'undue attention ... to events which are defined as crimes ... [and] distracts attention from more serious harm', such as harms caused by the state and powerful corporate social actors, acts which, as a result, are 'positively excluded' from any analysis of crime and criminality (2005: 9). Muncie argues that the social harm perspective:

> is particularly illuminating for the study of youth and crime because it forces recognition that a host of state – and corporate-initiated damaging events are far more endemic and can be far more devastating than those that make up the youth 'problem'. Moreover, much of the political and media concern over youth crime focuses on the exceptional or on recreational drug use, vandalism, brawls, anti-social behaviour, and so which by comparison would not seem to score as high on a scale of persistent social harm. (2009: 155)

Therefore this approach is important as it not only takes a more holistic position on the nature of social harm caused by different groups, and as such puts the social harm caused by young people in stark perspective, but it also raises questions regarding the groups on which social harm disproportionately impacts. As Hillyard and Tombs argue, 'it is clear that various forms of harms are not distributed randomly' (2005: 14). Exposures to such harms are differentially distributed by, for example, ethnicity and class, and these social harms, which can be deleterious to people's welfare from the cradle to the grave, threaten the community collectively.

Conclusion

Despite the pervasive influence of class-based inequalities the relationships between crime and inequality are often ignored (Grover 2008). The chapter has sought to explore explicitly the issues of structural disadvantage, youth, class and crime. In doing so it has illustrated some of the ways in which centrally important structural factors shape the lived experiences of working-class young people in the process of negotiating adolescent transition in modern-day Britain. However, while much has been made of New Labour's much vaunted rhetoric regarding eradicating child poverty by 2020, it is still a major determinant of children and young people's future life chances. Indeed in 2008 the Children's Commission for England identified poverty as 'the single most pernicious influence that is blighting the lives and prospects of our young people' which 'underpins most of the other social issues we are concerned with' (cited in Cassidy 2008).

This is particularly pertinent in relation to criminal justice. The chapter has not argued that there is a clear, direct or causal link between class inequality or poverty and criminality (Hirsch 2008) but it has argued that inequality and poverty shape young people's experiences of crime as both perpetrators and victims. As Kemshall argues, 'structural factors are still key determinants in the world of risk inhabited by young people' (2008: 31). However, these are best viewed, as Scraton and Haydon argue, as '"determining contexts" rather than mechanisms of total determination' (2002: 325). As Goldson argues, the links between poverty and delinquency are 'neither causal nor deterministic' but they are 'bound by an unmistakable corollary' (2001: 78).

Although it is apparent that the 'poor predate the poor' (Young 2007: 48), this chapter has also raised concerns regarding the extent to which the criminal justice system myopically focuses on the 'dangerous acts of the poor' (Reiman 1998 cited in Hillyard and Tombs 2005: 14) while ignoring the socially harmful and often criminal activities of more powerful social actors. It is also clear that there is an emerging body of evidence that children and families residing in working-class communities are the most vulnerable to the criminal and socially harmful activities of the powerful – it is this vulnerable group which are disproportionately the victims of such acts. However, as Sim argues, 'Tony Blair's three governments, like their conservative predecessors' have 'continued with the relentless focus on the conventional criminality of the powerless while simultaneously rolling back interventions for regulating the powerful' (forthcoming).

Notes

1   Colquhoun appears to acknowledge the impact of the material conditions of poverty in the 'causes' of crime. For him, the problem was not poverty itself; indeed, he identified poverty as having a positive impact in motivating the poor to work.
2   Goldson and Yates (2008) and Jamieson and Yates (2009) offer an analysis of youth justice policies during this period – period which while characterized by an assault on social rights, also saw the development of a range of progressive youth justice strategies.

References

Advocacy Committee of the Royal College of Paediatrics and Health (2007) *A Fair Deal for all Children. Equity in Child Health: A Policy Statement.* London: Royal College of Paediatrics and Health.

Anderson, B. (1983) *Imagined Communities: Reflections on the Origins and Spread of Nationalism.* London: Verso.

Bauman, Z. and Tester, K. (2001) *Conversations with Zygmunt Bauman.* Cambridge: Polity Press.

Boswell, G. (1995) *Young and Dangerous: The Backgrounds and Careers of Section 53 Offenders*. Aldershot: Avebury.

Bottrell, D. (2002) 'Working with "hardened criminals": a youth worker's perspective of perceptions of young people in a housing estate.' Paper presented to the 'Housing, crime and stronger communities' conference convened by the Australian Institute of Criminology and the Australian Housing and Urban Research Institute, Melbourne 6–7 May.

Box, S. (1983) *Power, Crime and Mystification*. London: Tavistock.

British Institute for Brain Injured Children (2005) *'Ain't Misbehavin': Young People with Learning and Communication Difficulties and Anti-social Behaviour*. London: British Institute for Brain Injured Children.

Bynner, J. (2002) *Young People's Changing Routes to Independence*. York: Joseph Rowntree Trust.

Byrne, D. (2005) *Social Exclusion* (2nd edn). Maidenhead: Open University Press.

Campbell, B. (1993) *Goliath: Britain's Dangerous Places*. London: Methuen.

Casey, L. (2004) 'Taking a stand', *Criminal Justice Matters*, 57: 6–7.

Cassidy, S. (2008) 'Failure on child poverty targets is "moral disgrace"', *Independent*, Monday 9 June.

Cavadino, M. and Dignan, J. (2007) *The Penal System: An Introduction*. London: Sage.

Cockburn, T. (2000) 'From "street arabs" to angels: working class children, competence and citizenship, 1850–1914', in J. Batseleer and B. Humphries (eds) *Welfare, Exclusion and Political Agency*. London: Routledge.

Cohen, S. (2002) *Folk Devils and Moral Panics* (30th anniversary issue). London: Routledge.

Davidson, R. and Erskine, A. (1992) 'Introduction', in R. Davidson and A. Erikson (eds) *Poverty Deprivation and Social Work: Research Highlights in Social Work 22*. London: Jessica Kingsley.

Davies, N. (1998) *Dark Heart: The Shocking Truth about Hidden Britain*. London: Vintage.

Dimon, C., Misch, P. and Goldberg, D. (2001) 'On being in a young offender institution: what boys on remand told a child psychiatrist', *Psychiatric Bulletin*, 29: 342–5.

Dorling, D. (2005) 'Prime suspect: murder in Britain', in P. Hillyard *et al.* (eds) *Beyond Criminology? Taking Harm Seriously*. London: Pluto Press.

Emsley, C. (2007) 'The history of crime and crime control institutions', in M. Maguire *et al.* (eds) *The Oxford Handbook of Criminology* (3rd edn). Oxford: Clarendon Press.

France, A. (2000) 'Towards a sociological understanding of youth and their risk taking', *Journal of Youth Studies*, 3: 317–31.

Furlong, A. and Cartmel, F. (1997) *Young People and Social Change: Individualisation and Risk in Late Modernity*. London: Open University Press.

Giddens, A. (2007) *Over to You, Mr Brown: How Labour can Win Again*. Cambridge: Polity Press.

Goldson, B. (1998) *Children in Trouble: Backgrounds and Outcomes*. Liverpool: University of Liverpool, Department of Sociology, Social Policy and Social Work Studies.

Goldson, B. (2001) 'A rational youth justice? Some critical reflections on the research, policy and practice relation', *Probation Journal*, 4: 76–85.

Goldson, B. (2005) 'Taking liberties: policy and the punitive turn', in H. Hendrick (ed.) *Children and Social Policy: An Essential Reader*. Bristol: Policy Press.

Goldson, B. and Chigwada-Bailey, R. (1999) '(What) justice for black children and young people?', in B. Goldson (ed.) *Youth Justice: Contemporary Policy and Practice*. Aldershot: Ashgate.

Goldson, B. and Yates, J. (2008) 'Youth justice policy and practice: reclaiming applied criminology as critical intervention', in J. Yates, with B. Stout and B. Williams (eds) *Applied Criminology*. London: Sage.

Griggs, J. and Walker, R. (2008) *The Costs of Child Poverty for Individuals and Society*. York: Joseph Rowntree Foundation.

Grover, C. (2008) *Crime and Inequality*. Cullompton: Willan Publishing.

Grover, C. (forthcoming) 'Child poverty', in K. Broadhurst *et al.* (eds) *Critical Perspectives on Safeguarding Children*. Chichester: Wiley-Blackwell.

Haines, K. and Drakeford, M. (1998) *Young People and Youth Justice*. London: Palgrave.

Hadley, E. (1990) 'Natives in a strange land: the philanthropic discourse of juvenile emigration in mid-nineteenth century England', *Victorian Studies*, 33: 7–29.

Hall, S., Critcher, C., Jefferson, T., Clarke, J.N. and Roberts, B. (1978) *Policing the Crisis: Mugging, the State and Law and Order*. London: Macmillan.

Hall, S., Winlow, S. and Ancrum, C. (2008) *Criminal Identities and Consumer Culture: Crime, Exclusion and the New Culture of Narcissim*. Cullompton: Willan Publishing.

Harvey, D. (2008) 'The right to the city', *New Left Review*, 53: 23–40.

Hewlett, S.A. (1993) *Child Neglect in Rich Nations*. New York, NY: UNICEF.

Hills, J. and Stewart, K. (2005) *Policies towards Poverty, Inequality and Exclusion since 1997*. York: Joseph Rowntree Foundation.

Hillyard, P., Sim, J., Tombs, S. and Whyte, D. (2004) 'Leaving a "stain upon the silence": contemporary criminology and the politics of dissent', *British Journal of Criminology*, 44: 369–90.

Hillyard, P. and Tombs, S. (2005) 'Beyond criminology?', in P. Hillyard *et al.* (eds) *Criminal Obsessions: Why Harm Matters more than Crime*. London: Crime and Society Foundation.

Hirsch, D. (2008) *Estimating the Costs of Child Poverty*. York: Joseph Rowntree Foundation.

House of Commons Home Affairs Committee (2007) *Black Young People and the Criminal Justice System*. London: HMSO (available online at http://www.parliament.the-stationery-office.co.uk/pa/cm200607/cmselect/cmhaff/181/181i.pdf).

Jamieson, J. (forthcoming) 'In search of youth justice', in K. Broadhurst *et al.* (eds) *Critical Perspectives on Safeguarding Children*. Chichester: Wiley-Blackwell.

Jamieson, J. and Yates, J. (2009) 'Young people, youth justice and the state', in R. Coleman *et al.* (eds) *State, Power, Crime*. London: Sage.

Katz, J. (1988) *Seductions of Crime: Moral and Sensual Attractions in Doing Evil*. New York, NY: Basic Books.

Kemshall, H. (2008) 'Risks, rights and justice: understanding and responding to youth risk', *Youth Justice*, 8: 21–37.

Killeen, D. (2008) *Is Poverty in the UK a Denial of People's Human Rights?* York: Joseph Rowntree Foundation.

Lader, D., Singleton, M. and Meltzer, H. (2000) *Psychiatric Morbidity among Young Offenders in England and Wales*. London: Office for National Statistics.

Law, A. and Mooney, G. (2006) '"We've never had it so good": the "problem" of the working class in devolved Scotland', *Critical Social Policy*, 26: 523–42.

Lister, R. (1990) *The Exclusive Society: Citizenship and the Poor*. London: CPAG.

MacDonald, R. and Marsh, J. (2005) *Disconnected Youth? Growing Up in Britain's Poor Neighbourhoods*. Basingstoke: Palgrave Macmillan.

Macilwee, M. (2006) *The Gangs of Liverpool: From Cornermen to the High Rip: The Mobs that Terrorised a City*. London: Milo.

McCauley, R. (2006) *Out of Sight: Crime, Youth and Exclusion in Modern Britain.* Cullompton: Willan Publishing.

Merton, R. (1957) *Social Theory and Social Structure.* New York, NY: Free Press.

Mills, C.W. (1959) *The Sociological Imagination.* New York, NY: Oxford University Press.

Mills, C.W. (1963, 1967) *Power, Politics and People: The Collective Essays of C. Wright Mills* (ed. I.H. Horowitz). New York, NY: Oxford University Press.

Mooney, G. (1999) 'Urban "disorders"', in S. Pile *et al.* (eds) *Unruly Cities?* London: Routledge.

Mooney, G. (2009) '"Problem populations" and what to do about them.' Paper presented at the Liverpool John Moores 'Criminology' seminar series, 24 March.

Muncie, J. (1999) *Youth and Crime: A Critical Introduction.* London: Sage.

Muncie, J. (2004) *Youth and Crime: A Critical Introduction* (2nd edn). London: Sage.

Muncie, J. (2009) *Youth and Crime: A Critical Introduction* (3rd edn). London: Sage.

Murray, C. (1990) *The Emerging British Underclass.* London: Institute of Economic Affairs, Health and Welfare Unit.

Pearson, G. (1983) *Hooligan: A History of Respectable Fears.* London: Macmillan.

Pearson, G. (2006) 'From peaky blinders to hoodies', *Criminal Justice Matters,* 65: 6–7.

Petersen, A. (1996) 'Risk, governance and the new public health', in A. Petersen and R. Bunton (eds) *Foucault, Health and Medicine.* London: Routledge.

Pitts, J. (2000) 'The new youth justice and the politics of electoral anxiety', in B. Goldson (ed.) *The New Youth Justice.* Lyme Regis: Russell House Publishing.

Pitts, J. (2008) *Reluctant Gangsters: The Changing Face of Youth Crime.* Cullompton: Willan Publishing.

Pitts, J. and Bateman, T. (2005) 'Youth crime in England and Wales', in J. Pitts and T. Bateman (eds) *The Russell House Companion to Youth Justice.* London: Russell House.

Poynting, S., Noble, G., Tabar, P. and Collins, J. (2004) *Bin Laden in the Suburbs: Criminalising the Arab Other.* Sydney: Sydney Institute of Criminology.

Reiner, R. (2007) 'Political economy', in M. Maguire *et al.* (eds.) *The Oxford Handbook of Criminology* (4th edn). Oxford: Clarendon Press.

Ruggiero, V. (2000) *Crime and Markets.* Oxford: Clarendon Press.

Scraton, P. and Haydon, D. (2002) 'Challenging the criminalization of children and young people: securing a rights based agenda', in J. Muncie *et al.* (eds.) *Youth Justice: Critical Readings.* London: Sage.

Sim, J. (forthcoming) *The Carceral State: Power and Punishment in a Hard Land.* London: Sage.

Singleton, N., Meltzer, H. and Gatwood, R. (1998) *Psychiatric Morbidity among Prisoners in England and Wales.* London: HMSO.

Social Exclusion Unit (2001) *Preventing Social Exclusion.* London: HMSO.

Social Exclusion Unit (2002) *Reducing Re-offending by Ex-prisoners.* London: Social Exclusion Unit.

Social Exclusion Unit (2004) *Breaking the Cycle: Taking Stock of Progress and Priorities for the Future.* London: Office of the Deputy Prime Minister.

Spalek, B. and King, S. (2007) *Farepak Victims Speak out: An Exploration of the Harms Caused by the Collapse of Farepak.* London: Centre of Crime and Justice Studies (available online at http://www.crimeandjustice.org.uk/farepakvictims.html).

Tombs, S. and Whyte, D. (2003) 'Unmasking the crimes of the powerful', *Critical Criminology: An International Journal,* 11: 217–36.

Tombs, S. and Whyte, D. (2007) *Safety Crime.* Cullompton: Willan Publishing.

Tombs, S. and Williams, B. (2008) 'Corporate crime and its victims', in B. Stout *et al.* (eds) *Applied Criminology*. London: Sage.

UNICEF (2007) *Child Poverty in Perspective: An Overview of Child Well-being in Rich Countries. Innocenti Report Card 7*. Florence: UNICEF Innocenti Research Centre.

White, R. and Cuneen, C. (2006) 'Social class, youth and crime', in B. Goldson and J. Muncie (eds) *Youth Crime and Justice*. London: Sage.

Willis, P. (1977) *Learning to Labour*. Westmead: Saxon House.

Wood, J. and Hine, J. (2009) 'Introduction: the changing context of work with young people', in J. Wood and J. Hine (eds) *Work with Young People: Theory and Policy for Practice*. London: Sage.

Yates, J. (2006) '"You just don't grass": youth, crime and "grassing" in a working class community', *Youth Justice*, 7: 195–210.

Yates, J. (2009) 'Youth justice: moving in an anti social direction', in J. Wood and J. Hine (eds) *Work with Young People: Theory and Policy for Practice*. London: Sage.

Yates, J. and Fyson, R. (2007) 'Anti social behaviour and young people with learning difficulties.' Paper presented at the National Association of Youth Justice annual conference, Harper Adams College, Shropshire, September.

Young, J. (2007) *The Vertigo of Late Modernity*. London: Sage.

Youth Justice Trust (2003) *On the Case: A Survey of over 1,000 Children and Young People under Supervision by YOTs*. Manchester: Youth Justice Trust.

2

Transitions to adulthood

Rachel Thomson

What does it mean to be an adult to young people growing up in the UK today? Becoming sexually active? Learning to drive? Earning a wage? Becoming a parent? This chapter will draw on a sociological and youth studies framework to explore the ways that the subjective and objective markers of adulthood have changed over the course of a generation: from a collective rite of passage to a fragmented and increasingly individualized process giving rise to a distinction between the extended transitions to adulthood of middle-class young people and the 'faster' or 'accelerated' transitions of more marginalized groups. The chapter draws on the Inventing Adulthoods study, a ten-year investigation of young people's transitions, in order to illustrate the importance of the subjective dimension of the transition to adulthood – feelings of competence, autonomy and recognition by others.

The changing shape of youth transitions

Today's generation of young people face the task of creating lives that are very different from those of their parents. The sequence of transition from childhood to adulthood is no longer to leave school, to enter work and to establish an independent home, partnership and family in fast succession. At the centre of this transformation is the effective disappearance of the youth labour market and a corresponding expansion of higher education. In 1954 just 6 per cent of the British population went to university. By 2010 the UK government aims that 50 per cent of young people will participate in higher education. This dramatic expansion initially privileged the middle class and girls, yet is increasingly impacting on working-class young people, who are often the first generation in their family to go to university.

The demand to remain in further education at least until the age of 18 means that there is an increasing body of disgruntled young people housed within educational institutions without being engaged seriously in a route towards qualification (Forsyth and Furlong 2003; MacDonald and Marsh 2005). Those who pursue higher education are faced with an extended dependency on parents who may not understand or be able to support them. Studies of trends in educational achievement suggest that girls out-perform boys, and minority ethnic groups out-perform the majority white population (Egerton and Halsey 1993; Modood and Acland 1998; Platt 2005).

Where transitions to adulthood were previously collective, one-step, linear and predictable, they are increasingly uncertain and non-linear. The sociologists Furlong and Cartmel capture this change through the metaphor of travel – with the 'train journey' transitions of the past giving way to the 'car journey' transitions of the present, in which drivers have the 'impression of having control over the timing and routing of their journeys and with the experience of passing other motorists' (1997: 6). But the social inequalities of the past have not disappeared, and it is argued that youth transitions in the UK are more starkly shaped by social class than many other European economies (Bynner 2001; Holdsworth 2004; Machin and Blanden 2004).

Extending their travelling metaphor, Furlong and Cartmel point out that 'what many of the drivers fail to realize is that the type of car which they have been allocated at the start of the journey is the most significant predictor of the ultimate outcome' (1997: 7). The expansion of higher education also impacts on the middle classes for whom privilege must be secured in new ways. As universities open up to non-traditional students, there is a corresponding inflation in what it takes to succeed, with the spectre of downward social mobility becoming a powerful presence in the middle-class psyche.

Unequal resources and the fast and slow tracks to adulthood

Reviewing the youth studies field for the Social Exclusion Unit, the sociologist Gill Jones (2006) characterizes transitions to adulthood as becoming more:

- *extended* (with economic independence deferred);

- *complex* (there is no longer a conventional timetable; dependence and independence may combine and critical moments make a difference);

- *risky* (involving backtracking, risk-taking and parent/child conflict);

- *individualized* (young people have more choice but are not equally able to capitalize on it), and

- *polarized* (with inequalities more sharply defined in relation to more elite 'slow track' transitions and a more risky 'fast track').

Although the period of dependence on family and public resources has been extended for a growing majority of young people, independence comes quickly for others. Longitudinal studies point towards a polarization of life chances between young people, played out through different inequalities of income, education, health and family support (Schoon and Bynner 2003). Commentators have characterized this in terms of the emergence of two distinct patterns of transition: a fast and a slow track (Bynner *et al.* 2002; Jones 2002). Both are patterns that have their roots in longstanding class cultural practices, associated with very different understandings of success and happiness (Thomson and Holland 2003). But where slow-track transitions were formerly the preserve of the middle classes they are increasingly being pursued by young people from working-class backgrounds. Fast-track transitions are now associated with social exclusion and, in policy terms, tend to be seen in terms of a loss of childhood rather than the acquisition of adult status. Gill Jones describes the fast and slow tracks as follows:

- **Slow track transitions** typically involve staying on in post-compulsory education and delaying entry into full-time employment and family formation (often until 30 or later). Slow track transitions involve many semi-independent statuses, requiring different levels of parental support. Slow track transitions, following longstanding middle-class practices are problematic for those without middle-class models of parental support. This is reflected in the number of 'broken' or 'fractured' transitions, which occur.

- **Fast track transitions** may typically involve leaving education at or before the minimum age, and risking unemployment or insecure and badly paid work. Failed fast track transitions may result in young people ending up not economically active (i.e. 'NEET'). They may also involve early family formation – including teenage pregnancy. The risk of involvement in problematic social behaviour – offending, abuse of drugs and alcohol – is also higher among this group. Fast track transitions follow a working-class pattern where young people are expected to be self-supporting, and are particularly problematic when they cannot be, because of low wages, unemployment or teenage motherhood. It is from this latter group that 'socially excluded' young people come (2006: 7).

Being and feeling grown-up: competence, recognition and investment

Whatever their background, the contemporary generation struggle to find ways in which to feel autonomous while also negotiating the extended forms of dependency that are a feature of the contemporary landscape. What it means to be grown-up is contested. Certain forms of experience are framed within policy terms as growing up too quickly – teenage parenthood, homelessness and involvement in criminal careers. Yet the cultural manifestations of extended youth are also problematized – such as the growth in a binge-drinking culture – as young adults who are unable to secure mortgages or to afford to start families spend what disposable income they have on partying (Hollands 1995; Jones and Martin 1999).

It is possible to think about the transition to adulthood in terms of both objective and subjective markers. Objective markers include forms of legal entitlement/responsibility (rights to vote, borrow money, claim independent benefits, drive, drink and consent), while subjective markers point to the importance of feelings of maturity and independence. In an in-depth study of 100 young people's transitions to adulthood in the UK, my colleagues and I tracked young people over time, asking them about those aspects of their lives and experiences that made them feel grown up, and attempting to understand the impact this had on their subsequent behaviour. As we sought to understand how young people invent adulthood over time we realized that they felt 'adult' in different ways in different contexts, and thinking of themselves as adult was related to their feelings of *competence* and the *recognition* that they received for that competence.

We described the major arenas of their lives where this was played out as *fields*, which we see as locations within which adult identities can be developed, such as education, work, leisure and consumption, and the domestic (which includes family, relationships and care). The balance between competence and recognition in these fields changes over time not only through changing circumstances and opportunities but also through investments in these fields made by young people in response to their experiences and investments made by others.

The following descriptions of the fields are drawn from the experiences of the participants in the study and show how dependence on one field may entail independence in another (Thomson *et al.* 2004; Henderson *et al.* 2007).

Education

Educational achievement brings with it rewards of recognition, which in turn encourage young people to invest more in this field in their construction of adulthood. The route would take them through school, qualification, to university and could lead to an adulthood associated with professional work. This was a route often, but not exclusively, associated with a middle-class background.

Failure to secure a sense of competence or recognition in the educational field, led to varied alternative trajectories – for example, pursuing an accelerated adulthood, with a traditional pattern of leaving school and entering work as soon as possible, starting a steady relationship and 'settling down'. The fields in which competence and recognition were sought in this case were work and the domestic. They might pursue an extended youth, having fun, failing in education, becoming a rebel. Some struggled to maintain a connection with education, perhaps following vocational courses that led nowhere while working in 'Mc jobs'. And finally they might find competence and recognition through investment in a criminal lifestyle that provided the kinds of financial reward that was not available to them through the local youth labour market.

Accelerated adulthood could be precipitated by various life events – a teenage pregnancy, family breakdown or bereavement, or coming out. As a result the young person might leave school and/or home and perhaps take on adult responsibilities. These trajectories might have been abandoned at later interviews or be the cause of regret in hindsight.

Work

Work was an attractive source of competence and recognition for those who were unsuccessful in education. Like many young people in the UK, most in the study undertook high levels of part-time work, but it was those who were unable to find a sense of recognition in education who were more likely to prioritize the demands of work in the competition for their time and energy. The young people who invested in education tended to see part-time work undertaken while at school as useful for financing a certain lifestyle, or for providing useful experience for the future. Those less invested in education were more likely to see part-time work as providing personal affirmation in their role as worker. The money allowed a degree of independence from their family, or contributed to family finances. The appeal of full-time wages and a working life evaporated quickly for many who took this route on leaving school, only to find themselves left behind by those following the higher education track.

Leisure and consumption

Consumption and leisure were important for the young workers – providing a field in which their spending power gave them a privileged position. Some young people, alienated from education, developed their leisure identities creatively, engaging in club culture and, through that, developing alternative careers, reworking traditional boundaries and accessing cultural and social capital. Young people were also involved in less commercial forms of leisure, such as community projects, self-help groups, organized youth movements and paramilitary activities. Again, these forms of activity gave young people experience of responsibility, competence and recognition that in biographical terms may have been highly significant in shaping their future trajectory.

Young people making a primary investment in education were more likely to defer commercially based leisure competences until they could 'afford' to enjoy them – possibly at university.

The domestic: family, relationships and care

We found that many young people took on an extremely high level of responsibility within the home, for childcare, housework and care of sick or unhappy parents. This was more typical of young women, although several young men also undertook forms of caring. Many of the working-class young people indicated a sense of competence through home and family and revealed a consciousness of the details of household budgets in their accounts, leading them to avoid placing additional financial or emotional burdens on their parents. This care for their families could give them a sense of self-worth and shape their plans for the future. If they thought their families could not afford it, they might curtail educational investment or plan to live close to parents whom they would expect to care for as they grew older.

Establishing a family of their own was also central to their imagined futures, with adulthood defined through the couple relationship and parenthood. This contrasts with more individualized orientations towards family life, in which young people considered parental support and higher education as a 'right', and where they deferred establishing a family life of their own to the distant future.

A biographical approach over time

This account of the different fields of young people's biographies shows how they are pulled by competing versions of adulthood: one stressing independence, autonomy and pleasure; and the other relationship, interdependence and care. The choices that confront young people are highly structured by gender, locality, ethnicity and social class. The choices that they make are highly consequential for subsequent processes of inclusion and exclusion. Investments in one field are likely to be associated with dis-investments in another. We only have so much energy, time and personal resources. So, for example, young people who do not experience themselves as competent at school are more likely to be attracted to forms of recognition available to them in work or in leisure. This is illustrated vividly by the case of Cheryl:

> Cheryl: 'You can't have the best of both worlds'
> At her first interview Cheryl was 16 years old, living at home with her parents and sister and studying for her GCSEs at school. At this point she looked to education as a source of personal development, expressing the hope that she would go on to take A levels and possibly on to a nursing

course. She expressed no ambitions to move out of her neighbourhood. Much of her energy went into an eight-month-old relationship with her 20-year-old boyfriend, through whom she vicariously accessed some of the material culture of adult life – a car, money and a social life. She also had two part-time jobs that together earned her £50 per week.

Cheryl's 18-year-old sister had recently had a baby, and this had provoked Cheryl to reflect on the kind of adulthood that she wanted for herself. She explained that she was in 'no hurry' to become an adult with all the associated responsibilities and in particular wanted to delay motherhood. At this point she was enjoying a life without commitments, but with many of the 'trappings' of adulthood made accessible through her boyfriend. Her investment in education was offset by feelings of maturity gained through her relationship and practices, such as cooking her boyfriend dinner and saving for joint holidays.

By her second interview this balance had shifted substantially. Having passed five GCSEs Cheryl decided to continue in a newly formed school sixth form, pursuing an NVQ course. She reported being very frustrated by the school's failure to recognize the greater maturity of the members of the sixth form. According to her the school treated them like children. At the same time her relationship with her boyfriend had become more domestic and 'adult-like'. As a couple they made regular visits to relatives and family, shared cosy nights in together where Cheryl would cook and talked about getting engaged and buying a car. Her plans for her future had also shifted. In this interview she was more focused on a future as a housewife, staying at home looking after children while her husband worked outside the home.

With more demands at school Cheryl had given up her part-time work and found it difficult being dependent on her parents and being treated as a child at school. While still committed to her educational training, she also talked about being tempted by the world of work and the financial and emotional independence that this seemed to offer. So although Cheryl was still attending school, the only arena of her life in which she experienced any adult-like competence, or was recognized as having any, was in her relationship with her boyfriend. However, the relationship became increasingly domestic, and Cheryl described her life as increasingly boring and routine.

At her third interview we discovered a very different young woman, for whom 'everything' had changed. The pressures and frustrations that were evident in her second interview had come to a head. Cheryl had left the sixth form two months before completing her NVQ to take up a full-time clerical job paying £140 per week. She explains that she 'just got claustrophobic you know with the school sort of treating us really like children'.

She explained this decision in terms of frustrations at her lack of freedom and spending power in comparison with her friends. The school had proved to be very inflexible in response to her situation. The headteacher denied a plea by the careers teacher for her to be allowed to complete the course in the evening:

> 'And I told her that I just wasn't happy and I wanted money and wanted to be able to enjoy myself, I didn't like having to still have to do things at night and all and parents were still treating me like children and all because I was still at school . . . But he just said you can't have best of both worlds.'

The decision to move into employment can be understood as the catalyst for a whole series of changes. In the same week that Cheryl took up her job she also moved out of her parental home, renting a room in the house of another woman who was working. Soon after this her relationship with her boyfriend came to an end, partly as a result of Cheryl's frustrations with his parents' refusal to treat their relationship as sufficiently adult. As a consequence Cheryl was no longer staying at home and living for the future but going out, partying and living for the moment. Work not only provided her with the material resources to become independent of her boyfriend and parents but also with access to social and cultural networks that made different forms of adulthood available to her. Significantly, in this interview Cheryl was again talking about university as a possible option for the future. She recognized that her recent choices may have made the route to university harder and longer, but for her the informal gains that she had made in this period were more significant than any that she would have made at school.

In many ways Cheryl's story is typical of many working-class young people in the Inventing Adulthoods study, for whom the educational pathway is seen as offering insufficient immediate rewards in contrast to the world of work and consumption that they see many of their peers enjoying. Parenthood can also provide an alternative site of competence, in a way that is particularly resonant for young women. If she had become pregnant, she might have easily been drawn into a local form of adulthood defined through parental and domestic responsibility. From a biographical perspective it becomes possible to understand the competing pull-and-push factors that affect young people's choices. Central to these is the pursuit of a sense of competence (of being good at something) and recognized by others as such. Cheryl gained a sense of competence both in her relationship and as a worker, yet at school she felt like a child. Insights gained by following an individual over time, through the different twists and turns of their transitions, encourage a move away from notions of good/bad or successful/unsuccessful transitions towards asking questions about resources and timing.

Within the Inventing Adulthoods study there were young people who became involved in various different kinds of 'trouble', often involving drinking and drugs and disaffection from schooling. In each of these biographies there was a logic to the young person's behaviour when understood in a holistic context and over time. As others have found, 'disengagement from schooling needs to be understood in terms of simultaneous and associated processes of engagement with street-based, peer networks' (MacDonald and Marsh 2005: 4). The extent to which young people are able to manage the transition to adulthood without harming themselves and/or others is mediated in large part by the resources on which they can draw, in terms of the environment within which they are living and the emotional resources of family and friends. Timing also makes a difference, as does the extent to which the young person is recognized and supported by significant adults around them. Young people growing up in poverty and in turbulent families are particularly vulnerable, and may struggle to realize their potential (MacDonald and Marsh 2005).

This chapter invites the reader to think about young people in the round and over time. By beginning with biography it is possible to rethink life experiences that are currently framed in terms of social exclusion as the consequences of young people's labours to be socially included and recognized as competent adults. By focusing on *becoming* rather than *being* it is possible to understand the pursuit of adulthood as an unfinished and emergent accomplishment that, in changing times, is likely to involve a resequencing of the traditional components of the 'package' that adulthood represents. This is a perspective that is urgently needed in a policy and practice climate in which biographical configurations are cast as 'anti-social behaviours': teenage parenthood, dropping out of education and involvement in criminal and drug subcultures.

The biographical approach recognizes the young people at the centre of these policy discourses, making sense of their choices through an understanding of their investments. More importantly, it provides a way of seeing the whole of young people's lives (including the limited character of their 'choices' and the critical role of timing in their biographies) in such a way that generates insights that could inform practice with young people. It is clear from Cheryl's case study that her decision to become a student makes sense and is rewarding. Yet it is also clear that there were a number of moments when alternative futures could have been supported. If policy-makers and practitioners wish to support young people to create different futures from those readily available to them, it is necessary to engage creatively and sensitively with the dynamic of investment, recognition and competence that underlies the biographical process.

Conclusion

In this chapter I have explored the meaning of adulthood in contemporary UK society. Youth transitions are shaped by historical forces and social location. Today's young people face a very different world from their parents and grandparents. For young working-class men and women it is no longer a matter of leaving school at 16 and walking into work. The expectation is increasingly that these young people will remain in education. This gives rise to a range of *biographical challenges* with which young people must contend: managing extended dependency on parents and family resources; balancing autonomy and dependence as adult status is acquired in a piecemeal way; maintaining a sense of belonging and security against the demand to expose the self to risks and new experiences; and negotiating the demands of deferred gratification against the acquisition of resources and recognition within the present (Thomson 2009). Those with the fewest resources to draw upon may experience acute conflicts which they are unable to escape or resolve, and alternative criminal careers may appear to offer immediate rewards.

References

Bynner, J. (2001) 'British youth transitions in comparative context', *Journal of Youth Studies*, 4: 5–24.

Bynner, J., Elias, P., McKnight, A., Pan, H. and Pierre, G. (2002) *Young People's Changing Routes to Independence*. York: Joseph Rowntree Foundation.

Egerton, M. and Halsey, A.H. (1993) 'Trends in social class and gender in access to higher education in Britain', *Oxford Review of Education*, 19: 183–96.

Forsyth, A. and Furlong, A. (2003) *Socio-economic Disadvantage and Access to Higher Education*. Bristol: Policy Press.

Furlong, A. and Cartmel, F. (1997/2006) *Young People and Social Change: Individualization and Risk in Late Modernity*. Buckingham: Open University Press.

Henderson, S., Holland, J., McGrellis, S., Sharpe, S. and Thomson, R. (2007) *Inventing Adulthoods: A Biographical Approach to Youth Transitions*. London: Sage.

Holdsworth, C. (2004) 'Family support and the transition out of parental home in Britain, Spain and Norway', *Sociology*, 38: 909–26.

Hollands, R. (1995) *Friday Night, Saturday Night: Youth Cultural Identification in the Post Industrial City*. Newcastle upon Tyne: University of Newcastle upon Tyne.

Jones, G. (2002) *The Youth Divide: Diverging Paths to Adulthood*. York: Joseph Rowntree Foundation.

Jones, G. (2006) *The Thinking and Behavior of Young Adults (Aged 16–25): A Literature Review for the Social Exclusion Unit*. London: Office of the Deputy Prime Minister and Social Exclusion Unit.

Jones, G. and Martin, C.D. (1999) 'The "young consumer" at home: dependence, resistance and autonomy', in J. Hearn and S. Roseneil (eds) *Consuming Cultures: Power and Resistance*. Basingstoke: Macmillan.

MacDonald, R. and Marsh, J. (2005) *Disconnected Youth? Growing up in Britain's Poor Neighbourhoods*. Basingstoke: Palgrave.

Machin, S. and Blanden, J. (2004) 'Educational inequality and the expansion of UK higher education', *Scottish Journal of Political Economy*, 51: 230–49.

Modood, T. and Acland, T. (1998) 'Conclusion', in T. Modood and T. Acland (eds) *Race and Higher Education*. London: Policy Studies Institute.

Platt, L. (2005) *Migration and Social Mobility: The Life Chances of Britain's Minority Ethnic Communities*. Bristol: Policy Press for JRF.

Schoon, I. and Bynner, J. (2003) 'Risk and resilience in the life course: implications for interventions and social policies', *Journal of Youth Studies*, 6: 21–31.

Schoon, I. and Parsons, S. (2003) 'Competence in the face of adversity: the impact of early family environment and long-term consequences', *Children and Society*, 16: 260–72.

Thomson, R. (2009) *Unfolding Lives: Youth, Gender and Change*. Bristol: Policy Press.

Thomson, R. and Holland, J. (2003) 'Making the most of what you've got: resources, values and inequalities in young people's transitions to adulthood', *Educational Review*, 55: 33–46.

Thomson, R., Holland, J., McGrellis, S., Bell, R., Henderson, S. and Sharpe, S. (2004) 'Inventing adulthood: a biographical approach to understanding youth citizenship', *Sociological Review*, 52: 218–93.

3

From child to adult: theoretical assumptions in ideas about growing up

Lindsay O'Dell

Introduction

> A major stumbling block in the path of those wishing to work for children in the UK is the status of children and childhood itself. (Mayall 2005: 79)

This chapter critically examines the notion of 'development' to look at ways in which moral agendas around about 'normality' are embedded and naturalized through our understandings of 'growing up'. Ideas from critical developmental psychology (for example, from Burman 2008) are used to demonstrate that development is not an inevitable, natural process but one which attends to the local and specific norms of the society in which young people develop. The chapter critically examines the construction of development as a progressive accumulation of skills acquired through a series of stages to examine how this construction sets up a 'normal' trajectory for development which can stigmatize and problematize young people who, for many reasons, fall outside the given norms. The chapter concludes by examining the implications of this for practice within a youth justice setting.

I. How do we develop?

While we all have ideas about how children develop, these are often derived from knowledge produced by developmental psychologists (Mayall 2005). The traditional, and still arguably dominant, view in developmental psychology is that development occurs through different stages; that we develop through a distinct process of progression from a less sophisticated stage to a more complex one. This is evident in our understandings of physical growth as well as for psychological, cognitive and other forms of development.

The key theories of development include Piaget's theory of cognitive development; Kohlberg's theory of moral development; and Erickson's psychosocial development. In Piaget's theory children develop through three stages: increasing cognitive abilities; learning to take another person's view into account; and developing abstract reasoning and logic. Piaget's theory has been extensively tested and re-evaluated, and the focus on cognitive development and skills remains an important area of practice, particularly with the cognitive skills training evident in youth justice practice (Pitts 2001). However, the basic premise of children being less developed than adults remains. The assumption of children as 'less' than adults – less developed and less competent – is discussed throughout this chapter.

Kohlberg's theory of moral development builds on Piaget's theory to suggest that children develop a view of morality progressing from self-interested action through to conformity to society's rules. Kohlberg argues that some people develop an individualized morality that transcends the law. This is usually explained by reference to people such as Mahatma Ghandi and Martin Luther King who were both seen to draw on a higher sense of morality in justifying their acts of civil disobedience.

2. Progression

The implicit assumption within a stage model of development is that development is a cumulative acquisition of skills, moving from undeveloped, less sophisticated and immature to the endpoint of 'adulthood'. While there are substantial differences between the developmental theories of Piaget and Erikson (such as the focus they place on the child developing cognition and a sense of identity), they share some basic similarities. Both assume that development is the acquisition of skills to equip an individual to live an autonomous, independent life and to operate as a rational, logical thinker capable of individual actions. However, Walkerdine (1993) argues that the endpoints of development, as we view them, are culturally and socially constructed, reflecting the individualistic values of western society, in which independence and autonomy are valued over interdependency and collectivist solutions. Thus the dominant view of childhood and development – conceived as an orderly progression through time – involves ideological assumptions. This remains persuasive, so that even psychologists who disagree with a stage-based view of development conceptualize the process as a progressive one.

Walkerdine and other academics (such as Morss 1992 and Vandenberg 1993), however, question the very notion of development as seen in this way. Instead, they emphasize the cultural factors behind the idea of development as a progression, arguing that this can be seen, in part at least, as a legacy of the cultural and scientifically 'positivist' movements arising from modernism, particularly evolutionary theory and changes in Judeo-Christian theology (Vandenberg 1993).

Along with new ideas in positivist science and theology, there was also a questioning of the traditional view that children are 'mini-adults'. For instance, work from the Child Study movement (a precursor of modern developmental psychology) argues that the view that children are qualitatively different from adults reflects the thinking of Victorian philanthropic movements which emphasized the need to protect children – 'saving' them from the harsh and inappropriate world of adult life. This can be seen in the call for compulsory education that arose from Victorian campaigns in which children were 'positioned' as ignorant or lacking in basic knowledge. It was also apparent in the changing perceptions of children and young people engaged in criminal behaviour and how the state should respond to this. Garland (1990: 201) argues that the move to see children and young people as different from adults set up the distinction of 'adult' and 'juvenile' justice.

The philanthropic intentions of the 'child savers' also produced unexpected effects, particularly with regards to the new status of the 'child'. Rose (1990), for example, argues that compulsory education served to produce compliant citizens and workers, and was part of new techniques for controlling the growing urban masses. In addition, he argues that the new welfare practices aimed at child welfare served to reinforce children's dependency on their families, particularly their parents, and to promote parental responsibility for children. The tension between family and young person, evident in the Victorian child-saving movements, is still very much in evidence today, particularly in the practice of parenting orders.

3.   The construction of the child

The dominant view of childhood today arises from this historical and psychological context which emphasizes development as progression through time. Childhood is seen to be a time of innocence, due to cognitive immaturity, and a period of dependence on adults, again due to an immaturity that requires protection of the child by adults. This fosters a model of intervention that ignores the 'voices' of children and excludes them from the decision-making process because they lack the knowledge and maturity of adults (Mayall 2005). The implications of this are discussed below with reference to how we view 'normal' and 'abnormal' development; and how we operate from an adult-centred perspective.

Mapping 'normal' and 'abnormal' development

The concept of 'abnormal' development is crucially important to youth justice because it frames the way children are thought about – about what are considered to be appropriate interventions. Implicit within stage-based the-ories of development is the view of a 'normal' pathway or trajectory of development which sets up expectations about how *all* children *should* develop (Burman 1994, 2008). Fleer (2006) argues that we see children in an age-graded way and use these classifications of different stages to generate expectations about how children and young people should behave. Thus, expectations about what is 'normal' at different ages serve to regulate normality and determine the nature of the professional intervention. For example, if a two-year-old child hits another child it is assumed to be age appropriate, something they will grow out of. However, if a 12-year-old hits a younger child the behaviour is seen very differently (usually from a risk-based perspective) and responded to accordingly. The 'de-juvenilization' of youth justice work (Pitts 2001) and debates about the age of criminal responsibility are made sense of in terms of age-related abilities. However, while age-related capabilities are often easy to note in young people, it is important to examine the context within which young people live in order to make sense of their actions in a more nuanced and informed way.

A further implication of the dominant view of development (as a cumulative progression of skills through time) is that it is seen to be vitally important to get the foundations of children's development right. Work in prevention, and in identifying early signs of problematic behaviour, rests upon the assumption of a clear developmental trajectory. However, the links between early childhood problems and outcomes in later life are by no means understood or clearly proved for all children (O'Dell 2003). There are many ameliorating factors that can have a significant impact on how seriously a child is affected in the long term (protective factors include being believed, supportive adults, supportive schooling, the temperament of the child). This is not to argue that negative life experiences and trauma in childhood are not harmful but to recognize that there are many factors that need to be taken into account in a child's life rather than automatically assuming that they will struggle with the effects of early experiences for their whole lives.

The aim of much work with children and young people is to observe (what is assumed to be) 'normal' development and to rectify any 'abnormal' behaviours (Rose 1990; Mayall 2005). Children who do not fit within this 'normal' developmental trajectory are seen in ways that define them as problems (Mayall 2005; Burman 2008). For example, a common way of describing children whose lives do not accord with normative ideas about families and the context in which they grow up is often referred to as having experienced a 'broken' childhood and to have symbolically 'lost out' on their childhood. Children and young people who transgress from the characteristics assumed as 'normal' are therefore subject to interventions which invoke the dual agendas of 'welfare' and 'prevention', seeing young people as victim and/or a threat (Griffin 1993; Mayall 2005; Meyer 2007). Children or young people who are not passive and dependent, such as child workers or teenage parents, evoke strong reactions because their activities are deemed to be incongruent with their chronological stage, transgressing the assumed activities (and stages) of childhood. Therefore children and young people whose behaviour defies the bedrock assumptions of childhood development are seen, symbolically, as 'lost children', and subject to protection (if they are viewed as a victim of circumstances) or punished (if they are seen to represent a 'risk' – in terms of posing a 'danger' to the public through serious or persistent offending). The boundary between victimhood and culpability is a tricky one in which strong emotional reactions are elicited.

We have strong emotional reactions to images of children who are seen as victims of their circumstances. Emotional reactions to crimes committed both by young people and against young people elicit a much higher level of emotional response than crimes by, or against, adults. This is partly because of the way offences by and against children involve a disruption in the taken-for-granted assumptions about children. The child as victim elicits a strong emotional concern to protect, but equally strong is the desire to correct misbehaviour. Therefore claiming to speak for the best interests of a child, when the child is positioned as a 'victim', conveys a strong message which is difficult to challenge. However speaking for a child who is seen to have transgressed dominant assumptions about the characteristics and capabilities of childhood remains difficult and is likely to be subject to challenge. A way of doing so in youth justice work is evident in the dichotomous construction of young people as both the 'offender' and 'victim' of their own problematic life events. However the focus for understanding and explaining this is attributed to individual psychopathology and thus action is based on work to transform individual young people. As a consequence, the focus on wider structural inequalities of opportunity and provision, which constitute a significant factor in explaining problematic behaviours, tends to be left out of the equation.

The dominant view of development is of children and young people as 'becomings' – whose importance lies in the fact that they will one day *become* adults. In viewing development as a progression through time we assume that we grow out of childhood and of children's knowledge. Authors such as Mayall (2005) and Mason (2005) argue that childhood skills and knowledge are lost, made invisible and devalued as a result of this. Hence: 'The construction of children as passive dependents – as not adults and therefore lesser beings than adults – enables adults to discount and marginalize children's knowledge' (Mason 2005: 96).

Conclusion

In this chapter I have argued that, while it seems self-evident that children do grow up, the ways in which we understand this process are currently dependent on outmoded and unreflective theory. This has led us to see childhood in a way which simplifies development into a set of 'stages', assuming a largely universal progression through time. Much child protection and youth justice work draws on this dominant construction of children as immature, deficient in adult skills and, thus, in need of intervention. In so doing, it raises concerns that we view children and young people – who for many reasons have experiences outside this conceptual framework – in potentially unhelpful ways. Children and young people live in a complex relationship balancing security with the need to take risks in developing their skills in autonomy and self-agency. As discussed, this contradiction is echoed in the criminal justice system in the operation of the two agendas of 'prevention' and 'welfare', where children are deemed to be morally responsible for their offending yet where the sentences imposed also suggest reform and moral training via rehabilitation programmes.

Garland (1990) stresses the value of theory in helping us to reflect on practice. In accounting for how children and young people develop, a helpful way of understanding is to draw on the theoretical work of Vygotsky (1986) developed in the discipline of cultural psychology. Here children are seen to develop in accordance with local, culturally specific knowledge, norms and practices. The emphasis is placed upon the child's active role in shaping and developing cultural tools (knowledge and practice relevant to their lives) and not on formal stages of development. Children are seen to develop in partnership and in relationships with others, often older or more skilled peers or family members. From this perspective the role of those working with children and young people is to attend to the lived realities of the young person and to understand the context within which this takes place. Here the principle of responsivity – being engaged with the world of the young person – is essential to devising intervention packages (where appropriate) that seek to work alongside them, developing a meaningful conversation between the practitioner and the young person, recognizing the different priorities and concerns of both.

References

Burman, E. (1994) *Deconstructing Developmental Psychology*. London: Routledge.

Burman, E. (2008) *Deconstructing Developmental Psychology* (2nd edn). London: Routledge.

Fleer, M. (2006) 'The cultural construction of child development: creating institutional and cultural intersubjectivity', *International Journal of Early Years Education*, 14: 127–40.

Garland, D. (1990) *Punishment and Modern Society*. Oxford: Oxford University Press.

Griffin, C. (1993) *Representations of Youth*. Cambridge: Polity Press.

Mason, J. (2005) 'Child protection policy and the construction of childhood', in J. Mason and T. Fattore (eds) *Children Taken Seriously in Theory, Policy and Practice*. London: Jessica Kingsley.

Mayall, B. (2005) 'The social condition of UK childhoods: children's understandings and their implications', in J. Mason and T. Fattore (eds) *Children Taken Seriously in Theory, Policy and Practice*. London: Jessica Kingsley.

Meyer, A. (2007) 'The moral rhetoric of childhood', *Childhood*, 14: 85–104.

Morss, J.R. (1992) 'Making waves: deconstruction and developmental psychology', *Theory and Psychology*, 2: 445–65.

O'Dell, L. (2003) 'Distinctly different? Descriptions of the sexually abused and ''non abused'' child', *Educational and Child Psychology*, 20: 22–33 (special edition: critical approaches to child protection).

Pitts, J. (2001) 'The new correctionalism: young people, youth justice and New Labour', in R. Matthews and J. Pitts (eds) *Crime, Disorder and Community Safety: A New Agenda?* London: Routledge.

Rose, N. (1990) *Governing the Soul: The Shaping of the Private Life*. London: Routledge.

Vandenberg, B. (1993) 'Developmental psychology, God and the good', *Theory and Psychology*, 3: 191–205.

Vygotsky, L.S. (1986) *Thought and Language*. Cambridge, MA: MIT Press.

Walkerdine, V. (1993) 'Beyond developmentalism', *Theory and Psychology*, 3: 451–69.

4

Sex 'n' drugs 'n' rock 'n' roll: young people as consumers

Mary Jane Kehily

Introduction

'Pint of lager, a whisky and an "E" please' orders Lip as he beats a path to the bar after a little local difficulty in the domestic sphere. The young character in the Channel 4 series *Shameless* seeks solace in the pub where the bar staff supplement their income with a spot of in-house dealing. The routine drug use of working-class life, as represented in the television series, conjures up a scene in which alcohol and ecstasy can be ordered at the local as an everyday event of no great significance to the unfolding drama. On the Chatsworth Estate drink and drugs exist as an integral part of everyday life, illustrating in a beautifully excessive televisual performance the shock and humour generated by a sustained focus on the unrespectable poor. Narrating the opening sequence of the programme, central character Frank Gallagher chants: 'Make poverty history – free drink and drugs now.' Drugs and alcohol were, in his account, kindly invented to facilitate working-class life – to keep us all going and calm us all down. Drunk, high and father of nine, Frank is proud to announce that Chatsworth residents would 'come on yer face for the price of a pint'.

The consumption practices of young people have long been the focus of policy initiatives and moral panic. Sex, drugs and rock 'n' roll, in particular, have become symbolic markers of youthful excess. In the 'new times' of accelerated globalization and hyper-consumption, however, young people can also be seen as valuable and compliant consumers of products and services. Young people are surrounded by commercial products that are made and marketed especially for them. In western societies the notion of the 'teenager' as a distinct phase in the life-cycle has been coupled with the emergence of a 'youth market'. In economic terms, young people can be seen as an important and influential consumer group. With the rise in manufacturing industries and the mass production of goods in the post-World War Two period, youth have been looked upon in marketing terms as a specific group with a disposable income. The 'teenager' has evolved as part of a generational cohort with a distinct style expressed in the conspicuous consumption of music, clothes and leisure activities (Griffin 1993; Springhall 1998).

In the globalized economy youth can be seen as the exemplar of a market segment, sharing common patterns of consumption across the world. A diverse range of products aimed at young people, such as clothes, television, music, sports equipment/facilities, books, magazines, mobile phones, MP3 player and games, are now regarded as part of the staple fare of teenage life. The advent of new technology has increased the range of products available to young people, expanding upon the battery of accessories and paraphernalia that become entwined in the cultural landscape of young lives. Much of the controversy surrounding young people and consumption centres upon the ways in which young people are viewed and positioned: are they innocent victims of aggressive economic forces needing protection or agentic experimenters and risk-takers needing control? To develop an understanding of young people as consumers it is important to ask the question: which young people? Socioeconomic circumstances, location and access to resources all have a bearing on young lives and their relationship to consumption.

Understanding consumption

In *Keywords* (1976), Williams explains that earlier meanings of the terms 'consumer' and 'consumption' had negative associations with destruction and waste. From the fourteenth to the seventeenth centuries consumption meant to 'destroy, to use up, to waste, to exhaust' (1976: 69). Consumption took on an economic meaning with the growth of industrialization in western societies during the nineteenth century. In this period consumption came to be understood as the opposite of production – the end point in a process which involved turning raw materials into products to be marketed and sold. In the twentieth century this use of the term grew with the economic boom of the post-World War Two period that made mass-produced goods widely available.

Consumption is now commonly understood to mean the purchase and use of manufactured goods, though aspects of the earlier meanings still persist. Production and consumption can be seen as social processes that involve individuals in making, using and remaking the resources they have available to them.

More recently the use of the terms has been expanded to embrace cultural as well as material products. O'Sullivan *et al.* (1994) offer the following definition:

> The act or fact of using up the products or yield of any industry in support of any process. Production and consumption are terms borrowed from political economy, and they are now widely used to describe the parties

to and the transactions of communication. Thus meanings, media output, texts and so on are said to be produced and consumed. Media professionals are seen as industrial producers while audiences or readers are seen as the consumers of meaning. (1994: 244)

In this definition notions of production and consumption have been applied to the world of culture, cultural products and communication. O'Sullivan and his colleagues suggest that we are all consumers of meanings and messages that saturate our everyday cultural worlds.

Furthermore, as consumers of messages we also *create* and produce meanings by interpreting them in ways that make sense to us as individuals. Daniel Miller (1997) highlights the significance of consumption in the cultural sphere by pointing out that 'consumption can be a means of creating authentic culture' (1997: 19). Miller suggests that consumption may be more important than production or distribution as it is fundamentally a social activity, providing a site for developing social relations. Following this approach to consumption and culture, it is possible to suggest that the social relationships engaged in practices of consumption also make subject positions available to young people. From this perspective characterizations of youthful femininity in late modernity, such as 'ladette' and 'can-do' girl (Aapolo *et al.* 2005) are brought into being in the realm of the cultural, where identities can be delineated and played out through forms of consumption and lifestyle. The chapter works with this contemporary understanding of consumption as part of a cultural process involving subcultural activity, identity and the negotiation of agency.

Consuming values

Early work on consumer culture inspired by the Frankfurt School of sociology in the 1930s tended to cast the practices of consumption in a negative light. Studies from the 1950s and early 1960s point to the many ways in which consumption serves the interests of manufacturers through processes whereby individuals become passive victims of consumer capital. This approach is reflected in the title of an influential study, *The Hidden Persuaders* (Packard 1957). This study, like others of the time, presents the expansion of mass production as a *bad thing in itself*, creating commodities which lack authenticity and meet 'false' needs. From this Marxian-inflected perspective, consumer needs can be understood as generated by marketing and advertising agencies, which have ideological control over our lives. A common theme of such studies is the emphasis on the power of production and its ideological hold over the individual, placing consumers in a passive position as the manipulated dupes of omnipotent and highly persuasive commercial forces.

This tendency to cast consumerism as a destructive force is reworked by Bauman, who argues that consumer 'freedom' has become a major medium of social control in late capitalism. Suggesting that consumerism has replaced work as the main instrument of social cohesion, 'the hub around which the life-world rotates' (1988: 76), Bauman concludes that consumer culture offers individuals freedom and individuality at a high price. For Bauman, the power of the consumer market lies in its enduring appeal to those who are controlled by it. Offering individuals choice, pleasure and seemingly endless 'model identities', the consumer market provides 'a substitute for permanently frustrated power ambitions, as the sole recompense for oppression at work, the only outlet for freedom and autonomy' (1988: 73).

By contrast much other contemporary work on consumption tends to position consumers as agentic individuals able to exercise choice, commonly pointing to the ways in which practices of consumption involve the creative reworking of meanings, identities and practices. It is interesting to note that, in countries where consumption has been regulated and restricted, the ability to consume the products of modern western capitalism may be seen as a new-found 'freedom'. The demise of communism in eastern Europe, as Pilkington *et al.* (2002) point out, has been marked by the opening up of new markets for western goods in contexts where the ability to consume has been viewed simultaneously as a form of liberation and a cultural imposition.

An early study of practices of consumption (Veblen 1899 [1970]) explored the world of the nouveau riche in late-nineteenth century America. Veblen's analysis suggests that this group bought products to impress others and were more concerned with issues of taste, display and status than with function or use value. Ideas of taste have been further explored in more recent work by Bourdieu (1984), who suggests that identities are produced through practices of 'distinction'. Bourdieu argues that culture is concerned with the processes of identification and differentiation that allow individuals to distinguish themselves from others. Through the practices of consumption individuals and groups exercise cultural capital, express taste and articulate a sense of identity. Such practices point to the potential for consumption to become a 'moral project' (Miller 1997: 47), a vehicle for the expression of priorities, judgement and choice. Bourdieu uses the concept of 'habitus' to capture a sense of the cultural environment that is structured in terms of taste and distinction, learnt in childhood and applied in later life.

The legacy of the Frankfurt School lives on in much contemporary commentary on young people and consumption. The consumption practices of children and young people can become the locus of attention in concerns about juvenile crime, anti-social behaviour and obesity. Young people's use of new technologies has been associated with seemingly new forms of bullying, violence and harassment known as 'happy slapping'. The rise in childhood and adolescent obesity is commonly discussed as the over-indulgence of a TV and fast-food generation. We may also recall that 'video nasties' were implicated in the murder of James Bulger. In popular discourse a recurrent motif suggests that young people's relationship to consumption is broadly regarded as 'toxic' (Palmer 2006), a lethal cocktail that damages children and young people and throws the whole ideal of childhood into crisis. Palmer's (2006) 'toxic childhood' thesis postulates that young people have come to associate happiness with the stuff of consumer culture and the desirous nature of consumption patterns: wanting things, buying things, having things bought for you have acquired misplaced prominence in children's lives, distorting notions of what happiness really is and how it can be achieved. Within these popular discourses parents are positioned as the besieged victims of 'pester power', reluctantly conceding to the demands of their avaricious offspring. A brief look at young people as consumers in relation to sex and drugs and rock and roll, however, refutes the idea of a golden age of innocence by pointing to the lived realities of young people's experience as a diverse quest for pleasure, sociability, protest and self definition.

Sex 'n'. . .

Young people and sex is a powerful combination for comment, concern and intervention. The sexual activity of young people functions symbolically as an incendiary device for moral panics and policy initiatives, providing 'proof' of young people's profligacy and the decline of moral order. In the UK and the USA, teenage pregnancy in particular is regarded as a social problem. The Social Exclusion Unit's report on teenage pregnancy in England (Social Exclusion Unit 1999) was followed by the setting up of the Teenage Pregnancy Unit, a cross-government initiative to reduce the under-18 conception rate by half by 2010. Among the range of strategies to reduce teenage pregnancy, the unit was established to provide support for young mothers, as well as offering sex and relationship education, easy access to contraception and life skills designed to delay early sexual activity. These interventions seek to address policy concerns regarding the long-term pattern of 'intergenerational transmission' that sees early motherhood repeated in subsequent generations.

However, the 'problem' of teenage pregnancy needs to be placed within the experience of first-time motherhood more generally. The trend in the UK and most western countries is towards later motherhood for the majority of women and early motherhood for a minority. Large-scale surveys, such as the Millennium Cohort Study in the UK, indicate that the age at which women become mothers reflects their socioeconomic status. Typically, women with higher education qualifications and professional careers delay the birth of their first child until their late 30s or early 40s, while for other women, motherhood comes early, in the mid-teenage years before education has been completed or a place in the labour market achieved (see Chapter 2). Placed in this context, teenage mothers appear *out of place* and, from certain perspectives, can be viewed as aberrant, deviant and excessive.

Skeggs (2004) analysis of social class and culture in contemporary Britain points to the enduring status of working-class women as embodying an overly abundant and unruly sexuality that places them dangerously close to the

45

reviled figure of the prostitute. In the past, Skeggs suggests, working-class femininity was redeemable through respectability. In the contemporary period, however, young working-class mothers inevitably fall on the other side of the respectability divide and 'are yet again becoming the abject of the nation' (2004: 23). As Walkerdine *et al.* (2001) point out, teenage pregnancy is largely a working-class affair. Of the 20,000 under 18-year-olds who become mothers every year, the majority are likely to be working class and disaffected from school. For middle-class girls, however, pregnancy is usually regarded as a disruption to the educative process and a barrier to educational success. Indeed, the goal of a professional career 'acts as a contraceptive for middle-class girls' (Walkerdine *et al.* 2001: 194).

Drugs 'n' . . .

Deliciously inspirational studies of the past, such as those of Howard Becker, Jock Young and the work of writers at the Centre for Contemporary Cultural Studies (CCCS), offer a historical trajectory that draws out the links between the past and present. Crucially, this body of work encourages us to reflect upon some key themes running through the literature. In contrast to bio-medical and pharmacological approaches, the pleasures of drug consumption are socially learnt. Drug cultures can function as 'emotional communities', especially as traditional sources of social integration, such as work and career, may be in decline. The language, symbolism and culture of drug consumption remain important to understanding drug use as a cultural practice that may or may not constitute a form of resistance. The contemporary world presents itself as immediately more complex, calling for a re-evaluation of previous studies and theoretical approaches. Processes of globalization and the changed sphere of leisure give the consumption of drugs increased visibility in late modernity.

Contemporary studies, such as Shiner and Newburn (1997) and Parker *et al.* (1998), present contrasting views of drug use as a normal everyday activity. While Parker *et al.* draw largely upon surveys to suggest that soft drug use and awareness of soft drugs are commonplace in contemporary times, Shiner and Newburn's empirical analysis questions the salience of this claim as overly general, not sufficiently attuned to the diverse views of young people and unsupported by statistical evidence. Significantly, the normalization thesis captures an *attitude* that invokes the omnipresence of drugs in everyday life – a view that can be seen in conversational terms as a dialogue with popular culture, redolent of portrayals in music, television and news media. An important feature of this seemingly new awareness of drugs as integral to everyday life is the claim to 'moral accommodation', a societal ease with the mundane presence of drugs in ways that eschew judgement, pathology or vilification. A more nuanced reading of the normalization thesis suggests that while drug use may be commonplace, the fault-lines of acceptability may be dependent upon what people do and what drugs are involved. A moral consensus, far from being judgement-free, points to the presence of a set of binaries that define the acceptable from the unacceptable: soft drugs/hard drugs; using/dealing; children/adults. While moral censure is delineated in different ways, it is commonly socially excluded drug users with criminal careers who receive negative attention.

Rock 'n' roll

In an influential collection of studies, *Resistance through Rituals: Youth Subcultures in Postwar Britain*, Hall and Jefferson (1976) trace an interest in youth subcultures as expressive forms of resistance that make connections between everyday experience, social class, culture and the wider society. Music can be regarded as central to young people's experience of and participation in youth subcultures. Engaging in subcultural activity involves young people in acts of 'articulation' – the bringing together of different elements to make sense of and speak to collective concerns. Hall and Jefferson suggest that working-class youth subcultures involve young people in a 'double articulation': first, dialoguing with their parents culture and, secondly, the broader culture of postwar social change. To view youth subcultures as adolescent rebellion is to underestimate the extent to which young people seek to speak to and comment upon generational change and social structures. Rather, from a cultural studies perspective, youth subcultures appear purposeful interventions, imbued with meaning. The productivity of subcultural formations may challenge youth justice perspectives, but an engagement with this idea may also be insightful and rewarding.

The increased commodification and commercialization of all areas of social life appears to have closed down the possibility of subcultural space for young people. Besides, the notion of a 'dominant culture' is also changing and fragmenting, creating multiple *cultures* rather than the mainstream and the subcultural. Steve Redhead's (1997) study asserted that subcultures have been replaced by 'clubcultures'. Redhead's analysis signals the impact of globalization on youth culture. Redhead defines clubcultures as global and fluid youth formations that are based upon the media and the niche marketing of dance music as a youth-culture-for-all. Redhead refers to clubbing as 'hedonism in hard times' (1997) – suggesting that it is both an escape from and a riposte to political realities.

Sarah Thornton (1995) provides a complementary approach to Redhead's in her study of club cultures. Thornton suggests that through engagement with different styles of dance music, young people define themselves in relation to their peers. Drawing upon the work of Bourdieu (1984), Thornton develops the idea of 'sub-cultural capital' to analyse the forms of taste and distinction that characterize the club scene.

Further studies have critiqued the concept of subculture and tried to find other terms to express young people's relationship to music, self-activity and self-expression. Contenders for the newly reconfigured subcultural crown include 'scenes', 'tribes' and 'neo-tribes'. 'Scenes' is a term used widely in studies of popular music to explore musical collectivities. 'Tribes' and 'neo-tribes' draw upon the work of Maffesoli (1995) to describe loose groups of young people whose stylized tastes and lifestyles come together during moments of shared interest. The consumption patterns of young people provide an insight into a diverse set of practices, constantly subject to change and redefinition.

Conclusion

This chapter has considered young people as consumers and discussed some of the ways in which their consumption practices have been treated and represented. While much youthful consumption can be regarded as benign expressions of a generational cohort, the consumption of sex, drugs and rock 'n' roll creates moments of adult anxiety within a historical trajectory that currently surfaces as 'toxic'. Studies of consumption point to the enduring struggle for meaning within this field: exploitation, agency and the exercise of taste, judgement and morality form a potent and contested mixture in the evaluation of what consumption practices *mean*. For young women engagement in sex and early pregnancy is viewed as a 'problem' requiring policy intervention. The ubiquity of drug use in some communities is also cast as a 'problem', particularly when it leads to social exclusion and criminal careers. Music, a key feature of youth subcultures, may be less regulated than sex or drugs. However, concern over, for example, rave culture and the lyrics of rap music indicates that this realm of consumption is not free from surveillance or potential intervention. Finally, the class-based character of adult concerns should be noted. Within the domain of youth and consumption, socio-economic status plays a part in constructing young people as in need of regulation and control.

References

Aapolo, S., Gonick, M. and Harris, A. (2005) *Young Femininity: Girlhood, Power and Social Change*. Basingstoke: Palgrave.

Bauman, Z. (1988) *Freedom*. Milton Keynes: Open University Press.

Bourdieu, P. (1984) *Distinction: A Social Critique of the Judgement of Taste*. Cambridge, MA: Harvard University Press.

Griffin, C. (1993) *Representations of Youth: The Study of Youth and Adolescence in Britain and America*. Cambridge: Polity Press.

Hall, S. and Jefferson, T. (1976) *Resistance through Rituals: Youth Subcultures in Postwar Britain*. London: Hutchinson.

Maffesoli, M. (1995) *The Time of the Tribes: The Decline of Individualism in Mass Society*. London: Sage.

Miller, D. (1997) 'Consumption and its consequences', in H. MacKay (ed.) *Consumption and Everyday Life*. London: Sage/The Open University.

O'Sullivan, T., Hartley, J., Saunders, D., Montgomery, M. and Fiske, J. (1994) *Key Concepts in Communications and Cultural Studies*. London: Routledge.

Packard, V. (1957 [1970]) *The Hidden Persuaders*. Harmondsworth: Penguin.

Palmer, S. (2006) *Toxic Childhood: How the Modern World is Damaging our Children and What We Can Do About It*. London: Orion.

Parker, H., Williams, L. and Aldridge, J. (1998) *Illegal Leisure: The Normalisation of Adolescent Recreational Drug Use*. London: Routledge.

Pilkington, H., Omel'chenko, E., Flynn, M., Blivdina, V. and Starkova, E. (2002) *Looking West: Cultural Globalization and Russian Youth*. University Park, PA: Pennsylvania State University Press.

Redhead, S. (1997) *Subcultures to Clubcultures*. Oxford: Blackwell.

Shiner, M. and Newburn, T. (1997) 'Definitely, maybe not? The normalisation of recreational drug use among young people', *Sociology*, 31: 511–29.

Skeggs, B. (2004) *Class, Self, Culture*. London: Routledge.

Social Exclusion Unit (1999) *Teenage Pregnancy*. London: HMSO.

Springhall, J. (1998) *Youth, Popular Culture and Moral Panics, Penny Gaffs to Gangsta-rap, 1830–1996*. Basingstoke: Macmillan.

Thornton, S. (1995) *Club Cultures: Music, Media and Subcultural Capital*. Cambridge: Polity Press.

Veblen, T. (1970 [1899]) *The Theory of the Leisure Class: An Economic Study of Institutions*. London: Allen & Unwin.

Walkerdine, V., Lucey, H. and Melody, J. (2001) *Growing up Girl: Psychosocial Explorations of Gender and Class*. Basingstoke: Palgrave.

William, R. (1976) *Keywords*. London: Fontana.

5

Bullying as abuse

Carrie-Anne Myers

Introduction

While narratives describing youths as a threat or as a problem to society are familiar in academic and popular publications, insufficient attention has been paid by either the policy community or the public to the experience of childhood and youth as a period of potential victimization at the hands of both adults and other young people. As a whole, adolescent victimization is: 'an area of victimization that is remarkably ill-served by the official statistics' (Anderson *et al.* 1994: 9). Encouragingly, there has been a growing body of work on children as victims (Feyerham and Hindelang 1974; Finkelhor 1979; Morgan 1988; Garofalo 1989; Best 1990; Morgan and Zedner 1992; Walker 1992; Abrahams 1994; Anderson *et al.* 1994), but its focus has primarily been on issues of child abuse, incest and the victimization of children in domestic and institutional settings. This chapter considers the victimization of young people within the context of bullying. It gives practitioners the opportunity to consider the wealth of literature on the topic and some of the practical tools that have been developed in the context of the education system to help them deal with the issue in practice within the youth justice system.

Defining child mistreatment, neglect or abuse is highly problematical (Corby 2000) and can lead to a number of definitions and understandings as to what it actually constitutes. As Corby argues:

> There is much debate over the merits and demerits of broad and narrow definitions. Professionals in the child protection field tend to adopt narrow 'operational' definitions relating particularly to minimal levels of parental care acceptable to society. Their concerns are focussed largely on physical abuse, neglect and sexual and emotional abuse within the family and in substitute care. Many academics take a broader view – they emphasize the quality of life that children and young people should be entitled to and locate the responsibility for enabling them to achieve this firmly within governments and social institutions. (2004: 207)

Such observations are interesting as they reflect the similar contrast within youth justice, where there is a tension between the individual treatment of the offender and the wider concern to address the environmental and structural factors and the needs of the community. Without question some children in familial and institutional settings are subject to horrifying levels of abuse, such as the cases of Victoria Climbié (2000) and Baby Peter (2008). While this mistreatment and neglect does, all too often, occur, it is legally prohibited and our society has numerous statutory procedures and cultural mores intended to identify, prevent and prohibit such behaviours. Although imperfect, these legal and social structures do exist to protect vulnerable children.

Nevertheless, despite this awareness, children do still experience a form of mistreatment and abuse, often publicly, with little exercise of censure or control. The adolescent as a victim has tended to be an overlooked concept, and becoming a victim at the hands of peers has been almost ignored, notably within the context of the youth justice system. This abuse can be physically and psychologically damaging with effects lasting into adulthood, yet it is normalized and minimized as part of the day-to-day experiences of childhood through the use of the, often dismissive, term bullying. This neglected but widespread form of mistreatment is the focus of this chapter and will help practitioners and others working with young people to consider the nor-malized, accepted levels of violence and mistreatment that occur on a daily basis among this age group.

Bullying

Bullying is a form of mistreatment and abuse that occurs predominantly in schools. What distinguishes it from 'common sense' views and ideas of mistreatment and abuse towards children and young people is its intra-group nature – that is to say, it is peer-on-peer victimization, the young people are the bullies, the victims and the perpetrators. Adults are often absent from this form of abuse: absent as perpetrators and as protectors.

Bullying is a ubiquitous but ambivalent term. It is used in everyday language in a variety of ways, each of which encompasses different events and involves different meanings. It can be seen as an 'umbrella' description for a range of quite disparate verbal, psychological, physical and violent interac-tions. Bullying research was pioneered by Olweus (1993). His definition is generally accepted to identify what actually constitutes bullying in an educational setting:

A student is being bullied or victimized when he or she is exposed, repeatedly and over time, to negative actions on the part of one or more other students. Also implied in bullying is an imbalance in strength (an asymmetric power relationship): the student who is exposed to the negative actions has difficulty defending him/herself and is somewhat helpless against the student or students who harass. In judging the seriousness of a particular sign, one must also consider the *frequency* with which the sign occurs. For example, many students are teased by peers occasionally, but, as a rule, it is only when it occurs relatively often (and in a nasty way) that it needs to be taken seriously. (1993: 54)

Subsequent studies have replicated versions of the bullying questionnaire Olweus designed to measure its extent within schools. This demonstrates its day-to-day, routine existence: 'schools are aggressive places, where bullying occurs much more frequently than teachers even think happen. Every piece of research demonstrates that teachers underestimate the amount of bullying when compared with the response of the pupils in the school' (Tattum and Herbert 1997: 47).

Studies in the UK have consistently found that a substantial number of primary and secondary-school children are the victims of bullying. The first large-scale survey of bullying in English schools by Whitney and Smith (1993) involved over 6,700 primary and secondary-school pupils, and it confirmed that bullying was extensive. Although levels of bullying varied from school to school, they did not find any primary schools where less than 19 per cent of the population reported having been bullied at some time during the term, with name-calling, being physically hit and being threatened as the most common types of direct bullying, and being isolated, being left out of groups and having rumours spread as the most common types of indirect bullying. Although some of these behaviours and experiences are minor in comparison with the extreme physical assaults on children such as Victoria Climbié, their impact on the well being of the young victim can be extreme, while the sheer numbers of children affected make the phenomenon shocking and important. Again, around one quarter of primary-school pupils in Whitney and Smith's study reported being bullied – this is a huge proportion of pupils experiencing abuse, a proportion that would not be tolerated in the adult population.

Further UK surveys confirm similar rates of persistent bullying to those of the Sheffield study. Glover *et al.* (2000), in a survey of 4,700 pupils in 25 secondary schools, found that *75 per cent* of pupils reported that they had been bullied 'sometimes', while more severe and repeated bullying was reported by approximately seven per cent of pupils. Through surveys and interviews carried out in 1996, 1998 and 2000 with over 7,000 respondents aged between 13 and 18 years, Katz *et al.* (2001) found that more than half of all respondents had been bullied at some time, with over ten per cent reporting that they had been bullied severely.

We have seen that bullying is pervasive in primary and secondary schools with anywhere between 25 and 75 per cent of students experiencing bullying and around 10 per cent of students being 'severely' bullied. It is worth considering at this point what we mean by 'severe' bullying. These are not childhood games that have gone too far; these are calculated and purposeful behaviours which, in the adult world, would constitute serious criminal offences. In Myers (2004) we see examples of severe bullying which would constitute criminal behaviour if they were perceived as 'offences' rather than 'bullying'. Brian, a 15-year-old pupil, describes his experiences and, in doing so, illustrates the serious physical and emotional harm that can arise from bullying:

> It was all the time really, just like it was in school, then it went out of school as well, it was just everywhere and then it like came to the house as well like vandalism. It was quite scary actually. You could actually see it escalating all the time and I was thinking, 'when's it ever going to stop?' And it actually got to the point where I was considering suicide, and all sorts of things, it was pretty bad. (2004: 138)

Simon (11 years old) provides another example of the extremes of victimization that bullying can involve. Significantly, he came to the interview with his hand in plaster and a sling. At the outset he informed me that he had fallen off of his skateboard and broken a few fingers. After an interview that lasted for approximately two hours, and once my tape recorder had been switched off, it emerged that his bully had caused his injury, by deliberately riding his skateboard over Simon's hand.

Previous research has documented the direct/indirect nature of school bullying, with boys opting for more direct and physical methods and girls more indirect (Bjorkvist *et al.* 1992; Ahmad and Smith 1994). As direct bullying is 'easier' and more 'obvious' to spot, it has been argued that it is a possibility that girls' bullying has been underestimated in the past (Smith and Sharp 1994a, 1994b).

More recently, Burman *et al.* (2002) considered patterns of violence among Scottish girls aged between 13 and 16 years. Only five per cent described themselves as being violent and the overall finding was that girls are slow to use physical violence. Instead, the researchers found that verbal abuse and intimidation to and from other girls and boys were everyday occurrences for girls and that girls reported that they often witnessed physical violence. Half the girls described the ability to 'stick up' for oneself in both physically violent and verbally abusive situations as extremely important. Many girls reported that they were able to recognize potentially violent situations and would take steps to avoid confrontation. The most prolific form of bullying that Myers (2006) found was performed by young people in mixed-sex groups, which would more often than not involve the public humiliation of victims. While girls tend towards indirect and non-violent bullying, the evidence shows that gender differences in acts of bullying are not clear cut and that both boys and girls are involved in its occurrence as perpetrators, victims and bystanders.

That children are aware of and anxious about their chances of being bullied is evidenced in research. Tattum and Herbert (1997) demonstrated how victimization is one of the most common worries of children transferring from primary to secondary schools. Despite the prevalence of bullying in our schools, and despite the seriousness of some acts of bullying, only about half the young people interviewed by Katz *et al.* (2001) said that they believed their school's anti-bullying policy was 'working'. This lack of faith in institutional and adult responses to bullying is deeply worrying. All professionals working with children and young people are charged with safeguarding their care, yet it seems that bullying and violence have become established problems within the education system of England and Wales.

The school as an institution and the problem of exclusion

As adults, if we experience mistreatment and abuse we are more or less able to seek recourse or, if that fails, to remove ourselves from the abusive situation. However, there are exceptions to this ability, such as instances of domestic violence and elder abuse. Children are compelled by law to attend school which, as we have seen, can be a site of abuse in the form of bullying, in which many young people feel that adults do little or nothing to protect them:

> One often forgotten, though central, feature of schooling is that it is *compulsory*. While discussions of the development of compulsory education since 1870 are frequently couched in liberal and democratic arguments to do with the beneficial effects of the dissemination of literacy and knowledge, we should not forget that educational institutions also contain a real substratum of coercion. Today, although schooling generally operates with the consent of the pupils, if that consent is withdrawn, school can be experienced as a much more coercive and total institution. (Muncie 1984: 135)

Clearly the compulsory nature of school means it is hard for bullied children to escape the abusive situation without resorting to truancy – which often attracts discipline and punishment and makes the young person vulnerable to exclusion.

Research has illustrated the important role of the school in socializing young people for later life (Graham and Bowling 1995; Goldblatt and Lewis 1998), and a clear link has been established between school violence and offending behaviour (Devlin 1997). Indeed, according to Graham (1988), children's experiences at school are second only to the influence of the family on pupils' propensity to offend. Overall, research indicates that factors such as low academic achievement, poor school attendance and difficult behaviour in school are associated with anti-social and criminal behaviour in young people (Flood-Page *et al.* 2000). This association between school lack of achievement and offending has been demonstrated consistently in longitudinal studies

(Farrington and Loeber 1999) and cross-sectional local research (Haines *et al.* 2001). The school often responds to these incidences by excluding pupils.

Children who are most vulnerable to exclusion are likely to live in districts or in circumstances of disadvantage. As Britton *et al.* (2002) indicate, young people most at risk may be missed or ignored by official agencies. Exclusion serves to enhance that risk. The social correlates and consequences of exclusion are a matter of considerable concern, as school exclusion and truancy are increasingly being linked to adolescent drug use and youth offending in the UK (Haines and Case 2003). It must be pointed out that a number of *victims* will often play truant to remove themselves from a negative school experience and, in very extreme cases, will be taken out of the school or moved for their own protection to stop levels of bullying that may be occurring against them. This will increase the chance of exclusion. Thus the victims are punished for their victimization.

Haines and Case (2003) found that traditional approaches to the reduction of exclusion tend to be conducted in isolation, with schools and LEAs acting independently, without a necessary framework binding services together in a coherent manner. In addition, most school reform efforts have fallen short because they have neglected to take the time or risk to try to change the foundation of the school and its culture (Piperato and Roy 2002). Therefore, for those who are working with children and young people the 'problem' behaviour which is highlighted as a consequence of bullying may not be as clear cut as thought. It may well be the case that the 'excluded persistent truant' was actually a victim within the education system.

Policy responses to tackle bullying

Clearly these are important issues and it would be a misrepresentation to say there has been no policy response. School bullying and violence have been high on the government's agenda since the Department for Education and Skills (2000) launched its nationwide anti-bullying strategy, *Bullying: Don't Suffer in Silence*. Subsequently, a number of interventions have been introduced as part of schools' pastoral care systems to combat bullying, and finding effective ways of intervening is crucially important (Salmivalli 2001). Such initiatives have been largely in response to the United Nations Convention on the Rights of the Child (1990), the Children Act 2004 – which saw the production of *Every Child Matters* (2004) – and the updated *Youth Matters* (DfES 2005). These policies are designed to take full account of the views of young people, and every school in England and Wales must have an anti-bullying policy. Current statutory guidance can be found at the Department for Children, Schools and Families' website (http://www.dcsf.gov.uk).

As a result of the ongoing research and the subsequent government response, there have been a number of interventions introduced into schools to tackle bullying. These are predominantly whole-school approaches to improve the school environment and surrounding community (Cowie *et al.* 2008). They all follow a similar rhetoric of restorative justice and are based on restorative practice. The aim is to remain inclusive and to make the pupils themselves responsible for the consequences of peer-group actions on the ethos of the school learning environment. For the purpose of this chapter peer-support schemes are used as an example. Peer support takes a number of forms including befriending, mediation/conflict resolution and counselling-based approaches. Peer supporters are usually volunteers, often self-nominated, and members of the peer group play a part in their selection (Cowie and Wallace 2000).

Through the use of basic listening skills, empathy for the other's point of view, a problem-solving approach to interpersonal difficulties and a willing-ness to take a supportive role, peer support and mediation schemes facilitate positive peer relations (Cremin 2002, 2004). Where programmes have been evaluated, the responses are usually positive and are reported to result in a substantial decrease in the incidence of problem behaviours in the schools (Cowie 1998; Naylor and Cowie 1999; Cowie *et al.* 2002).

Naylor *et al.* (2001) found that pupils were more likely to tell someone that they were being bullied in schools where there was a well established system of peer support in place. Overall, peer-support schemes have become increasingly widespread and are strongly supported by practitioners (for example, see CHIPS – http://www.nspcc.org.uk/Inform/resourcesfor teachers/CHIPS/chips_wda55379.html). Peer support encourages a sense of social responsibility; it unites the bullies, victims and the bystanders in the same space and focuses them on a common goal of creating a positive school environment for all; and it provides opportunities for young people to be active, responsible citizens and to support their peers (Cowie and Hutson 2005).

However, in some contexts peer support is not effective – see, for example, the study by Cowie and Olafsson (2001) on the failure of a peer-support system in a very aggressive inner-city school. This was also documented by Hewitt *et al.* (2002) who examined levels of criminal violence in the community and compared it with the level of violence in six inner-city schools. They found that a key factor was the relationship between the school and its social setting. Those schools that demonstrated the greatest violence resilience were those that emphasized the value of fostering good relationships within the school, and between the school and the community. They also noted that, while racism and sexism were addressed by schools to some extent, homophobic behaviour was scarcely addressed at all. Homophobic name-calling was endemic in all the schools in the study. None the less, research continues to question the effectiveness of these anti-bullying policies and consistently records its regular, daily occurrence. Furthermore, 'new' forms of bullying are emerging which will briefly be considered.

Cyberbullying

Cyberbullying is a form of covert psychological bullying conveyed through electronic media, such as mobile phones, web-logs and websites, and online chatrooms. This development is particularly pernicious since bullies can remain anonymous by hiding behind screen names and can quickly reach a wide audience of peers. Notably, the victim of cyberbullying can be reached at home and at all hours of the day or night. The 'Anti-bullying' week 19–23 November 2007, amid a fanfare of national media attention, identified 'cyberbullying' as a particular cause for concern.

British academic interest in cyberbullying originated in 2001 (Smith *et al.* 2008) as the use of electronic devices by young people increased (Slonje and Smith 2008), providing 'a new arsenal of weapons for violence in schools' (Shariff 2005). Despite this interest, academic research into the phenomenon is still in its early stages. Cyberbullying is a rapidly expanding form of often normalized mistreatment and abuse that our young people are being confronted with on a daily basis. Coupled with the ever-present existence of bullying, it would appear to be the case that this is a problem which is far from being cured.

Conclusions

Clearly bullying is a widespread phenomenon which can affect a large number of children and young people. There are policies which are rolled out at the government level to tackle school bullying but, as we have seen, these are not always effective and it has to be remembered that a large number of young people are not in the conventional education system. There is a movement towards adopting more mediating and restorative approaches to resolving bullying in schools. However, the community, the youth justice system and the school would benefit from sharing best practice between them.

A school is not an isolated place; rather, it is located in a community. The level and type of normalized violence in a school, namely bullying, will interact with the level and type of normalized violence in that community. The solutions to school violence must include solutions to juvenile violence in the community in which the school is located (Redding and Shalf 2001). As we have seen, there are a number of links and relationships which overlap and which must be considered. What is clearly emerging is a two-way relationship that requires action in partnership rather than as stand-alone agencies. Furthermore, there must exist a willingness to create opportunities for young people and the adults who work with them to connect with one another rather than closing down avenues of communication through the lack of understanding which can often result from professional affiliations.

References

Abrahams, C. (1994) *The Hidden Victims: Children and Domestic Violence*. London: National Childrens Home.

Ahmad, Y. and Smith, P.K. (1994) 'Bullying in schools and the issue of sex differences', in J. Archer (ed.) *Male Violence*. London: Routledge

Anderson, S., Kinsey, R., Loader, I. and Smith, C. (1994) *Cautionary Tales: Young People, Crime and Policing in Edinburgh*. Avebury: Ashgate.

Best, J. (1990) *Threatened Children: Rhetoric and Concern about Child Victims*. Chicago, IL: University of Chicago Press.

Bjorkvist, K., Lagerspetz, K.M.J. and Kaukainen, A. (1992) 'Do girls manipulate and boys fight? Developmental trends in regard to direct and indirect aggression', *Aggressive Behaviour*, 18: 117–27.

Britton, L., Chatrik, B., Coles, B., Craig, G., Hylton, C. and Mumtaz, S. (2002) *Missing Connexions: The Career Dynamics and Welfare Needs of Black and Minority Ethnic Young People at the Margins*. London: Policy Press.

Burman, M.J., Brown, J.A., Tisdall, K. and Batchelor, S.A. (2002) *A View from the Girls: Exploring Violence and Violent Behaviour. Violence Research Programme Research Findings*. Swindon: Economic and Research Council.

Corby, B. (2000) *Child Abuse: Towards a Knowledge Base* (2nd edn). Buckingham: Open University Press.

Corby, B. (2004) 'The mistreatment of young people', in J. Roche *et al.* (eds) *Youth in Society* (2nd edn). London: Sage.

Cowie, H. (1998) 'Perspectives of teachers and pupils on the experience of peer support against bullying', *Educational Research and Evaluation*, 4: 108–25.

Cowie, H. and Hutson, N. (2005) 'Peer support: a strategy to help bystanders challenge school bullying', *Pastoral Care in Education*, 23: 40–4.

Cowie, H., Myers, C.A., Hutson, N. and Jennifer, D. (2008) 'Taking stock of school violence: risk, responsibility and regulation', *Education and Urban Society*, 40: 494–505.

Cowie, H., Naylor, P., Talamelli, L., Chauhan, P. and Smith, P.K. (2002) 'Knowledge, use of and attitudes towards peer support', *Journal of Adolescence*, 25: 453–67.

Cowie, H. and Olafsson, R. (2001) 'The role of peer support in helping the victims of bullying in a school with high levels of aggression', *School Psychology International*, 21: 79–95.

Cowie, H. and Wallace, P. (2000) *Peer Support in Action*. London: Sage.

Cremin, H. (2002) 'Circle time: why it doesn't always work', *Journal of the National Primary Trust*, Spring: 23–9.

Cremin, H. (2004) 'Missing the point of the circle', *Emotional Literacy Update*, September.

Devlin, A. (1997) 'Offenders at school: links between school failure and aggressive behaviour', in D. Tattum and G. Herbert (eds) *Bullying: Home, School and Community*. London: David Fulton.

DfES (2002) *Bullying: Don't Suffer in Silence* (2nd edn). London: HMSO.

Farrington, D.P. and Loeber, R. (1999) 'Risk factors for delinquency over time and place', *Youth Update*, 17: 4–5.

Feyerham, W.H. and Hindelang, M.J. (1974) 'On the victimization of juveniles: some preliminary results', *Journal of Research in Crime and Delinquency*, 11: 40–50.

Finkelhor, D. (1979) *Sexually Victimized Children*. New York, NY: Free Press.

Flood-Page, C., Campbell, S., Harrington, V. and Miller, J. (2000) *Youth Crime: Findings from the 1998/99 Youth Lifestyles Survey*. London: Home Office.

Garofalo, J. (1989) 'Victimization and the fear of crime', *Journal of Research in Crime and Delinquency*, 16: 80–97.

Glover, D., Gough, G., Johnson, M. and Cartwright, N. (2000) 'Bullying in 25 secondary schools: incidence, impact and intervention', *Educational Research*, 42: 141–56.

Goldblatt, P. and Lewis, C. (1998) *Reducing Offending: An Assessment of Research Evidence on Ways of Dealing with Offending Behaviour*. London: Home Office.

Graham, J. (1988) *Schools, Disruptive Behaviour and Delinquency: A Review of Research. Home Office Research Study* 96. London: HMSO.

Graham, J. and Bowling, B. (1995) *Young People and Crime*. London: Home Office.

Haines, K. and Case, S. (2003) 'Promoting positive behaviour in schools: the Youth Social Audit', *Youth Justice*, 3: 86–101.

Haines, K., Jones, R. and Isles, E. (2001) 'The causes and correlates of school exclusion: can targeted social provision prevent school breakdown?', in *Promoting Positive Behaviour in Schools. Spotlight* 58. Cardiff: Wales Office for Research and Development.

Hewitt, R., Epstein, D., Leonard, D., Mauthner, M. and Watkins, C. (2002) *The Violence-resilient School: A Comparative Study of Schools and their Environments*. ESRC Violence Research Programme, Research Findings (available online at http://www1.rhbnc.ac.uk/sociopolitical-science/vrp/Findings/rfhewitt.PDF).

Katz, A., Buchanan, A. and Bream, V. (2001) *Bullying in Britain: Testimonies from Teenagers*. London: Young Voice.

Morgan, J. (1988) 'Children as victims', in M. Maguire and J. Pointing (eds) *Victims of Crime: A New Deal*. Milton Keynes: Open University Press.

Morgan, J. and Zedner, L. (1992) *Child Victims: Crime, Impact and Criminal Justice*. Oxford: Clarendon Press.

Muncie, J. (1984) *The Trouble with Kids Today: Youth and Crime in Post-war Britain*. London: Hutchinson.

Myers, C.A. (2004) 'A qualitative analysis of the social regulation of violence in a Cornish school, 1999–2003.' Unpublished thesis, London School of Economics and Political Science.

Myers, C.A. (2006) 'Schoolbags at dawn: the role of gender in incidents of school violence', in F. Heidensohn (ed.) *Gender and Justice: New Perspectives*. Cullompton: Willan Publishing.

Naylor, P. and Cowie, H. (1999) 'The effectiveness of peer support systems in challenging school bullying: the perspectives and experiences of teachers and pupils', *Journal of Adolescence*, 22: 467–79.

Naylor, P., Cowie, H. and del Rey, R. (2001) 'Reported coping strategies of some UK secondary school girls and boys to being bullied', *Child Psychology and Psychiatry Review*, 6: 114–20.

Olweus, D. (1993) *Bullying at School*. Oxford: Blackwell.

Piperato, D.F. and Roy, J.R. (2002) 'Transforming school culture'. Plenary speakers at 'Dreaming of a new reality', the third international conference on 'Conferencing, circles and other restorative practices', 8–10 August, Minneapolis, MN.

Redding, R.E. and Shalf, S.M. (2001) 'The legal context of school violence: the effectiveness of federal, state and local law enforcement efforts to reduce gun violence in schools', *Law and Policy: Special Issue on School Violence*, 23: 297–343.

Salmivalli, D. (2001) 'Peer-led intervention campaign against school bullying: who considered it useful, who benefited?', *Educational Research*, 43: 263–78.

Shariff, S. (2005) 'Cyber-dilemmas in the new millennium: school obligations to provide student safety in a virtual school environment', *McGill Journal of Education*, 40: 457–77.

Slonje, R. and Smith, P.K. (2008) 'Cyberbullying: another main type of bullying?', *Scandinavian Journal of Psychology*, 49: 147–54.

Smith, P.K., Mahdavi, J., Carvalho, M., Fisher, S., Russell, S. and Tippett, N. (2008) 'Cyberbullying: its nature and impact in secondary school pupils', *Journal of Child Psychology and Psychiatry*, 49: 376–85.

Smith, P.K. and Sharp, S. (eds) (1994a) *School Bullying: Insights and Perspectives*. London: Routledge.

Smith, P.K. and Sharp, S. (1994b) 'The problem of school bullying', in P.K. Smith and S. Sharp (eds) *School Bullying: Insights and Perspectives*. London: Routledge.

Tattum, D. and Herbert, G. (eds) (1997) *Bullying: Home, School and Community*. London: David Fulton.

Walker, M. (1992) *Surviving Secrets: The Experience of Abuse for the Child, the Adult and the Helper*. Milton Keynes: Open University Press.

Whitney, I. and Smith, P.K. (1993) 'A survey of the nature and extent of bully/victim problems in junior/middle and secondary schools', *Educational Research*, 35: 3–25.

Web resources

Children Act (2004) (http://www.everychildmatters.gov.uk/strategy/guidance/).

CHIPS: ChildLine in Partnership with Schools and the NSPCC (National Society for the Prevention of Cruelty to Children) (http://www.nspcc.org.uk/Inform/resourcesfor teachers/CHIPS/chips_wda55379.html).

Department for Children, Schools and Families (http://www.dcsf.gov.uk).

Every Child Matters (2004) (http://www.everychildmatters.gov.uk/).

United Nations Convention on the Rights of the Child (1990) (http://www.unicef.org/crc/).

Youth Matters (2005) (http://www.dfes.gov.uk/publications/youth/).

Part II

Research, Knowledge and Evidence in Youth Justice

Introduction

Rod Earle

Perhaps one of the most compelling injunctions arising from the reconfiguration of youth justice in the last 15 years has been to take research evidence seriously. Practitioners, policy-makers and academics are increasingly focused on an expanding evidence base to inform 'effective practice' (see Stephenson *et al.* 2007). In this part our contributors interrogate this process.

For Barry Goldson, the recent proliferation of 'research-based evidence' in youth justice involves the sequestration of a variety of ways of knowing about young people for the narrow purposes of their control. Goldson provides readers with an invaluable assessment of the ways in which contemporary policy and practice derive or diverge from criminological and sociological knowledge. In noting the long heritage of studies on youth and deviance, Goldson suggests that criminology owes a debt to marginalized youth and goes further by indicating a way in which this debt may be settled, or at very least not added to. Five core principles are set out to guide the development of a 'youth justice with integrity'. Youth justice practitioners and policy-makers may be challenged by the demand for 'the conceptual and institutional decriminalization of social need'. However, Goldson's concerns about early intervention and the rising prominence of what might be seen as 'prehabilitation' are not to be dismissed lightly. Rising to the challenges posed by his five principles offers a rich vision for a future informed by more than the 'selective' or 'privileged' evidence and research that currently holds sway in youth justice.

These themes are developed by Jo Phoenix who also argues that there is no shortage of information about young people's law-breaking, either in the academic or the popular press. What concerns Phoenix is that only very rarely are the voices of young people themselves heard, let alone those of the practitioners who engage with them. They are listened to even less. In their place Phoenix finds a growing platform of research driven by predetermined policy objectives. These crowd the youth justice stage, confining the inconveniently complex and contradictory experiences of youth to the wings. In this chapter we find an appeal to reject self-referential and self-justifying technocratic research concerned only with the efficacy and interior of the youth justice system, and to look beyond its boundaries. Phoenix might endorse an approach to research and the production of knowledge that Les Back (2007) describes in his book *The Art of Listening*. This is reflexive research that is prepared to abandon the seductive dream of 'sociological omnipotence' (Bourdieu 2000: 2) that so preoccupies the 'new youth justice' (Goldson 2000). With its tendencies towards naked instrumentalism, criminology, among all the social sciences, has most to gain from addressing the question originally posed over 25 years ago by the social theorist Albert O. Hirschman (1982: 143): 'after so many failed prophesies is it not in the interests of social science to embrace complexity, be it at some sacrifice of its claim to predictive power?'

In youth justice research the 'embrace of complexity' has too often been avoided in preference to an epistemological compulsion towards the predictive, the positivistic, at the expense of the hermeneutic. In presenting such a compelling indictment of contemporary youth justice research, Phoenix raises profound theoretical and methodological questions about the way 'official research', such as that promoted by the Home Office and the Youth Justice Board, routinely excludes the views and narratives of the very people that it needs to understand.

The developments considered by Goldson and Phoenix operate in a specific global context that is explored by Richard Hester. Drawing from contemporary critical sociology and recent events, Hester takes up the paradox of the simultaneous heightened presence of 'the local' and 'the global' in all aspects of human experience. While recognizing that globalization is a plural, rather than a singular, process composed of many disparate trajectories, it is the pre-eminence of certain features that concerns Hester. Just as the neo-liberal economic model of deregulation has dominated some aspects of globalization, so the 'what works' agenda and, specifically, the risk–need–responsivity model has come to the fore in the youth justice systems of anglophone countries. Hester dryly notes that these countries also 'top the league tables in terms of incarcerating young people'. Using the example of Croatia, Hester warns of the dangers of contexts and principles 'lost in translation' as a globalized market in 'youth justice solutions' emerges out of the science of risk.

For at least two of the older editors of this volume Risk was, for many years, simply a board game played on wet afternoons in their school holidays. Now, according to the sociologist Ulrich Beck (1992), risk is the structuring determinant of both social and personal life (and about as much fun!). In Chapter 9, Stephen Case explores how a specific conceptualization of risk has come to dominate the field of practice and policy in youth justice. The procedures of risk assessment using the Asset data-collection instrument are considered in some detail and their ethical implications weighed up, and largely found wanting. The latest development in risk-based assessment and intervention in the form of the Youth Justice Board's 'scaled approach' is considered as the latest manifestation of investment in what Case characterizes as the 'evidential myth'. Case is a constructive critic, however, and urges practitioners and critics to engage in 'a radical reorientation of risk assessment', refining the approach to suit local and more personalized needs in favour of its current managerial and actuarial priorities.

This series of informed critical engagements with research, evidence and knowledge in youth justice is concluded with a reflection by Wendy Stainton Rogers on more fundamentally philosophical themes. Asking 'What can we know, and how can we know it?', Stainton Rogers invites readers to consider critically the traditions of modernist thinking and the challenges of the postmodern. To assist readers in 'thinking about how we think', she offers a guide to the 'logics of inquiry'. To encounter questions of epistemology and ontology in a handbook of youth justice may seem both odd and challenging. They are infrequent intellectual visitors but considerations of whether the reality of objects of knowledge, such as 'youth', 'children' and 'crime', can be independent of the processes of knowledge that produce and reproduce them are often implicitly present in critical discussions of youth justice. Bhaskar (1971/89) describes this presence as 'intransitive' – i.e. grammatically invisible. However becoming more conscious of the presence of these ontological and epistemological questions is pivotal to assessing the possibilities of change (Cain 1992: 129).

References

Back, L. (2007) *The Art of Listening*. Oxford: Berg.

Beck, U. (1992) *Risk Society: Towards a New Modernity*. London: Sage.

Bhaskar, R. (1971/89) *The Possibility of Naturalism*. Brighton: Harvester.

Bourdieu, P. (2000) *Pascalian Meditations*. Cambridge: Polity Press.

Cain, M. (1992) 'Realist philosophy and standpoint epistemologies or feminist criminology as a successor science', in L. Gelsthorpe and A. Morris (eds) *Feminist Perspectives in Criminology*. Buckingham: Open University Press.

Goldson, B. (2000) *The New Youth Justice*. Lyme Regis: Russell House Publishing.

Hirschman, A. (1982) *Shifting Involvements: Private Interest and Public Action*. Princeton, NJ: Princeton University Press.

Stephenson, M., Giller H. and Brown, S. (2007) *Effective Practice in Youth Justice*. Cullompton: Willan Publishing.

6

Research-informed youth justice?

Barry Goldson

Introduction

This chapter critically reviews the relationship between research and youth justice policy and practice. It is argued that 'youth' has comprised a key focus of official inquiry and academic criminology for the best part of two centuries. The knowledge produced by such activity, together with the lessons offered by substantial practice experience and the provisions of international human rights instruments, provides a basis for research-informed youth justice. In this way, five core policy and practice principles are identified and discussed. The chapter proceeds to signal the means by which the enduring politicization of youth justice serves to undermine research-informed approaches and, in so doing, to distort the processes of policy formation and practice development.

Criminology and youth

From the time when 'juvenile delinquency' was first officially recognized as a discrete 'social problem' in the early part of the nineteenth century, to the emergence of a spectrum of modern-day concerns – ranging from 'disorderly' and/or 'anti-social' behaviour to violent crime and youth gangs – a preoccupation with 'youth' has provided a core focus for criminological research. Indeed, it is difficult to conceive and conceptualize contemporary criminology without acknowledging the central significance of 'youth' as a subject of inquiry and investigation.

Theorizing and studying urban 'zones', processes of 'cultural transmission' and 'differential association', gang formations and 'street-corner society' (see, for example, Park and Burgess 1925; Thrasher 1927; Shaw 1929; Sutherland 1939; Shaw and McKay 1942; Whyte 1943), together with notions of 'anomie', 'strain' and 'subculture' (see, for example, Mays 1954; Cohen 1955; Merton 1938, 1957; Cloward and Ohlin 1961; Matza 1964; Downes 1966; Parker 1974), largely centred on youth. Equally, sociological analyses of deviance and deviants and the problematization of 'labelling' processes, negative social reaction, stigma and the potentially counterproductive tendencies of formal criminal justice interventions are deeply rooted in the study of youth (see, for example, Tannenbaum 1938; Kitsuse 1962; Becker 1963; Erikson 1966; Lemert 1967; Schur 1971, 1973).

'Youth' has also been crucial to developing our understanding of the emergence, consolidation and consequences of 'moral panic' and the related processes of demonization and othering (see, for example, Cohen 1973; Hall *et al.* 1978; Pearson 1983; Scraton 1997). Furthermore, critical analyses of youth crime, youth justice and youth criminalization have served to expose and illuminate the manifest injustices of 'justice' processes, frequently shaped – if not determined – by the structural relations of class, 'race' and gender (see, for example, Cunneen and White 2002; Goldson and Muncie 2006a).

In sum, 'youth' is deeply embedded within and across criminology; from its classicist and positivist foundations, through multiple realist, radical, critical and cultural perspectives and, more recently, to the 'new penology' (Feeley and Simon 1992) and emphases on risk management, assessment and actuarialism. Youth, and by definition youth justice – however inadequate the term might be – is key to criminology. It pervades its traditions, its past, its present and no doubt its future.

Applying criminological knowledge: towards research-informed policy and practice

The centrality of youth within criminological research has produced a deep reservoir of knowledge. Furthermore, the accumulated lessons that can be drawn from national and international youth justice practice experience, together with the provisions that underpin the international children's human rights framework,[1] offer additional insights (Goldson and Muncie 2006b). In other words, the combination of criminological knowledge, practice experience and core human rights instruments provides a robust knowledge base that lends itself – at least potentially – to a 'principled youth justice' or a 'youth justice with integrity' (Goldson and Muncie 2006c, 2007). For the purposes here, five core principles are pivotal.

First, is the principle that policy and practice should comprehensively address the social and economic conditions that are known to give rise to social antagonism, harm, human distress, crime and criminalization, particularly poverty and inequality (Wilkinson and Pickett 2009). Youth justice systems around the world characteristically process (and punish) the children of the poor. This is not to suggest that all poor children commit crime, or that only poor children offend, but the corollaries between child poverty, social and economic inequality, youth crime and criminalization are undeniable.

Notwithstanding the New Labour government's 'historic pledge' to end child poverty, more than a decade after its landslide general election victory in 1997 a staggering 2.9 million children continue to endure poverty in the UK (Brewer *et al.* 2009). Perhaps more significantly, there is evidence of 'an apparent loss of policy momentum' with regard to tackling child poverty (Hills *et al.* 2009: 5). Indeed, when account is taken of key measures of 'wellbeing', children in the UK are more disadvantaged than their counterparts in any of the 21 OECD (Organization for Economic Co-operation and Development) countries surveyed by UNICEF (2007). Furthermore, in the face of deepening economic recession, 'multi-dimensional poverty' (Tomlinson and Walker 2009) threatens to compromise further the 'wellbeing' of children and young people. Such conditions are key to understanding the problems both experienced – and sometimes perpetuated – by identifiable sections of the young. There is clearly a need to reinvigorate comprehensive policies to eradicate child poverty, to address social polarization and inequality and, in so doing, to alleviate the social and economic contexts within which youth crime and processes of child criminalization are often located.

Secondly, and closely related to the first point, is the principle of universality. This requires dispensing with conditionality and instead providing holistic services that promote the rights, meet the needs and safeguard the wellbeing of *all* children and young people. It necessitates closing the contradictory fractures that have opened between 'every child matters' priorities, on the one hand, and 'no more excuses' imperatives on the other hand (Goldson and Muncie 2006c). It amounts to implementing comprehensively redistributionist and genuinely inclusionary strategies that address explicitly the practical realities and complexities of children's lived experiences. In essence this requires the conceptual and institutional decriminalization of social need. 'Normal' social institutions – including families (however they are configured), 'communities', youth services, leisure and recreational services, health provision, schools, training and employment initiatives – must be adequately resourced and supported. The industrial-scale expansion of the youth justice system should be curtailed and resources redirected to generic 'children first' services. If for no other reason, this is necessary because, as Bateman and Pitts (2005: 257) have observed, 'those factors which appear to be most closely associated with persistent and serious youth crime . . . are those which are least amenable to intervention by agents of the youth justice system'. One of the most ambitious and comprehensive research analyses of youth crime prevention programmes in the world, for example, demonstrated that, even for 'serious, violent and chronic juvenile offenders', some of the most effective responses emanate from initiatives that are located *outside* the formal youth justice system (decriminalization), build upon children's and young people's strengths as distinct from emphasizing their 'deficits' (normalization) and adopt a social-structural approach rather than drawing on individualized, criminogenic and/or medico-psychological perspectives (contextualization) (Howell *et al.* 1995).

Thirdly, is the principle that children and young people should, whenever possible, be diverted away from the formal youth justice apparatus. Diversion is the antithesis of early intervention and net-widening. Perhaps counter-intuitively, research and practice experience shows that diversion is an effective strategy in terms of youth crime prevention (see, for example, Bell *et al.* 1999; Goldson 2000; Kemp *et al.* 2002; Pragnell 2005). McAra and McVie (2007) – on the basis of their detailed empirical research in Edinburgh – conclude that the deeper that children and young people penetrate youth justice systems the less likely they are to 'desist' from offending: 'the key to reducing offending lies in minimal intervention and maximum diversion' (2007: 315). This central conclusion is consistent with research evidence that has developed over half a century (see, for example, Becker 1963; Matza 1964; Lemert 1967; Schur 1971, 1973; Thorpe *et al.* 1980).

Perhaps the most effective diversionary strategy is literally to remove children and young people from the reach of the youth justice system altogether, by significantly raising the age of criminal responsibility. There are strong grounds to support this proposition, not least evidence from jurisdictions where the age of criminal responsibility is substantially higher than it is in the UK jurisdictions and where 'it can be shown that there are no negative consequences to be seen in terms of crime rates' (Dunkel 1996: 38).

Fourthly, is the principle of deinstitutionalization or decarceration. Youth justice interventions that are ineffective in terms of reducing youth crime, that aggravate the very issues that they ostensibly seek to resolve and/or that are known to be damaging and harmful are, by definition, irrational and should be scaled down if not abolished. This particularly applies to penal institutional-ization/incarceration.

Research-based critique of child imprisonment draws attention to its enormous fiscal expense and the spectacular failings of custodial institutions when measured in terms of youth crime reduction and community safety. In 2003–4, for example, child imprisonment in England and Wales alone cost £293.5 million. The Prison Reform Trust (2008) noted that the Youth Justice Board spends up to 70 per cent of its annual budget on custody or, to put it another way, it spends ten times more on child imprisonment each year than it invests in crime prevention programmes. Such expense yields very little positive return. A Parliamentary Select Committee, for example, reported that reconviction rates stand at 80 per cent with regard to released child prisoners (House of Commons Committee of Public Accounts 2004).

Further concern regarding youth custody derives from a knowledge of its compound effect upon the typically damaged biographies and vulnerabilities of child prisoners. The conditions and treatment typically endured by child prisoners routinely violate their emotional, psychological and physical integrity. Furthermore, a major independent inquiry led by Lord Carlile (2006) exposed deeply problematic practices, including the excessive use of physical restraint, solitary confinement and strip searching. High rates of self-harm among child prisoners, together with the deaths of 30 children in penal institutions in England and Wales between 1990 and 2007 (Goldson and Coles 2008), perhaps signal the most serious questions.

Fifthly, are the related principles of depoliticization and tolerance. The politicization of youth crime and justice serves both to legitimize 'ill-considered but attention grabbing tough-on-crime proposals' (Tonry 2004: 2) and to 'institutionalize intolerance' (Muncie 1999). Such reactive politicization not only negates knowledge – derived from research and practice experience – but it also distorts policy formation. Furthermore, it is based upon a skewed reading of public opinion itself. Indeed, while the public tends to have a more pessimistic view of youth crime than is justified by the official crime statistics, people are also significantly less recriminatory and punitive than is often supposed (Hough and Roberts 2004). Furthermore:

> When the nature of public attitudes is explored in depth using sophisticated research methods, quite different results emerge compared to the often-cited rudimentary surveys ... [T]here is little evidence to support the view that harsh penal and criminal policies are favoured as a means of addressing offending behaviour. (Hancock 2004: 63)

And:

> Close analysis would suggest that there is something of a 'comedy of errors' in which policy and practice is not based on a proper understanding of public opinion. (Allen 2002: 6)

A genuinely research-informed approach to youth justice requires policy-makers to remain cognizant of the complexities of public opinion. Moreover, senior politicians have a responsibility to inform public opinion as distinct from simply reacting to oversimplified and fundamentally erroneous interpretations of it. Ultimately this requires the depoliticization of youth justice and the development of more progressively tolerant, human rights compliant, non-criminalizing, inclusionary and participative policy and practice strategies.

The rhetoric and reality of 'evidence-based' approaches

Just a decade has passed since the *Modernising Government* white paper proposed that policy should be informed routinely by evidence and subject to regular evaluative scrutiny and audit (Cabinet Office 1999). This implied that the government had committed itself to 'professional' policy-making soundly based on research, knowledge and experience of 'what works'. It appeared to signal a rational shift from 'opinion-based' to 'evidence-based' policy formation and practice development.

Indeed, the *rhetoric* of 'evidence-based' policy and 'what works' rationales has gained prominence within key aspects of modern youth justice discourse. The *reality*, however, is that the mechanics of youth justice policy formation are far more complex. It is not practical to engage with the detail here (for a fuller discussion see Goldson and Muncie 2006a), although it is particularly important to highlight the processes of selective filtering that are applied. This occurs where some 'evidence' is privileged and emphasized, while other 'evidence' is marginalized or 'forgotten'. Such *subjective* and *selective*, as distinct from *objective* and *scientifically comprehensive*, processes are clearly problematic and they seriously compromise the notion of a genuinely research-informed youth justice.

Conclusion

The key to understanding the obstacles that impede processes of research-informed policy formation and practice development is located within the continuing *political* significance of youth justice. In this way, politicization ultimately eclipses and obscures knowledge derived from research and practice experience. According to Garland (2001: 172), this is symptomatic of:

> A new relationship between politicians, the public and penal experts . . . [whereby] politicians are more directive, penal experts are less influential, and public opinion becomes a key reference point . . . [Youth] justice is now more vulnerable to shifts of public mood and political reaction . . . and expert control of the policy agenda has been considerably reduced.

It follows, therefore, that the selective interpretation and application of research and practice-based knowledge mean that certain youth justice policies continue to be driven by *political* motivation as distinct from theoretical purity, empirical integrity or 'what works' effectiveness.

Notes

1 For the purposes of youth justice four key children's human rights instruments are particularly significant: the *United Nations Standard Minimum Rules for the Administration of Juvenile Justice* (the 'Beijing Rules' 1985); the *United Nations Guidelines for the Prevention of Juvenile Delinquency* (the 'Riyadh Guidelines' 1990); the *United Nations Rules for the Protection of Juveniles Deprived of their Liberty* (the 'JDL' or 'Havana' Rules' 1990); and, perhaps most important of all, the *United Nations Convention on the Rights of the Child* (the 'UNCRC' 1989).

References

Allen, R. (2002) '''There must be some way of dealing with kids'': young offenders, public attitudes and policy change', *Youth Justice*, 2: 3–13.

Bateman, T. and Pitts, J. (2005) 'Conclusion: what the evidence tells us', in T. Bateman and J. Pitts (eds) *The RHP Companion to Youth Justice*. Lyme Regis: Russell House Publishing.

Becker, H. (1963) *Outsiders: Studies in the Sociology of Deviance*. London: Macmillan.

Bell, A., Hodgson, M. and Pragnell, S. (1999) 'Diverting children and young people from crime and the criminal justice system', in B. Goldson (ed.) *Youth Justice: Contemporary Policy and Practice*. Aldershot: Ashgate.

Brewer, M., Browne, J., Joyce, R. and Sutherland, H. (2009) *Micro-simulating Child Poverty in 2010 and 2020*. London: Institute of Fiscal Studies.

Cabinet Office (1999) *Modernising Government*. London: HMSO.

Carlile, Lord (2006) *The Lord Carlile of Berriew QC: An Independent Inquiry into the Use of Physical Restraint, Solitary Confinement and Forcible Strip Searching of Children in Prisons, Secure Training Centres and Local Authority Secure Children's Homes*. London: Howard League for Penal Reform.

Cloward, R. and Ohlin, L. (1961) *Delinquency and Opportunity: A Theory of Delinquent Gangs*. New York, NY: Free Press.

Cohen, A. (1955) *Delinquent Boys: The Culture of the Gang*. New York, NY: Free Press.

Cohen, S. (1973) *Folk Devils and Moral Panics: The Creation of the Mods and Rockers*. London: Paladin.

Cunneen, C. and White, R. (2002) *Juvenile Justice: Youth and Crime in Australia*. Oxford: Oxford University Press.

Downes, D. (1966) *The Delinquent Solution: A Study in Subcultural Theory*. London: Routledge & Kegan Paul.

Dunkel, F. (1996) 'Current directions in criminal policy', in W. McCarney (ed.) *Juvenile Delinquents and Young People in Danger in an Open Environment*. Winchester: Waterside Books.

Erikson, K. (1966) *Wayward Puritans: A Study in the Sociology of Deviance*. New York, NY: Wiley.

Feeley, M. and Simon, J. (1992) 'The new penology: notes on the merging strategy of correction and its implications', *Criminology*, 30: 449–74.

Garland, D. (2001) *The Culture of Control*. Oxford: Oxford University Press.

Goldson, B. (2000) 'Wither diversion? Interventionism and the new youth justice', in B. Goldson (ed.) *The New Youth Justice*. Lyme Regis: Russell House Publishing.

Goldson, B. and Coles, D. (2008) 'Child deaths in the juvenile secure estate', in M. Blyth *et al.* (eds) *Children and Young People in Custody. Researching Criminal Justice Series*. Bristol: Policy Press.

Goldson, B. and Muncie, J. (eds) (2006a) *Youth Crime and Justice*. London: Sage.

Goldson, B. and Muncie, J. (2006b) 'Rethinking youth justice: comparative analysis, international human rights and research evidence', *Youth Justice*, 6: 91–106.

Goldson, B. and Muncie, J. (2006c) 'Critical anatomy: towards a principled youth justice', in B. Goldson and J. Muncie (eds) *Youth Crime and Justice*. London: Sage.

Goldson, B. and Muncie, J. (2007) 'Youth justice with integrity: beyond Allen's "new approach"', in Z. Davies and W. McMahon (eds) *Debating Youth Justice: From Punishment to Problem Solving?* London: Centre for Crime and Justice Studies.

Hall, S., Critcher, C., Jefferson, T., Clarke, J. and Roberts, B. (1978) *Policing the Crisis: Mugging, the State and Law and Order*. Basingstoke: Macmillan.

Hancock, L. (2004) 'Criminal justice, public opinion, fear and popular politics', in J. Muncie and D. Wilson (eds) *Student Handbook of Criminal Justice and Criminology*. London: Cavendish Publishing.

Hills, J., Sefton, T. and Stewart, K. (2009) 'Poverty, inequality and policy since 1997', in *Findings*. York: Joseph Rowntree Foundation.

Hough, M. and Roberts, J. (2004) *Youth Crime and Youth Justice: Public Opinion in England and Wales*. Bristol: Policy Press.

House of Commons Committee of Public Accounts (2004) *Youth Offending: The Delivery of Community and Custodial Sentences. Fortieth Report of Session 2003–4*. London: HMSO.

Howell, J., Krisberg, B., Hawkins, J. and Wilson, J. (eds) (1995) *Serious, Violent and Chronic Juvenile Offenders: A Sourcebook*. London: Sage.

Kemp, V., Sorsby, A., Liddle, M. and Merrington, S. (2002) *Assessing Responses to Youth Offending in Northamptonshire. Research Briefing* 2. London: Nacro.

Kitsuse, J. (1962) 'Societal reaction to deviant behaviour', *Social Problems*, 9: 247–56.

Lemert, E. (1967) *Human Deviance, Social Problems and Social Control*. Englewood Cliffs, NJ: Prentice Hall.

Matza, D. (1964) *Delinquency and Drift*. New York, NY: Wiley.

Mays, J.B. (1954) *Growing up in the City: A Study of Juvenile Delinquency in an Urban Neighbourhood*. Liverpool: Liverpool University Press.

McAra, L. and McVie, S. (2007) 'Youth justice? The impact of system contact on patterns of desistance from offending', *European Journal of Criminology*, 4: 315–45.

Merton, R. (1938) 'Social structure and anomie', *American Sociological Review*, 3: 672–82.

Merton, R. (1957) *Social Theory and Social Structure*. New York, NY: Free Press.

Muncie, J. (1999) 'Institutionalised intolerance: youth justice and the 1998 Crime and Disorder Act', *Critical Social Policy*, 19: 147–75.

Park, R. and Burgess, E. (eds) (1925) *The City*. Chicago, IL: University of Chicago Press.

Parker, H. (1974) *View from the Boys: A Sociology of Down-town Adolescents*. Newton Abbot: David & Charles.

Pearson, G. (1983) *Hooligan: A History of Respectable Fears*. Basingstoke: Macmillan.

Pragnell, S. (2005) 'Reprimands and final warnings', in T. Bateman and J. Pitts (eds) *The RHP Companion to Youth Justice*. Lyme Regis: Russell House Publishing.

Prison Reform Trust (2008) *Bromley Briefings: Prison Factfile*. London: Prison Reform Trust.

Schur, E. (1971) *Labelling Deviant Behaviour: Its Sociological Implications*. New York, NY: Harper & Row.

Schur, E. (1973) *Radical Nonintervention: Rethinking the Delinquency Problem*. Englewood Cliffs, NJ: Prentice Hall.

Scraton, P. (1997) *'Childhood' in 'Crisis'?* London: UCL Press.

Shaw, C. (1929) *Delinquency Areas*. Chicago, IL: University of Chicago Press.

Shaw, C. and McKay, H. (1942) *Juvenile Delinquency and Urban Areas*. Chicago, IL: University of Chicago Press.

Sutherland, E. (1939) *Principles of Criminology*. Philadelphia, PA: J.B. Lippincott.

Tannenbaum, F. (1938) *Crime and the Community*. New York, NY: Columbia University Press.

Thorpe, D., Smith, D., Green, C. and Paley, J. (1980) *Out of Care: The Community Support of Juvenile Offenders*. London: George Allen & Unwin.

Thrasher, F. (1927) *The Gang: A Study of 1,313 Gangs in Chicago*. Chicago, IL: University of Chicago Press.

Tomlinson, M. and Walker, R. (2009) *Coping with Complexity: Child and Adult Poverty*. London: Child Poverty Action Group.

Tonry, M. (2004) *Punishment and Politics: Evidence and Emulation in the Making of English Crime Control Policy*. Cullompton: Willan Publishing.

UNICEF (2007) *Child Poverty in Perspective: An Overview of Child Well-being in Rich Countries*. Florence: UNICEF.

Whyte, W. (1943) *Street Corner Society: The Social Structure of an Italian Slum*. Chicago, IL: University of Chicago Press.

Wilkinson, R. and Pickett, K. (2009) *The Spirit Level: Why More Equal Societies Almost Always Do Better*. London: Allen Lane.

7

Whose account counts? Politics and research in youth justice

Jo Phoenix

This chapter is about how, since the late 1990s, UK governmental priorities and objectives have structured a particular relationship between knowledge production (i.e. research) and professional practice, such that youth justice research and practice now serve the demands of policy. In order to contextualize this discussion, the chapter starts by recounting an abridged history of the relationship between governmental objectives, policy, practice and research during the 1980s. The basic argument is that, whereas academic inquiry and knowledge production continue to exist outside the realm of government and are not necessarily linked to the development of professional practice, research within these realms is increasingly *utilitarian* and *instrumental* in character. Simply, 'official' research on youth justice (i.e. that which is funded and/or consumed by government or governmental organizations) is used more and more primarily to legitimate the direction and effect of successive political interventions into the field of professional practice and, more specifically, the system expansion that has occurred in the last ten years. Hence, 'official' research on young lawbreakers and youth justice is narrowly focused and excludes questions outside the framework of specific policy or practice innovations, just as youth justice practice is increasingly 'disciplined' by the dictates of these claims to knowledge that underpin policy.

Shifting histories in the research–practice–policy relationship

In relation to both adult and youth justice, the 1980s marked a watershed in the UK. The rhetoric of successive Conservative governments regarding adult offenders eschewed research and knowledge production in favour of a more or less 'common sense' approach. Michael Howard's oft-quoted line that 'Prison works. It ensures that we are protected from murderers, muggers and rapists, and it makes many who are tempted to commit crime think twice' (6 October 1993, Conservative Party conference speech) exemplified the belligerent public stance of the then Conservative government. Rejecting academic and research knowledge, politicians at the time drew on a series of assumptions derived from a neo-classicist tradition of thinking. In brief, writers such as Wilson (1975), Gottfredson and Hirschi (1990) and Murray (1990) all claimed that the findings of previous generations of social researchers were misguided.

As proof, they pointed to the dramatic increases in official and recorded crime rates from the 1950s–1970s in the USA and UK which occurred even while there were dramatic increases in the standards of living. According to these authors offending was a result of rational choice, the loss of self-control, the decline in moral standards of a society and/or the simple fact that, to paraphrase Wilson (1975), 'wicked people exist' and all that can or should be done with them is to separate them from innocent law-abiding citizens. With that, politicians and policy-makers had a ready-made rationale for ignoring previous generations of social and psychological research.

The message coming from these politically conservative thinkers was simple and one which chimed with the staunchly conservative political regimes in the USA and UK. Politicians both sides of the Atlantic could (and did) lose official interest in any question of causation, or in the connections between individuals' social context and their environment and the distribution and variation of lawbreaking or the influence of specific economic, political, ideological or social conditions on the processes of criminalization and punishment of particular groups of young lawbreakers.

Despite the harsh public rhetoric about adults and away from the public gaze, youth justice during the 1980s bore witness to what future commentators might come to call a momentary historical anomaly (Hendricks 2002): a decade in which practitioners, professionals, academics and government worked together to create progressive practices and policies in England and Wales for young people in conflict with the law. In real terms the period from 1982 to 1992 saw youth justice practices and policies framed by a call for minimum necessary state intervention in addition to community supervisions that operated as true *alternatives* to custody (Goldson 1997). Together, this had the effect of dramatically reducing the numbers of young people in the system and/or in state custody.

These policies had their origins in the radical and critical scholarship of the 1960s and 1970s which argued for radical non-intervention (see Empey 1982; Muncie and Wilson 2004) on the basis that youthful lawbreaking was 'normal' (cf. Matza 1969); that all empirical evidence indicated that young people 'grew out of crime'; and that official state reactions and responses to crime do not stop crime but, rather, consolidate a 'deviant' identity (cf. Schur 1975). These scholars also demonstrated how processes of differential criminalization lead to specific populations of young people (usually those already excluded and marginalized) being targeted for criminal justice interventions, the result of which often acted to further their marginalization and exclusion. Indeed, it was this understanding of youthful lawbreaking that underpinned the Labour Party's (1964) report, *Crime: A Challenge To Us All*, in which it was claimed that it is only the misdeeds of working-class young people that come to the attention of the criminal justice system, that criminal prosecution was not necessary for relatively low-level offences and that children committing more serious offences were in need of guidance and help rather than prosecution.

As Hendricks (2002) suggests, the period 1982–92 is most likely explained not as a result of policy-makers and politicians 'listening' to the research of the previous generations but, rather, as a happy coincidence or confluence of interests. In a context in which public spending on youth custody and justice interventions was escalating beyond control, a means to achieve one of the key objectives of Thatcherism (i.e. a reduction of public expenditure) was to support the decarcerative and decriminalizing impulses of professionals and practitioners. But, as Hendricks (2002) and Pitts (2001) also argue, this period of progressive policy and practice came to an end with the murder in 1993 of the toddler, James Bulger, by John Venables and Robert Thompson, both 10 years old. At that point, the same 'common sense' and punitive logic that framed adult penal policies (zero tolerance, incapacitation and so on) came to dominate the call for something 'to be done' about youth crime.

The point of this short history is not to tell a tale of the demise of progressive policies and work with young people but, rather, to highlight how little research has mattered in the shaping of youth penal and justice policies and practices in the recent past. As exemplified by the key moments of change, youth justice research did not shift or drive a different policy or practice agenda, although the lessons and messages of research may well have been used by politicians, policy-makers and professionals in their calls to do things differently and so on. There is, however, one notable exception: *Misspent Youth* (Audit Commission 1996) which formed the basis of the then landmark Crime and Disorder Act 1998. This made two notable claims: that a quarter of all crimes were committed by young people and that youth crime cost the public £1 billion per annum. Ignoring the *research*, which justified the progressive youth justice practices of the 1980s, *Misspent Youth* drew on the *political logic* that underpinned support for those practices (i.e. cost effectiveness, efficiency, value for money). Ironically, then, the same logic which permitted progressive practice also underpinned its opposite: massive system expansion, recriminalization and increasing levels of incarceration of younger and younger young people for relatively less serious offences.

Evidence-based policy and evidence-based practice or policy-based evidence and policy-driven practice?

Since then much has changed – especially in relation to the place of research in youth justice. One of the key strategies in New Labour's modernizing agenda was 'evidence-based policy' which claimed radically to reconceive the relationship between knowledge production, policy and practice. Instead of policies based on old political ideologies and dogma, New Labour portrayed itself as a 'thinking government' in which policy would frame practice and both would be based on evidence of 'what works'. The white paper entitled *Modernising Government* (1999) put forward the new formula for policy-making: 'policy decisions should be based on sound evidence. The raw ingredient of evidence is information. Good quality policy making depends on high quality information, derived from a variety of sources – expert knowledge; existing domestic and international research; existing statistics; stakeholder consultation; evaluation of previous policies' (Cabinet Office 1999: 31).

Such was the centrality of this formula that, when addressing the main independent funding organization of social research in the UK, the Economic and Social Research Council, the then Home Secretary David Blunkett declaimed:

> This government has given a clear commitment that we will be guided not by dogma but by an open-minded approach to understanding what works and why. This is central to our agenda for modernizing government: using information and knowledge much more effectively and creatively at the heart of policy-making and policy delivery. (2 February 2002)

As he had already indicated, the task for researchers was simple. Become useful or risk being irrelevant:

> It is . . . a question of improving the focus, relevance and timeliness of research, making it more accessible and intelligible to users, ensuring the research funding processes encourage this, and breaking down the barriers of mutual suspicion between social researchers and those in government. Many feel that too much social science research is inward-looking, too piecemeal, rather than helping to build knowledge in a cumulative way, and fails to focus on the key issues of concern to policy-makers, practitioners and the public, especially parents. (Blunkett 2000)

Noting that there are a variety of evidence-based policy models, others have since claimed New Labour's version of evidence-based policy is based on an instrumental rationality model in which policy-makers seek merely to *manage* the economic and social realms in an apolitical, technical and more or less mechanistic way (Sanderson 2002).

This position is a form of government that has come under tremendous critique by political scientists. Dryzek claims that evidence-based policy-making, as currently understood, is little more than 'the policy sciences of tyranny' (1989: 98). Lasswell (1951) argued that it amounts to government by technocratic policy-making. Wells (2007) astutely notes that New Labour's version of evidence-base policy is a form of government that relies on a strong central state, commanding and controlling, auditing, inspecting and monitoring.

In relation to youth justice, evidence-based policy translated into a 'what works' approach to interventions. As Stephenson *et al.* write: 'The headline message from government is that "what matters is what works" and that practice should be derived from the latest and most reliable research findings' (2007: 1). In practice, these research findings are the mass of evaluation studies that are now conducted on every conceivable officially sanctioned practice and policy development with young people in conflict with the law. As will be demonstrated below, this growth in 'administrative criminology' is defined by a narrow set of definitions, research problems and questions – and importantly one based on a fundamental inability to ask some of the far-reaching questions about criminal justice interventions into the lives of young lawbreakers.

Hence, the last decade has seen a huge level of Home Office and Youth Justice Board (YJB) investment and spending on research in order to create knowledge where, so the official story goes, none existed that could tell practitioners and policy-makers what worked (i.e. as though the previous generations of social and psychological research simply did not exist). Consider this: a mere 164 Home Office research studies were published in the three decades between 1969 and 1996. In comparison, 503 were published in the decade of 1997–2007. Making up this figure are 154 Home Office research studies, an additional 236 research studies published as online-only publications and 113 specialist youth justice research publications currently available through the YJB. By any account this is a tremendous outpouring of 'research'. Yet, despite this productivity, there is the troubling empirical reality that, regardless of the claims of that research to have established 'what works', the numbers of those coming into the system continue to rise as do the numbers of those being incarcerated. As noted by Carlen in relation to adult prisons, much of this youth justice 'research' has become a:

> lucrative and staple source of financing for many newcomers into the prison industry, who appear not to be at all unwilling to legitimate the use of imprisonment by reference to the 'effectiveness' of their 'programmes' in reducing crime. The verity of the 'programmers'' claim to 'success' are often 'proven' by dubious self-report questionnaire evidence from prisoners that a programme 'works' – usually in terms of changing prisoners' understanding of their offending behaviour. (Indeed in view of all these 'programmers' and 'counsellors' claiming to have to found the philosopher's stone in relation to changing offending behaviour, it is truly amazing that the prisons have not been emptied by now!). (2002: 120)

What Carlen is asserting is (1) that much of the 'research' produced in the last decade has not necessarily been framed by the sort of social understandings, theoretical frameworks or methodological demands of social research (cf. Pawson and Tilley 1997); (2) that research on justice and penality has become an industry *which generates its own demand and then supplies it*; and, more importantly, (3) that 'what works' research, by definition, cannot challenge its own terms of reference.

While Carlen was discussing adult prison policy and research, the same applies to youth justice. 'What works' research into youth justice interventions is, by definition, incapable of calling into question its own terms of reference. The research 'agenda' is based on a number of strongly held assumptions: that youth crime is a problem; that the problem of youth crime is one best located within specialized youth (criminal) justice agencies; and that interventions with young people, while varying in degrees of 'effectiveness', are socially and politically necessary. With that, the one piece of 'evidence' that policy-makers cannot collect, the one question that 'what works' research into youth justice practice and policy cannot ask, is arguably the most fundamental question: are *justice* interventions in *young* people's lives desirable? Instead, youth justice practitioners and policy-makers are treated to an almost endless stream of research demonstrating, *inter alia*, the technocratic efficacy of the various practice and policy developments to date.

So, for instance, research indicates that bail support and supervision schemes have a 'significant impact in ensuring that young people attend court' (YJB 2005c) and that the assessment tool, ASSET, demonstrates a relatively high level of reliability and validity in identifying factors likely to increase a young person's risk of reoffending (Baker *et al.* 2003). Alternatively, research consumers are informed that 'effective strategies' for addressing anti-social behaviour among young people are complex. More, research consumers are also informed that practitioners' own views of anti-social behaviour measures depend on whether they view their role as enabling change in the young people or supporting community protection from young people's misdeeds (YJB 2006).

Taking a broader view, YJB research indicates that, despite their controversy, parenting orders do have a role, if only to reach the vulnerable or needy parents of young lawbreakers who might never come forward for support of their own accord (Ghate and Ramella 2002). Or, in relation to persistent offenders, practitioners are often ill-equipped to conduct proper assessments, that interventions seem to have little rationale and that any interventions put in place should be targeted to specific needs/risks and be implemented earlier (YJB 2005b). More specifically still, research confirms that cognitive-behaviour programmes seem to reduce reoffending rates in the short term (YJB 2004b) and that, regardless of the relatively high reoffending rates, mentoring schemes act to increase young people's self-confidence (2008c).

The question here is not whether the research is credible: such interventions as parenting orders, cognitive-behavioural programmes, mentoring schemes, acceptable behaviour contracts and anti-social behaviour orders are most probably benign and capable of producing the effects that the research indicates. The point I am making is that such a programme of official research is not intended to deal with the Janus-like contradiction between, on the one hand, the seemingly positive impact that involvement with youth justice workers has on young people (as evidenced in the official research) and, on the other, the tremendously damaging impact that it can also have (as evidenced in massive system expansionism, up-tariffing and high rates of child incarceration).

This is not simply a question of the lack of 'ethical' direction in the official research. Rather, the issue is that the very conditions in which knowledge is produced about young lawbreakers and youth justice occlude important questions by bracketing off and obscuring other research knowledge about bullying, self-harming, mental health difficulties, attempted suicides, questions over the use of restraint in custodial settings, the disproportionately high rates of dual-heritage boys, children with mental health issues and/or learning difficulties coming into the system, and what this all means in relation to England and Wales' capacity to protect and ensure the rights of children. Nor is such a research programme capable of questioning whether criminal justice systems are the most appropriate place to be addressing issues such as education (YJB 2005b), cognitive deficits (YJB 2004b), parenting skills (Ghate and Ramella 2002), lack of self-confidence (YJB 2005a) or relationship building (Ghate and Ramella 2002; YJB 2005a, 2005b, 2004b). Finally, and most worryingly, such a research programme cannot *explain* why, despite having established programmes that are evaluated as 'working' to prevent youth offending and to reduce reoffending, the last ten years has seen a year-on-year rise in the total numbers of young people being processed through the youth justice service.

Hillyard *et al.* (2004) argue that New Labour's hunger for 'research' is highly partial and selective. As they note in a carefully detailed article on the relationship between criminological knowledge production and the state, policies on the 'crimes of the powerful', such as corporate killing and deaths in the workplace, have not been subject to the same type of scrutiny as the more conventional 'justice' interventions targeted, primarily, at working-class or disadvantaged youth. In a similar vein, it could be argued that attempts to regulate more stringently the activities of the financial sector of the City remain relatively under-researched in comparison with the scrutiny of young people in the inner city. Their argument is that the expansion of 'research' on crime and criminal justice has been of a particular nature and in a particular direction – utilitarian (i.e. research which is 'useful' to 'stakeholders' and the community, often conducted by academics within universities, often on behalf of government agencies, and by and large lacking any critical voice).

This is not the same as Blunkett's earlier warning to academics that their research risks being seen as irrelevant unless it can communicate a message to policy-makers and practitioners. Rather, Hillyard *et al.* (2004) are claiming that the utility of current 'official' criminal justice research is that it serves to maintain and legitimate highly particularized, official definitions of 'the problem', as well as defining the parameters in which it must be addressed. For instance, 'the problem' of 'troublesome' 'youths' (and occasionally troublesome practitioners – see below) is individualized and separated from its social context. Setting the parameters in this way means that the social, economic and political conditions young people inhabit are largely ignored and the view promoted that it is the young people themselves who must change and adjust to their social, personal and economic conditions in order that they make more law-abiding choices in the future.

In a final twist in the official tale, this partial and self-generating research programme into youth justice then forms the foundation of knowledge upon which policies regulating and governing the practitioners are based (and then subsequently evaluated). The performance targets, guidance on 'effective practice' and national standards that 'guide' practitioners (and against which youth justice teams are measured) are set in reference to the same technocratic, highly selective and self-referential research agenda that monitors the policy changes and practice innovations. In other words, official knowledge governs not just what is done with young lawbreakers but how 'troublesome' practitioners are dealt with (as not working towards targets, standards and so on). It is not only the 'young offenders' who are the objects of this disciplining process.

Conclusion

This chapter has sought to unpick the contemporary research–policy–practice relationship. It argued that the *political rhetoric* of evidence-based policy positions research as part and parcel of the evidence base upon which policy should be constructed. However, in *practice* the last ten years have borne witness to the expansion of policy-based evidence where, tautologically, specific policy interventions are assessed and evaluated as 'working' and – because they 'work' – they then form the basis of justification and rationale for the policies and interventions implemented. Inherently self-referential, this 'official' youth justice research then squares the circle, becoming the 'evidence' that youth justice practice and policy reforms of the last ten years have 'worked'. It also forms the 'evidence' for the creation of a set of dictates about 'effective practice' which in turn underpin national standards and the very performance measures over which individual youth justice services are held to account and through which local innovation and professional discretion are held in check.

At the risk of repetition, research on 'what works', by its nature and its inability to call into question the key terms of reference (i.e. the notion of the youth *offender* and the primary aim of the system as being the *prevention of offending*), serves the organizational function of legitimating the massive expansion of youth justice at the same time as providing the foundations of further policy innovations (and expansionism) and the guidelines on 'effective practice' that drive the work of practitioners.

This chapter has focused only on the research–policy–practice relationship and, in so doing, it has left unaddressed a number of related and important questions. First among these is the question of how practitioners can and do respond to these conditions given that one *effect* of evidence-based policy has been the governance (by targets) of practitioners' judgement, discretion and ability to innovate practice. Is possessing a critical understanding of official research enough, or indeed the only way of stepping outside contemporary official discourse? Is it possible to work *within* youth justice and be considered a 'radical practitioner'? Should there be attention and focus given to working *creatively* with governmental, official understandings and policies pertaining to young people in trouble with the law? In short, how and in what ways can youth justice practitioners generate debate and actually challenge the implications of evidence-based policy and the research that underpins it?

References

Audit Commission (1996) *Misspent Youth*. London: HMSO.

Baker, K., Jones, S., Roberts, C. and Merrington, S. (2003) *The Evaluation of the Validity and Reliability of the Youth Justice Board's Assessment for Young Offenders*. London: Youth Justice Board.

Blunkett, D. (2000) 'Influence or irrelevance: can social science improve government?' Speech to the Economic and Social Research Council, 2 February (available online at www.bera.ac.uk).

Cabinet Office (1999) *Modernising Government* (Cm 4310). London: HMSO.

Carlen, P. (2002) 'Carceral clawback: the case of women's imprisonment in Canada', *Punishment and Society*, 4: 115–21.

Chapman, T. and Hough, M. (1998) *Evidence Based Practice: A Guide to Effective Practice* (*HM Inspectorate of Probation*). London: Home Office.

Dryzek, J. (1989) 'Policy sciences of democracy', *Polity*, 22: 97–118.

Empey, La Mar T. (1982) *American Delinquency: Its Meanings, its Construction*. Chicago, IL: Dorsey Press.

Ghate, D. and Ramella, M. (2002) *Positive Parenting: The National Evaluation of the Youth Justice Board's Parenting Programme*. London: Youth Justice Board for England and Wales.

Goldson, B. (1997) 'Children in trouble: contemporary state responses to juvenile crime', in P. Scraton (ed.) *Childhood in Crisis?* London: Taylor & Francis.

Gottfredson, M. and Hirschi, T. (1990) *A General Theory of Crime*. Stanford, CA: Stanford University Press.

Hendricks, H. (2002) 'Constructions and reconstructions of British childhood: an interpretive survey from 1800 to the present', in J. Muncie *et al.* (eds) *Youth Justice: Critical Readings*. London: Sage.

Hillyard, P., Sim, J., Tombs, S. and Whyte, D. (2004) 'Leaving a stain upon the silence: contemporary criminology and the politics of dissent', *British Journal of Criminology*, 44: 369–90.

Labour Party (1964) *Crime: A Challenge to Us All*. London: Labour Party.

Lasswell, H.D. (1951) 'The policy orientation', in D. Lerner and H.D. Lasswell (eds) *The Policy Sciences*. Palo Alto, CA: Stanford University Press.

Mazta, D. (1969) *Becoming Delinquent*. Englewood Cliffs, NJ: Prentice Hall.

Muncie, J. and Wilson, D. (2004) *Student Handbook of Criminology and Criminal Justice*. London: Routledge.

Murray, C. (1990) *The Emerging British Underclass*. London: IEA Health and Welfare Unit.

Pawson, R. and Tilley, N. (1997) *Realistic Evaluation*. London: Sage.

Pitts, J. (2001) *The New Politics of Youth Crime: Discipline or Solidarity*. London: Palgrave.

Sanderson, I. (2002) 'Making sense of "what works": evidence based policy making as instrumental rationality?', *Public Policy and Administration*, 17: 61–75.

Schur, E.M. (1975) *Radical Non-intervention: Rethinking the Delinquency Problem*. Englewood Cliffs, NJ: Prentice Hall.

Stephenson, M., Giller, H. and Brown, S. (2007) *Effective Practice in Youth Justice*. Cullompton: Willan Publishing.

Wells, P. (2007) 'New Labour and evidence based policy making, 1997–2007', *People, Place and Policy Online*, 1: 22–9.

Wilson, J.Q. (1975) *Thinking about Crime*. New York, NY: Vintage.

Youth Justice Board (2004a) *National Standards for Youth Justice Services*. London: YJB.

Youth Justice Board (2004b) *Cognitive Behaviour Projects: A National Evaluation of the Youth Justice Board's Cognitive Behaviour Projects*. London: YJB.

Youth Justice Board (2005a) *National Evaluation of Youth Justice Board Mentoring Schemes*. London: YJB.

Youth Justice Board (2005b) *Persistent Young Offenders: A Retrospective Study*. London: YJB.

Youth Justice Board (2005c) *National Evaluation of Bail and Support Schemes*. London: YJB.

Youth Justice Board (2006) *A Summary of Research into Anti-Social Behaviour Orders Given to Young People between January 2004 and January 2005*. London: YJB.

Youth Justice Board (2008a) *Youth Justice Planning Framework, 2008/2009*. London: YJB.

Youth Justice Board (2008b) *Research Strategy, 2008–2011*. London: YJB.

Youth Justice Board (2008c) *Monitoring Performance and Improving Practice*. London: YJB.

8

Globalization, power and knowledge in youth justice

Richard Hester

There's more to the picture than meets the eye. Hey, Hey, My My.
(Neil Young and Crazy Horse, 'My My, Hey Hey (Out of the Blue)', from
the album, *Rust Never Sleeps*, Reprise Records 1979)

Introduction

The 2008 global 'economic crash' brought home starkly the fact that we live in a world that is economically, politically and socially linked. In recent times the power of these global economic ties was illustrated when the government of the world's largest superpower, the USA, was held to ransom by unfettered, international money markets.

Globalization is a word that can mean many things to many people, not only in the sense of economic and political globalization, although this is perhaps its most commonly accepted interpretation, but also in the sense of the social impact of these processes. Globalization is essentially a recognition that the world is becoming, metaphorically, a smaller place; as Giddens (1990) put it, a process of 'distanciation', a shrinking of time and space. If we so desire, within seconds, we can know what is happening in Wall Street, Rodeo Drive, Pennsylvania Avenue or Tiananmen Square in the same way a Londoner 100 years ago might have been aware, via the grapevine of talk and gossip, of events in Threadneedle Street, Bond Street, Downing Street or Parliament Square. It really does matter more and more what happens on the other side of the world for no other reason than the potential and real consequences felt in our immediate lives. Paradoxically through a 'business' metaphor sometimes referred to as 'glocalization', the significance of how the 'local' interprets the 'global' is of growing importance.

In parallel with the more general concerns of globalization, but with a much narrower focus, understanding what is going on in youth justice in England

and Wales demands an understanding of the global as well as the local and the relationship between these processes. Of more direct interest to the youth justice practitioner, this process of globalization can be seen as having 'permeated criminology' (Muncie 2005). There are many examples: globalization has impacted on the relationship between criminal law and human rights (Hollan 2000); on the criminology of the 'Other', such as vagrants, travellers and those seen as occupying 'the margins' of mainstream society (Aas 2007; Weber and Bowling 2008); and, indeed, on in the practice of youth justice itself (Muncie 2001, 2005, 2008).

The process of globalization is by no means neutral; nor is it simple. If the technology of 'late modernity' allows the possibility for this 'shrinking world' through cyberspace or access to the Internet, then politics, legislation and economics can impact in ways which are both complex and contradictory. It has, for example, been argued by Muncie (2005) that globalization has resulted in three distinct, but related, processes that impact on the way in which youth justice 'systems' are organized:

- *A shift away from welfare.* Here Muncie suggests 'a loss (or at least a major reconfiguration) of the social' so that 'policies based less on principles of social inclusion and more on social inequality, deregulation, privatization, penal expansionism and welfare residualism' (2005: 36) are the result of market-driven, neo-liberal policy formulation. This idea is further elaborated in Muncie (2008) with reference to a 'punitive turn' that appears to be a characteristic of 'western' nation-states, explained by the globalization of neo-liberal policy and a consequent shift in state/market relations leading to more exclusionary policies and ultimately to an increase in the incarceration of children and young people.

- *A process of policy transfer* whereby nation-states search for the 'holy grail' of 'what works' in reducing offending. This transfer, of course, has many difficulties. Transferring, for example, an ideal such as restorative justice from one side of the world is not the same thing as shipping industrial machinery or bauxite. The meaning is sometimes lost or shifted in translation.

- *Human rights and the rights of the child*, potentially antagonistic to the first point above and occurring under the rubric of globalization, is the process by which a raft of conventions has sought to 'bring into line' the way in which nation-states treat their children and specifically how they treat troublesome children. Perhaps the most important and well known is the UN Convention on the Rights of the Child (UNCRC). Notably, Article 3.1 of the UNCRC states that for all legal actions 'the best interests of the child should be a primary consideration'. However, this raft also includes the UN Standard Minimum Rules for the Administration of Justice (1985) (the Beijing Rules), the UN Standard Minimum Rules for Non-custodial

Measures (1990b) (the Tokyo Rules) and the UN Guidelines for the Prevention of Juvenile Delinquency (1990a) (the Riyadh Guidelines).

There is, not surprisingly, a substantial difference between what these conventions hope to achieve and their actual implementation at a national or local level. For example, the impact of the UNCRC is arguably differently interpreted and implemented even within the UK. This is unquestionably the case across all nation-states, particularly those involved in armed conflict. These generally homogenizing processes are found in the 'multilateral treaties concerning human rights, ascertaining standards in the field of substantive and procedural criminal law, which states by their legislation should observe' (Gardocki 1986: 703–4 cited in Hollan 2000: 240) and thus can, and do, impact on the delivery of youth justice systems in many nation-states.

The problems associated with the imposition of these apparently homogenizing 'child centred' global processes are as varied as they are abundant. For example, in Bosnia Herzegovina it was not until early 2008 that responsibility for a co-ordinating body was given to 'the Ministry of Human Rights and Refuges to ensure a children's rights approach' (Morris 2008: 204). In the case of New Zealand, doubts remain as to the level of commitment needed to safeguard the rights of children involved in the restructured youth justice system (Lynch 2008: 225). Generally, however, these issues vary from simple legislative compliance to difficulties in implementation and, of course, in political will.

What works and the risk–need–responsivity model

Within this complex set of relations in and between nation-states, this chapter focuses on one specific aspect of particular relevance to the youth justice practitioner: the development of a set of influential 'knowledge claims' clustered around the so-called 'what-works agenda'. The 'what-works agenda' and, specifically, the risk–need–responsivity (RNR) model, presently dominates youth justice policy in England and Wales (for more on this topic, see Chapter 9 this volume). Suffice to say here that one aspect of the globalization of youth justice practice has been the widespread incorporation of the RNR model into youth justice practice on the premise that it is 'evidence based'.

However, notwithstanding the contested claims around the veracity of the 'what works' evidence, several academic commentators (Robinson 2001; Farrant 2006) have questioned the way in which this 'knowledge base' has *limited*, rather than *extended*, the capacity for practitioners to explore a wider knowledge base and, consequently, to extend their ability to intervene effectively (in both cases the focus was on adult offenders). Essentially, when seen in the light of power relations between policy-makers and practitioners, the notion of 'what works' can be seen as a *dis*empowering force acting on, and consequently felt by, practitioners. Thus rather than providing what, on the surface, appears to be a solution to practice dilemmas, such as how to design programmes of effective interventions, a strict adherence to these 'scientifically established' 'principles of effective practice' serves also to constrain practitioners within narrow and prescribed limits. By offering 'solutions out of a can' the effect is thus to limit further reflection on the efficacy of both individual practice and the specific context in which this practice is located.

If this alone was not enough to provide both policy-makers and practitioners with some difficulty, issues of policy transfer provide yet another level of complexity in which the intended 'ideology' behind these principles (often cloaked in more neutral terms such as 'effective' or 'evidence based') is lost in translation. In the substantial literature on the subject of policy transfer (Nellis 2000; Muncie 2001; Newburn 2002), most illuminate the problems of the seductive siren call of such widely trumpeted 'success stories'. Thus the implementations of restorative justice, for example, are sometimes indistinguishable, in practice, from a government's stated objectives to redress the victim–offender balance in favour of the victim that stem from entirely different concerns and social or political constituencies.

In the case of the RNR model, one example of the process of policy transfer might be the difficulty in translating the ideas and specifics of policy reform and implementation, as developed in Scotland, for example, to a 'developing democracy' such as Croatia.

Lost in translation: RNR in Croatia

As Ratkajec has observed in the context of meeting the needs of children at risk in Croatia: '[global changes, as well as those specifically relating to Croatian society] influence both the phenomenon of the behavioural disorders and the intervention systems designed to address these' (2009: 1). In her paper, Ratkajec suggests that the implementation of interventions is 'always contextually influenced' (2009: 2) and thus, in a 'transitional' state such as Croatia, it is easy to see that there are both risks and opportunities for the development of methodologies imported from other nation-states. While recognizable elements, such as the words 'risk' and 'need', are evident in the literature of this emerging democracy, the *full* translation of these ideas and the way they fit in with prevailing sources of practice and knowledge may not be complete or exact.

Knowledge production and what comes to be regarded as expertise in youth justice do not occur on a level playing-field. It is interesting to note the asymmetry of knowledge production in the context of anglophone countries, especially the rich and populous USA and Canada in the case of RNR. It is more than a little ironic that these two countries, who top the league tables in terms of incarcerating young people, dominate in the production of research literature. As such they pose a clear and present danger of obscuring other conceptualizations of youth justice and its relationship to welfare and children's rights.

Knowledge and power

While Ratkajec suggests that matching the needs of children with a process of risk assessment will ultimately be helpful in respecting their rights, this may not be the case. It may be that by these two global processes are incommensurable or at least antagonistic. The very process by which 'what works' knowledge is globalized has an effect that runs counter to an approach to children that is first and foremost 'children centred'. Child-centred approaches are at risk of being marginalized by the more pressing needs to show results that reduce recidivism effectively and efficiently.

Francis Bacon's assertion that 'knowledge is power' (1597) predates the origins of the new youth justice system in England and Wales by exactly 400 years, and yet the relation between knowing something and being able to do something is not always so simple or straightforward. Power can be claimed and contested in the same way that knowledge can: '[Individuals] are always in the position of simultaneously undergoing and exercising power. They are not only its inert or consenting target; they are also the elements of its articulation' (Foucault 1980: 98).

For youth justice practitioners, 'knowing' about both the local and the wider context of offending, being aware of the structural inequalities that often propel young people into the criminal justice system, matters a great deal. In turn, the knowledge base and consequent action of youth justice practitioners directly impact on the lives of the children and young people with whom they work. Recognizing these links between power and knowledge in the context of the globalization of youth justice practice is essential if practitioners are to influence the way in which young people respond to interventions. Put another way, youth justice practitioners could helpfully reflect on the following:

- The direct impact of globalization on the wellbeing of children and young people in their area.

- The extent to which young people have the power to influence their local communities.

- The practitioner 'knowledge base' in the context of the globalization of youth justice practice.

- The 'transferability' and 'appropriateness' of any intervention model to local conditions.

From these reflections it follows that practitioners might be positively influenced as much by a 'rights based' approach as by a 'what works' approach. However, this relationship between power and knowledge in the context of youth justice practice can work in a number of ways. 'Centralizing' and 'managerial' approaches to the teaching of youth justice practitioners can limit the overarching knowledge necessary to take professional and critical decisions based on holistic and informed views (see Robinson 2001). Knowledge can empower both practitioners and the young people with whom they work, and it can act as a counterpoint to contest the excluding power of 'what works' knowledge.

Finally, in the context of knowledge–power relations, we need to be careful to avoid the development of systems that become part of a process leading to further surveillance. The thirst for knowing more and more about the lives of others in order to drive the 'risk-prevention machine' risks itself feeding the carceral leviathan by sucking more and more 'at-risk children' into the youth justice system. There is some irony that another 'global knowledge', concerned with addressing the rights of children may be a last counterpoint to this process as a result of the issues of 'data protection' and 'human rights' gaining greater political ascendancy.

Conclusions

Globalization and youth justice practice may seem, on the face of it, nothing to do with each other. However, it is the author's contention that, in order to be an effective youth justice practitioner, it is not enough just to acquire a narrow knowledge of how to do certain things. It is equally important to reflect, actively and collectively with colleagues, on why certain approaches and ideas around practice are developing. Often we read that 'research suggests this' or 'the evidence suggests that'. It is sometimes worth seeing the wider picture in terms of how some research seems to have more grip than others (for more discussion on this topic, see Chapter 6 this volume).

George Orwell once said that 'One of the aims of totalitarianism is not merely to make sure that people will think the right thoughts, but actually to make them less conscious' (1946: 383). While this chapter is not in any way implying insidious 'totalitarian processes' are swamping youth offending teams, it is suggesting very strongly that youth justice practitioners should be more, rather than less, conscious and critical of the global forces that can, and do, influence their (local) practice and the conditions that prevail in the communities in which they work.

References

Aas, K.F. (2007) 'Analysing a world in motion: global flows meet the criminology of the other', *Theoretical Criminology*, 11: 283–303.

Farrant, F. (2006) 'Knowledge production and the punishment ethic: the demise of the probation service', *Probation Journal*, 53: 317–33.

Foucault, M. (1980) *Power/Knowledge: Selected Interviews and Other Writings, 1972–7.* London: Longman.

Giddens, A. (1990) *The Consequences of Modernity*. Cambridge: Polity Press.

Harper, G. and Chitty, C. (2005) *The Impact of Corrections on Re-offending: A Review of 'What Works'. Home Office Research Study* 291. London: Home Office.

Hollan, M. (2000) 'Globalisation and conceptualisation in the sphere of international criminal law', *Acta Juridica Hungarica*, 41: 225–46.

Lynch, N. (2008) 'Youth justice in New Zealand: a children's right's perspective', *Youth Justice*, 8: 215.

Morris, C. (2008) 'Developing a juvenile justice system in Bosnia and Herzegovina: rights, diversion and alternatives', *Youth Justice*, 8: 197–213.

Muncie, J. (2001) 'Policy transfers and what works: some reflections on comparative youth justice', *Youth Justice*, 1: 27–35.

Muncie, J. (2005) 'The globalization of crime control – the case of youth and juvenile justice', *Theoretical Criminology*, 9: 35–64.

Muncie, J. (2008) 'The "punitive turn" in juvenile justice: cultures of control and rights compliance in western Europe and the USA', *Youth Justice*, 8: 107.

Nellis, M. (2000) 'Law and order: the electronic monitoring of offenders', in D. Dolowitz (ed.) *Policy Transfer and British Social Policy*. Buckingham: Open University Press.

Newburn, T. (2002). 'Atlantic crossings: policy transfer and crime control in the USA and Britain', *Punishment and Society*, 4: 165–94.

Orwell, G. (1946) 'Politics and literature', in *The Penguin Essays of George Orwell*. Harmondsworth: Penguin Books.

Ratkajec, G. (2009) 'Matching the interventions to the needs of children and youth at risk', *IUC Journal of Social Work Theory and Practice* (available online at http://www.bemidjistate.edu/academics/publications/social_work_journal/issue17).

Robinson, G. (2001) 'Power, knowledge and what works in probation', *Howard Journal*, 40: 235–54.

United Nations (1985) *The UN Standard Minimum Rules for the Administration of Justice (the Beijing Rules)*. New York, NY: United Nations.

United Nations (1990a) *Guidelines for the Prevention of Juvenile Delinquency (the Riyadh Guidelines)* (available online at http://www.un.org/documents/ga/res/45/a45r112.htm).

United Nations (1990b) *Standard Minimum Rules for Non-custodial Measures (the Tokyo Rules)* (available online at http://www.unhchr.ch/html/menu3/b/h_comp46.htm).

Weber, L. and Bowling, B. (2008) 'Valiant beggars and global vagabonds: select, eject, immobilize', *Theoretical Criminology*, 12: 355–75.

9

Preventing and reducing risk

Stephen Case

From the 1990s onwards, the spectre of the 'risk society' (Beck 1992) began to exert an increasing influence on official responses to young people perceived to be 'problematic'. Rapid globalization, wide-ranging social changes and socio-economic uncertainty have encouraged a preoccupation with unpredictability and 'risk' – particularly the risk ostensibly presented by young people to themselves and others (see Goldson 2003). Consequently, risk-based responses have pervaded youth justice policy and practice to the point that the notion of risk (factors) underpins all work with young people who enter the youth justice system.

New Labour: the party of risk?

In 1992, the Labour Party began to dominate the 'law and order' debate with the Conservatives, thanks in no small part to their sound bite: 'Tough on crime? Tough on the causes of crime.' In 1996, the *Misspent Youth* review characterized the youth justice system (YJS) under the Conservatives as inefficient, ineffective and uneconomical when agencies worked with young people and worked with each other (Audit Commission 1996). The report concluded that a realigned and reorientated the YJS should prioritize the prevention of youth offending by measuring risk factors[1] and by targeting their reduction through risk-focused early intervention. Upon taking power in 1997, Labour brought 'risk' to the forefront of public attention by emphasizing the danger/threat that young people allegedly posed to adults and the consequent imperative for state intervention to ensure public protection. Accordingly, in the Crime and Disorder Act 1998 (s. 37) the primary aim of the YJS became the prevention of youth offending. The emerging *risk factor prevention paradigm* (RFPP) resonated strongly with New Labour's risk-focused aspirations: 'The basic idea . . . is very simple: Identify the key risk factors for offending and implement prevention methods designed to counteract them' (Farrington 1997: 606).

The RFPP had a clear practical appeal to policy-makers and youth offending team (YOT) practitioners working in a political climate increasingly obsessed with accountability, transparency, risk aversion, defensible practice and cost effectiveness, particularly because it has provided an 'evidence-based' paradigm within which to work with young people entering the YJS (Stephenson *et al.* 2007). Indeed, the risk factor research on which the RFPP was based (i.e. the identification of correlations between psychosocial risk factors and future offending) was gathering significant steam internationally as a widely replicated and ostensibly validated approach to investigating and understanding youth offending.

Through the RFPP, the Labour Party committed to *actuarialism* – predicting offending and planning intervention using risk assessment. Governmental faith in the efficacy of actuarialism has been manifested and enacted in the development of risk assessment instruments for use in the YJS of England and Wales. Actuarialism and the RFPP marked a significant change for a youth justice practice traditionally dominated by welfare versus justice debates. The culture shift towards a focus on quantitative risk factors signified the introduction of Labour's managerialist, technicist and interventionist 'third way' approach to youth justice and to understanding youth offending.

Asset: predicting reconviction

Following the Crime and Disorder Act 1998, the Oxford University Centre for Criminology was commissioned to develop 'a common approach to the process of assessment [that] can assist practitioners ... [as] the basis for arriving at judgements and making decisions' (YJB 2003: 5). What emerged in April 2000 was the Asset risk assessment instrument. The Asset core profile form is completed by YOT practitioners following an interview with a young person aged 10–17 entering the YJS.

Asset measures current/recent exposure to 'dynamic' risk factors (i.e. those factors able to be changed) in 12 areas of risk that can be broadly considered 'psychosocial': *psychological* (emotional/mental health, perception of self/others, thinking/behaviour, attitudes to offending, motivation to change) and *social* (living arrangements, family/personal relationships, education/training/employment, neighbourhood, lifestyle, substance use, physical health). The Asset core profile is supplemented by sections relating to indicators of vulnerability, indicators of serious harm to others, positive (protective) factors and a 'What do you think?' self-assessment profile completed by the young person (see YJB 2007).

Since its inception, however, Asset has been the subject of intense debate between proponents and critics with regards to its content, methodology and practicality, with critics seeming to have the louder voice, if not the upper hand. The following criticisms are noted.

Factorization

Risk measures in Asset are the result of the crude factorization (quantification) of dynamic, multifaceted experiences, characteristics, circumstances, attitudes, behaviours, processes. For example, potentially complex neighbourhood problems (e.g. racial and ethnic tensions, tensions between the community and the police) are reduced to a quantitative judgement of their aggregated (combined) association with 'the likelihood of further offending' on a five-point scale (where 0 = no association and 4 = very strong, clear and direct). This procedure is unlikely to produce valid measures of risk for young people because so much quality, nuance and individualized meaning is 'washed away' through minimalist data analysis. Furthermore, the measurement of statistical relationships between risk factors and offending has been supplanted by (prescribed and subjective) practitioner judgements that offer little objectivity with which to reflect, validate or explain any substantive, real-world relationships between risk and offending (see Case and Haines 2009).

Marginalization of young people's perspectives

Asset makes only a limited attempt to integrate young people's qualitative views of risk into the assessment process, in favour of an adult-led assessment and intervention process that equates to 'a prescription without a consultation' (Case 2006: 174). The 'What do you think?' section appears as something of an afterthought here – not taken into account when practitioners make their judgements of risk (YJB 2008) and often neglected and ignored by practitioners (see Annison 2005).

The neglect of young people's differing constructions of risk casts further doubt over the validity and meaningfulness of the risk factors measured and targeted by risk assessment in the YJS (see Case 2006) because Asset fails to resonate with the lived realities of young people and is, therefore, lacking in responsivity. An issue for practitioners is, of course, what store to place on young people's (possibly deluded, exaggerated, biased) constructions of risk and how to reconcile these views with the evidence from practitioner-completed sections. However, to neglect to consider young people's perspective entirely is surely something that few practitioners would countenance as a valid, practical and ethical approach to risk assessment.

Evidence-based or technicized practice?

Proponents have argued that Asset offers practitioners detailed, structured and reliable evidence of risk to support their decision-making and to inform intervention (see, for example, Baker 2005). However, critics have accused

Asset of prioritizing rigid and impersonal management targets and aggregated statistics over the actual needs of individual offenders (e.g. Smith 2003). An even more frequent criticism has been that Asset may inculcate mechanized, depersonalized, tick-box risk assessment (see, for example, Souhami 2007), equating this to the 'technicization', 'bureaucratization', 'routinization' and even 'zombification' of youth justice practice (see Pitts 2001).

Such technicization of practice and aggregation of individualized data have also been criticized for having 'insufficient sensitivity to individual, social and temporal differences relating to age, gender, ethnicity, socio-economic status, local area . . . cultural, political or historical context' (Case 2007: 93). However, Baker (2005), an architect of the original aggregated (combined) instrument, has argued that Asset is not intended to be a comprehensive, stand-alone assessment but, rather, should be employed to complement other information sources available to the practitioner. She has subsequently recommended (when writing the source document for the updated Assessment Planning Interventions and Supervision (APIS) key element of effective practice for the Youth Justice Board (YJB)) 'an approach to assessment that encourages contextualization of each individual young person's circumstances' (YJB 2008: 12), mainly through giving greater attention to contextual influences on risk in the Asset evidence box.

Developmentalism and psychosocial bias

Despite emphasizing that practitioners should avoid 'relying on a favourite or fashionable theory' (YJB 2003: 103–4), the YJB has dictated (through the APIS guidance) that risk assessments be informed by three specific (developmental) explanations of offending behaviour: the *criminal careers model* (Farrington 1997), the *theory of age-graded informal social control* (Sampson and Laub 1993) and *interactional theory* (Thornberry 1987). Each theory explains offending as the predetermined product of exposure to psychosocial risk factors at different developmental stages (particularly in childhood) and, therefore, privileges risk factors located within the individual. As such, the YJB has promoted an 'evidence-based' (although highly prescriptive and reductionist), risk-based practice underpinned by the developmental determinism of 'individual, family, school and peer group influences and neglecting the role of wider structural and socio-political factors' (Case 2007: 93).

Even recent calls for contextualization have prioritized the influence of context on psychosocial risk factors rather than considering the independent influence of socio-structural context on offending. Consequently, Asset risk assessment 'conveniently individualizes offending' (Whyte 2009: 94) and it can be argued that practitioner autonomy, professional discretion and the operation of 'reflective' practice have been somewhat superseded by practical and theoretical duress.

Predictive utility or futility?

Evaluations have identified the main benefit of Asset to be high levels of *predictive validity* – the successfully prediction of reconviction outcomes in 67 per cent of cases after one year and 69 per cent of outcomes after two years (Baker *et al*. 2002, 2005); levels that have remained impressively consistent across subgroups of young offenders, such as females and black and ethnic minorities (Baker *et al*. 2005).

   However, these levels of predictive validity have elicited an equally 'predictable' criticism regarding Asset's high rate of *false positives* (those young people predicted to reoffend who do not) and *false negatives* (those predicted not to reoffend who do). Both practically and ethically, there is a clear potential for false-positive young people to be caught in a (widening) net of unmerited and possibly criminalizing interventions, while false negatives could fall through the cracks of risk assessment and be deprived of vital intervention and support because they are not deemed sufficiently 'risky' or indeed go on to commit serious offences.

What does Asset predict?

Asset risk factors predict *reconviction*, which does not equate to predicting *reoffending* because the former excludes the 'dark figure' of crime that is unreported by the public/offender and unrecorded by the police. This is potentially problematic because, for example, there may be a tangible, yet unmeasured, difference in exposure to risk between reoffenders (recidivists?) who have been reconvicted and those who have yet to be caught. Reconviction (plus the damaging effects of contact with official criminal justice agencies – see McAra and McVie 2007) may be, in reality, a risk factor for reoffending, rather than an outcome of exposure to risk. Therefore, young people could be entering the YJS already disadvantaged, more likely to be reconvicted (compared with 'reoffenders') because of the risk factors that brought them into the system and, thus, more likely to be further criminalized by risk assessment.

Onset: the pre-emptive strike

Despite serious methodological and theoretical criticisms of Asset, risk assessment in the YJS has been neither modified nor abandoned. Rather, the net of risk assessment has been widened to 'include' young people who have not been convicted but are considered to be 'at risk' of future offending. This demonstrates the government's conviction that: 'the risk factors for those on the cusp of entering the criminal justice system are, broadly speaking, the same as for those young people who have entered it' (Ashford 2007: 6).

Accordingly, the Onset referral, assessment and intervention process was introduced in April 2003 for use with young people aged 8–13 considered to be 'at risk' of offending (yet not officially recorded as offenders). Onset focuses on risk factors for the onset of offending (hence the tool's name) rather than for reoffending or reconviction (the focus of Asset) and it is used to underpin risk-focused, 'pre-offending' preventative intervention. The Onset process is initiated by a key stakeholder referral to a youth inclusion and support panel (YISP)[2] or youth inclusion programme (YIP)[3]. The Onset rating scale mirrors that used in Asset, as do the psychosocial domains within which risk is measured. Practitioners use Onset risk ratings to inform an intervention plan detailing appropriate (risk-focused) responses to the risk presented by a young person. Therefore, in terms of content, methodology and practical use, Onset can be seen to resemble a scaled-down, little-brother version of Asset.

Onset and Asset: variations on a theme?

The emergence of Onset has been premised on a presumed, yet ill-advised and non-evidenced, homogeneity with Asset regarding developmental, deterministic understandings of the risk-offending relationship (i.e. exposure to risk in childhood predicts later offending), despite the target behaviours for each instrument (offending and reconviction) being neither synonymous nor equivalent. Notwithstanding this disparity, risk assessment in the YJS has drawn on the same 'established' body of risk factors and (developmental) explanatory theories to populate both instruments and to understand the relationship between 'predictive' risk factors and offending.

The onset of ethical concerns

Young people receiving Onset-informed interventions are targeted on the basis of what they are judged (statistically) likely to do, rather than what they have actually done in respect of actual offending. Not only does this raise significant concerns about due process but there is also a danger that Onset could foster an overemphasis on risk and engender fatalistic views of certain young people as 'high risk' and inevitably 'pre-criminal', in turn pigeonholing specific (e.g. socially disadvantaged) youth populations and exposing them to invasive, predetermined interventions (see Goldson and Muncie 2006), suffering a similar fate to the false positives identified by Asset.

This is not to argue that early intervention in the lives of disadvantaged and 'in need' children and young people is ineffective or unwarranted, although it does raise questions about the nature of intervention. Clearly, there are many advantages to interventions promoting health, wellbeing, quality of life and access to opportunities for young people and strong evidence that these can help encourage positive, prosocial behaviour (see Catalano *et al.* 2004).

However, the link between *risk-focused* early intervention (in childhood) and the prevention of youth offending is extremely difficult to justify from extant criminological evidence. Moreover, *risk-focused* early intervention is an approach that is potentially stigmatizing and exclusionary. This latter concern has been acknowledged by the public distancing by David Farrington and David Utting from pre-emptive risk assessment: 'Even if there were no ethical objections to putting "potential delinquent" labels round the necks of young children, there would continue to be statistical barriers ... This demonstrates the dangers of assuming that anti-social five year olds are the criminals or drug abusers of tomorrow' (Sutton *et al.* 2004: 5).

The scaled approach to youth justice

The Audit Commission's report, *Youth Justice 2004* (the follow-up to *Misspent Youth*), concluded that 'YOTs should make better use of Asset to determine the amount as well as the nature of interventions with individuals using a scaled approach' (2004: point 142), a conclusion supported by a subsequent HMIP inspection of YOTs (2006). The YJB response was not to reject risk-based approaches to assessment and intervention, however, but to consolidate risk assessment through the 'scaled approach' to youth justice.

The scaled approach involves 'tailoring the intensity of intervention to the assessment' of risk (YJB 2009: 6). A young person's Asset score is placed into one of three risk categories: standard, enhanced, intensive. The risk category determines the young person's 'risk of reoffending' (even though Asset is intended to predict the risk of reconviction rather than reoffending) and the category dictates different aspects of the consequent youth justice response, including:

- the *sentence* proposed to the court;
- the proposed *frequency of contact* between the young person and a YOT practitioner (in the first three months of the order); and
- the suggested intervention *content*.

The scaled approach is, therefore, intended to enable YOT practitioners more effectively to target/tailor their time, resources and interventions to individual risk levels through the strategic and consistent utilization of Asset risk assessment scores.

However, several methodological and practical criticisms can be levelled at the Scaled Approach as currently conceived, particularly the following:

- *Heightened deprofessionalization*: YOT practitioners could be compelled to work within this mechanistic version of the RFPP as if it were evidence based (which it arguably is not) and in a more prescribed, uncritical and

deprofessionalized manner than they have (allegedly) utilized previously to assess risk and to apply risk-focused interventions.

- *Disproportionate intervention*: interventions may be disproportionate to the offence committed (e.g. too intensive for low-risk offenders who have committed a serious offence and vice versa). Although the YJB has acknowledged that 'practitioners should . . . consider whether there are any factors that indicate the intervention level may need to be increased or decreased' (YJB 2009: 9), the scaled approach does seem to suggest an inflexible and prescriptive match between intervention and assessed risk level. From a needs-based, welfarist perspective, the consequence could be an unconstructive incentive scheme encouraging needy young people to demonstrate sufficient levels of risk and deficit (possibly in collusion with well meaning practitioners) in order to qualify for much-needed intervention (see Goldson 2005), while young people measured to be 'low risk' (but potentially high need) could be deprived of the support to which they should be entitled.

- *A non-evidence base*: the scaled approach assumes that 'dynamic' risk factors are amenable to change through intervention programmes, contrary to the evidence from the early research that underpins the developmental crime prevention approach (e.g. Glueck and Glueck 1930; Cabot 1940; Bottoms and McClintock 1973), which suggested that early risk-focused intervention has little positive effect on the risk of offending and that maturation has a greater influence on desistance from offending than the reduction of risk factors. Furthermore, other studies have identified deleterious effects of risk-focused youth justice intervention on young people (see McCord 1978; McAra and McVie 2007). Consequently, the scaled approach could be accused of standing as an 'evidence based' approach that is actually based on evidence that undermines the entire process and potential of risk-focused intervention.

Risk assessment: perpetuating an evidential myth

The expressed purpose of YJS risk assessment has been to identify risk factors as suitable targets for interventions, in line with political objectives to 'nip crime in the bud' and reflective of the methodological premise of the RFPP. However, these risk factors are not necessarily 'predictors' or 'causes' in the experimental, clinical and explanatory sense. Instead, they are merely *correlates* with offending. Any conclusions that these risk factors predict, cause or explain offending have been therefore based on imputation, typically because risk factors are measured at an earlier stage than offending – so *A* is assumed to influence *B*. Identifying correlates, however, tells us little about the nature and direction of the risk-offending relationship. Furthermore, risk assessment in the YJS has been promoted and extrapolated without critical discussion of the potential implications of:

- measuring the same narrow body of psychosocial risk factors against different target variables (reconviction and offending); and

- attempting to understand the relationship between risk factors and these different target variables in the same developmental and deterministic manner.

Perhaps the most alarming oversight has been the failure to evaluate critically the ostensible (yet dubious) 'evidence base' that underpins risk assessment in the YJS. The resultant practice context has all but coerced practitioners into making subjective and under-informed judgements about how risk factors influence offending and how different risk-focused interventions might 'work'. Risk assessment in the YJS has simultaneously embodied the aggregated, deindividualized and prescriptive nature of actuarial justice and the subjective and individualized nature of clinical judgements (Case and Haines 2009) – offering an 'oversimplified technical fix' to a complex social reality (Stephenson *et al.* 2007).

What now for risk assessment?

Practitioners reading this could be forgiven for becoming disillusioned with the validity and utility of the risk assessment processes that they are compelled to work within. What is encouraged, however, is not fatalism and rejection but a critical re-evaluation of risk assessment as currently conceived. I have argued elsewhere for policy-makers and practitioners to consider a radical reorientation of risk assessment towards a contextualized approach that emphasizes individual, localized and intra-offending differences in risk profile, along with considering the independent impact of socio-structural risk factors on offending (Case 2006). However, the degree to which the current system enables practitioners to embark upon a 'radical' reorientation of their practice is moot, so the responsibility for creating the time, space and systems for this to happen probably rests more appropriately with policy-makers. Indeed, appeals to contextualization have been reflected in the recent source document that underpins the updated APIS guidance to practitioners (YJB 2008).

Furthermore, I have argued vehemently for more intensive consultation with young people in the YJS within a needs and rights-based inclusionary and promotional assessment framework that acknowledges the serious limitations of risk-based approaches and refocuses practitioners towards using professional judgement/experience to promote young people's welfare needs and positive outcomes/behaviours (see also Whyte 2009). It is hoped, therefore, that reorientated (risk) assessment processes could help to inform interventions that are 'sensitive and responsive to expressed need, thus limiting the criminalizing and stigmatizing potential of unwarranted and invasive interventions' (Case 2006: 177).

Notes

1 Taken to mean 'prior factors that increase the risk of occurrence of events such as the onset, frequency, persistence or duration of offending' (Farrington 2002 cited in YJB 2008: 11).

2 Multi-agency panels containing representatives from different agencies (typically from statutory agencies, such as the police, education, health and social services) working with young people aged 8–13 years old (or 14–18-year-olds in the case of the YISP+ programme). Onset is used to identify young people who are 'at risk' of offending. Following risk assessment, YISP staff seek to ensure that these young people and their families can access mainstream services at the earliest possible stage (although participation is voluntary).

3 Tailor-made programmes for 8–17-year-olds (junior YIPs for 8–12-year-olds, senior YIPs for 13–17-year-olds) living in 114 of the most socially deprived/ high-crime and therefore most 'high risk' neighbourhoods in England and Wales. YIPs seek to engage with the 50 young people in each neighbourhood measured by Onset to be most 'at risk' of offending by delivering preventative, risk-focused intervention to young people, their families and communities (YJB 2006).

References

Annison, J. (2005) 'Risk and protection', in T. Bateman and J. Pitts (eds) *The RHP Companion to Youth Justice*. Lyme Regis: Russell House Publishing.

Ashford, B. (2007) *Towards a Crime Prevention Strategy*. London: YJB.

Audit Commission (1996) *Misspent Youth: Young People and Crime*. London: Audit Commission.

Audit Commission (2004) *Youth Justice 2004*. London: Audit Commission.

Baker, K. (2005) 'Assessment in youth justice: professional discretion and the use of Asset', *Youth Justice*, 5: 106–22.

Baker, K., Jones, S., Roberts, C. and Merrington, S. (2002) *Validity and Reliability of Asset*. London: YJB.

Baker, K., Jones, S., Roberts, C. and Merrington, S. (2005) *Further Development of Asset*. London: YJB.

Beck, U. (1992) *Risk Society: Towards a New Modernity*. London: Sage.

Bottoms, A.E. and McClintock, F.H. (1973) *Criminals Coming of Age: A Study of Institutional Adaptation in the Treatment of Adolescent Offenders*. London: Heinemann.

Cabot, R. (1940) 'A long-term study of children: the Cambridge-Somerville Youth Study', *Child Development*, 11: 143–51.

Case, S.P. (2006) 'Young people "at risk" of what? Challenging risk-focused early intervention as crime prevention', *Youth Justice*, 6, 171–9.

Case, S.P. (2007) 'Questioning the "evidence" of risk that underpins evidence-led youth justice interventions', *Youth Justice*, 7: 91–106.

Case, S.P. and Haines, K.R. (2009) *Understanding Youth Offending: Risk Factor Research, Policy and Practice*. Cullompton: Willan Publishing.

Catalano, R., Berglund, M., Ryan, J., Lonczak, H. and Hawkins, D. (2004) 'Positive youth development in the United States: research findings on evaluations of positive youth development programs', *Annals of the American Academy of Political and Social Sciences*, 59: 98–124.

Farrington, D.P. (1997) 'Human development and criminal careers', in M. Maguire *et al.* (eds) *The Oxford Handbook of Criminology* (2nd edn). Oxford: Oxford University Press.

Glueck, S. and Glueck, E. (1930) *500 Criminal Careers*. New York, NY: Alfred Knopf.

Goldson, B. (2003) 'Tough on children: tough on justice.' Paper presented at the Centre for Studies in Crime and Social Justice (Edge Hill) in collaboration with the European Group for the Study of Deviance and Social Control, Chester.

Goldson, B. (2005) 'Taking liberties: policy and the punitive turn', in H. Hendrick (ed.) *Child Welfare and Social Policy*. Bristol: Policy Press.

Goldson, B. and Muncie, J. (2006) *Youth Crime and Justice*. London: Sage.

HMIP (2006) *Joint Inspection of Youth Offending Teams of England and Wales*. London: HMIP.

McAra, L. and McVie, S. (2007) 'Youth justice? The impact of system contact on patterns of desistance from offending', *European Journal of Criminology*, 4: 315–45.

McCord, J. (1978) 'A thirty year follow-up of treatment effects', *American Psychologist*, March: 284–9.

Pitts, J. (2001) 'Korrectional karaoke: New Labour and the zombification of youth justice', *Youth Justice*,1: 3–16.

Sampson, R.J. and Laub, J.H. (1993) *Crime in the Making: Pathways and Turning Points through Life*. Harvard, MA: Harvard University Press.

Smith, R. (2003) *Youth Justice: Ideas, Policy and Practice*. Cullompton: Willan Publishing.

Souhami, A. (2007) *Transforming Youth Justice: Occupational Identity and Cultural Change*. Cullompton: Willan Publishing.

Stephenson, M., Giller, H. and Brown, S. (2007) *Effective Practice in Youth Justice*. Cullompton: Willan Publishing.

Sutton, C., Utting, D. and Farrington, D.P. (2004) *Support from the Start: Working with Young Children and their Families to Reduce the Risks of Crime and Antisocial Behaviour*. London: DfES.

Thornberry, T.P. (1987) 'Toward an interactional theory of delinquency', *Criminology*, 25: 863–92.

Whyte, B. (2009) *Youth Justice in Practice: Making a Difference*. Bristol: Policy Press.

Youth Justice Board (2003) *Assessment, Planning Interventions and Supervision*. London: YJB.

Youth Justice Board (2006) *YIP Management Guidance*. London: YJB.

Youth Justice Board (2007) *ASSET Young Offender Assessment Profile* (available online at http://www.yjb.gov.uk/en-gb/practitioners/Assessment/Asset.htm).

Youth Justice Board (2008) *Assessment, Planning Interventions and Supervision* (source document). London: YJB.

Youth Justice Board (2009) *Youth Justice: The Scaled Approach. A Framework for Assessment and Interventions. Post-consultation Version Two*. London: YJB.

10

What can we know, and how can we know it?

Wendy Stainton Rogers

Introduction

Is youth crime getting worse or getting better? Does the 'scaled approach' (YJB 2009) target those most in need of help – or merely stigmatize the most deprived? Does locking up young offenders act as a deterrent or is it just a breeding ground for greater criminality? Those working in youth justice are constantly beset by claims and counter-claims to 'know' the answers to this kind of question, and it can be hard to know what and whom to believe. Yet practice and policy in youth justice need to be properly informed by valid and reliable evidence. The question is: how do we obtain evidence of this kind, and, when we get it, how do we know if we can trust it?

This chapter is intended to explore what constitutes reliable and valid 'evidence' – what we *can* know and what is entailed in that knowing. For all the claims of certainty behind the 'scientific facts' that are presented to us, even hard-core scientists acknowledge that there is never any absolute certainty about the things we 'know'. We laugh about the way our ancestors believed that the earth is flat and malaria was caused by 'bad air', but perhaps we should also wonder what will make our descendants laugh at us. What facts that we are currently convinced we 'know for certain' will they regard as preposterous?

In order to get to grips with these questions, I begin by going back to the very basics. I do this first by examining the underlying philosophical accounts of 'knowing' (called epistemologies) and the assumptions about our being-in-the-world (called ontologies) on which they are based. Then, I explore three distinctive 'logics of inquiry' – the underlying logical assumptions behind different approaches to gaining and validating knowledge.

Two paradigms: modernism and postmodernism

Notice I have talked about epistemologies and ontologies in the plural. This is because scholars adopt different, conflicting, paradigms. In this chapter I concentrate on just two of them:

- A 'natural science' (often called a *modernist*) paradigm, where the world is seen as arising from natural (including astrological, geological, biochemical and evolutionary) processes that are defined by scientific laws and is systematic and observable. Here rigorous hypothesis-testing research methods are regarded as the only means by which researchers can determine what constitutes reliable and valid knowledge.

- A 'social constructionist' (sometimes also called a *postmodern*) paradigm, where the world, as we know it, is seen as entirely the product of human meaning-making. Here interpretational methods are regarded as the means by which researchers can gain insight into how and why people behave as they do, as individuals, communities and societies.

Modernism

Broadly, modernism is the coherent set of assumptions that constitute the 'philosophy of science' as practised in the natural sciences, such as biology, chemistry and physics. Modernism is also the paradigm for the mainstream social sciences that inform youth justice, especially psychology but also criminology and sociology.

Modernist ontology

Mainstream social sciences assume a positivist ontology, where the social world is a system outside of and independent from people's thoughts and feelings and actions. Equally, the forces going on within each person's experience (their thoughts and feelings, motivations and concerns, beliefs and values) are seen to operate at an individual level, separate from the social world. Crucially, though, both elements (the social world and people living their lives within it) are seen to be made up of scientifically established related elements: social and economic forces (such as class and poverty) operating externally *upon* people; and psychological and psychodynamic factors (such as intelligence, impulsivity and personality) operating *inside* people's minds.

Modernist ontology assumes that these are real things, ones that social scientists can study in order to gain a greater understanding of the laws that govern the workings of social influence and human nature. The goal is to establish how these scientific laws work in just the same way as physicists have for the laws of gravity, motion and so on. Within the modernist paradigm, intelligence and personality are held to be enduring and stable human qualities that can be objectively measured, making it possible for people to be categorized – as 'more' or 'less' intelligent, say, or extrovert rather than introvert. Equally, socio-economic status is regarded as something that can be objectively and accurately classified and its impact on outcomes, such as criminality, predicted with some accuracy.

Modernist epistemology

Modernist epistemology is based upon positivism and empiricism. At its purest and most simple, positivism holds that if proper, rigorous, systematic scientific research methods are used, it is possible to discover reliable, factual knowledge about the world-as-it-really-is. Today few scientists claim that this is ever entirely possible. Since human perception and understanding are fallible, scientists will always be somewhat selective and biased by their preconceptions (Chalmers 1999). However, most scientists take a strong realist position. They believe that it is possible progressively to pin down 'the facts' and get close enough to reality to, at least, solve problems such as identifying cures for cancer and explaining the origins of the universe.

To pursue this goal, scientists seek to discover knowledge empirically; that is, through the systematic collection, analysis and interpretation of objective data that they can observe directly and, usually, measure, in ways not biased or distorted by subjective prejudice or ideology. The modernist conviction is that criminologists and psychologists can, through the proper use of scientific research methods, identify, for example, the reasons why young people engage in criminal behaviour – and, furthermore, they can use this knowledge to devise interventions that will reduce such criminality. It is further assumed that particular interventions can be evaluated – demonstrated to 'work' (or not) – as long as the evaluative process follows properly the appropriate scientific procedures and uses the right controls. In other words, objective evidence can be gained, and this evidence can be used to determine effective practice.

Postmodernism

Postmodernism often receives a bad press – portrayed as, variously, impossible to understand, irrational, 'arty-crafty' nonsense and so on. People often use the word 'postmodern' to describe, say, films that break the rules (for example, by having time go backwards) or interior design made up of a pastiche of styles, origins and materials put together in an ironic way, with, for example, the very elegant juxtaposed with the most gaudy and kitsch. You may think, then, that it is hardly a paradigm for informing youth justice.

However, used in relation to deeper questions of ontology and epistemology in youth justice, postmodernism takes on a far more serious role and refers, most notably, to its rejection of modernism's claims to rationality and, especially, to 'objectivity' in the way research is conducted.

Postmodern ontology

Postmodern ontology is based on the assumption that the social world only exists when and because people make it. The social world, in this view, is continually being created and recreated by people acting collectively together. Furthermore, there is not a single, homogeneous social world but a complex diversity of social worlds which operate differently. In this ontology, things gain their reality only because people *make* them real – and, so made, they can have the same impact as if they were real.

For instance, many cultures have rules about appropriate behaviour in relation to honour. One such is the principle of 'izzat' (a south Asian term referring to codes of family honour), which has a potent influence on how people live and, in some situations, how they die (for instance, in 'honour killings'). Another instance is the concept of 'treason' used to justify the execution of 'shell-shocked' soldiers who deserted in World War One – who today might be treated as suffering from 'post-traumatic stress disorder'. Everything we know about and experience, from furniture to terrorism, is made into a 'thing' ('thingified', if you like, though the correct term is 'reified') in ways that make it possible for people to make sense of the world and live their lives within it.

Postmodern epistemology

Knowledge, in postmodern terms, is constructed through human meaning-making. This principle is encapsulated in the term *social constructionism*. One of the key texts in this perspective was Berger and Luckmann's (1966) *The Social Construction of Reality*. A more recent and in many ways more approachable introduction to social constructionism is *Social Constructionism* by Vivien Burr (1995). In this she makes the point:

> It is through the daily interactions between people in the course of social life that our versions of knowledge become fabricated. Therefore social interaction of all kinds, and particularly language, is of great interest to social constructionists. The goings-on between people in the course of their everyday lives are seen as the practices during which our shared versions of knowledge are constructed. Therefore what we regard as 'truth' (which of course varies historically and cross-culturally) i.e. our current accepted ways of understanding the world, is a product not of objective observation of the world, but of social processes and interactions in which people are constantly engaged with each other. (1995: 4)

Burr stresses here that knowledge is not an absolute or universal truth but is always contextual. Researchers adopting a social constructionist approach are often more interested in gaining insight into the social consequences of social reality being constructed in contexts, and, most importantly, the impact this has upon how people can act and how they are treated. Rather than seeking out 'facts', they ask questions such as: what actions does this version of social reality make possible? In what ways does it constrain what people can do? Who gets their own way? Who is exploited?

Logics of inquiry

This section examines three different 'logics of inquiry', a term originated by Blaikie (2000) and which I find useful for 'getting back to basics' – examining the fundamentally different logics that lie behind our attempts to gain knowledge. Here I outline, discuss and give examples of the three key logics of inquiry used to gain evidence to inform policy and practice in youth justice:

- induction

- deduction

- abduction.

By and large, induction and deduction are generally adopted within the modernist paradigm. Abduction occurs in both modernist and postmodern research.

Induction

Induction can be seen as consisting of four main stages:

1. Facts are comprehensively observed, measured and recorded.

2. These facts are analyzed, compared and classified to look for trends and patterns. For example, the data are statistically analysed to look for correlations.

3. From this analysis, generalizations are inferred about the relationships between the measured and recorded facts.

4. These generalizations are tested by further observation of the facts.

Inductive studies are usually referred to as *descriptive research*. In them a situation is created or a naturally occurring event is observed, and the researcher seeks merely to record what happens in a dispassionate manner. By observing regularities in what happens, it is possible to come up with a hypothesis about what is 'going on'.

A good example here is the use of descriptive statistics about the personal qualities and circumstances of young people who engage in crime. The aim is to identify the risk factors that predispose young people to crime and, in this way, to inform interventions to prevent offending and reoffending (Farrington 1996).

Deduction

The philosopher of science, Carl Popper (1959), outlined how the principle of *hypothetico-deductivism* is the basis of scientific experiments – making deductions from the testing of hypotheses. Popper stressed that, to gain empirical knowledge, it must be possible to make logical and unequivocal predictions about cause and effect. He argued specifically that, while induction can generate hypotheses, it cannot test them – this requires a deductive approach. Furthermore, Popper argued, deduction is based on falsification – putting a rule or a theory's predictions to the test in ways that allow for them to be disproved. Popper's argument can be applied to modernist social science research and summarized as follows:

1. The social world operates in a lawful manner, and the aim is to discover these laws.

2. This is done by generating theories, and from these making predictions in the form of hypotheses about cause and effect. By conducting experiments we can find out if the predictions are true or not, and hence if the laws are invalid.

3. Hypothesis testing cannot unequivocally establish these laws – but it can allow us to disprove (and thus reject) false predictions and hence theories, thereby moving gradually closer to the truth.

4. But we have no way of knowing for certain when we have arrived at a true theory, so even those theories that have survived testing must be regarded as provisional.

This may still seem an odd thing to do. Was Popper really arguing that researchers should set out deliberately to prove that their theories are wrong? What he was saying was that studies *must* be designed in such a way that the hypothesis *can* be falsified. Popper famously illustrated his approach with the example of the black swan. For thousands of years Europeans had observed millions of white swans. Using inductive evidence, we could come up with the theory that all swans are white. However, exploration of Australasia introduced Europeans to black swans. Popper's point is this: no matter how many observations are made which confirm a theory there is always the possibility that a future observation could refute it. Induction cannot yield certainty.

Popper's proposal is an alternative scientific method based on falsification. However many confirming instances there are for a theory, it only takes one counter-observation to falsify it: only one black swan is needed to repudiate the theory that all swans are white. Science, according to Popper, progresses when a theory is shown to be wrong and a new theory is introduced which better explains the phenomenon. For Popper, the scientist should attempt to disprove their theory rather than attempt continually to prove it.

Abduction

Abduction is a term most associated with the writings of the philosopher, Charles Sanders Pierce. Pierce (1955) defined abduction as the process of forming an explanatory hypothesis. Abductive research offers an opportunity to work on hunches and to construct theory rather than test it. Peirce used the term to contrast against the deductive *testing* of hypotheses. By 'forming explanatory hypotheses' he meant that abduction is a process of identifying specific occurrences in research data and then working out the most plausible explanation for them.

A good example is the way that Alexander Fleming discovered penicillin. He was doing experiments on bacteria and was growing them on agar gel in a pile of lidded glass dishes. He came into the lab one day and saw that, in some of the dishes in which the bacteria were growing, the gel was ruined because it had gone mouldy. He was about to throw them away when he noticed that there was a clear ring around the mould. What could this ring mean? What could explain it? He soon came to the conclusion that the mould was producing something to kill the bacteria – and, in this way, antibiotics were discovered.

Thomas Kuhn (1970) has written eloquently about the role of such abductive reasoning in science. He argued that, while science is usually 'a highly cumulative enterprise, eminently successful in its aim, the steady extension of the scope and precision of scientific knowledge', this is not the only way. Sometimes scientists (such as Fleming) come across things that surprise them. When this happens, Kuhn says, they have to shift from testing hypotheses to creating them: 'New and unsuspected phenomena are … repeatedly un-covered by scientific research, and radical new theories have again and again been invented by scientists' (1970: 53).

Abductive research involves either homing in on disjunctions and discrep-ancies – that which is surprising or intriguing because it does not fit into pre-existing frameworks – or creating conditions where researchers can be surprised. Just as Sherlock Holmes would always reach a point of identifying the crucial clue – such as 'the dog that did not bark' – abductive research looks for anomalies, inconsistencies and incongruities in what has been examined.

And, just like Sherlock Holmes, the researcher now has to puzzle out what can possibly account for the anomaly.

One of the most powerful advocates of abductive research is Gary Shank (1998). Shank argues that researchers should give up trying to be 'scientific' by concentrating on inductive or deductive logic. Instead, he says, they should concentrate on developing the skills needed to conduct research into meaning. And abduction, he says, is the way to go. Researchers do not need to wait to be surprised – though they should treasure serendipitous surprises when they happen. Surprises can be *made* to happen. Shank claims that 'we tend to see the world not in terms of truth, but in terms of significance. This means that we experience not a world of facts, but of signs' (1998: 856). And so, he argues, we should devise methods based upon semiotics – the study of signs, symbols and meaning. Shank recommends 'a semiotic strategy that uses an abductive focus' since this is 'general enough to address basic issues, while being sensitive enough to the complex and manifold issues of meaning' (1998: 853).

An example is Christine Piper's (2000) in-depth analysis of the assumptions about children's interests within current law in England and Wales. Her analysis is very much about unpicking the taken-for-granted:

> Assumptions are those ideas, events and principles which are taken for granted as being true. They are no longer – or may have never been – subject to critical scrutiny, either because they appear self-evident or because it is assumed they have been proven to be 'true'. Spelling them out, thinking about their provenance and querying their validity is therefore not necessary. Indeed, the existence of a strong and widely held assumption may preclude the possibility of individuals thinking about the basis of the assumption: it simply does not cross their minds to do so because they do not recognize the existence of an alternative way of thinking. (2000: 261)

Piper goes on to say 'I think we may have reached that stage in the family justice system in recent years', declaring the key purpose of her paper – to scrutinize the assumptions about children's best interests upon which contemporary English family justice law is based.

In her paper she identifies an anomaly – that the law (as instantiated both by legislation and by legal practice) holds two very differing and conflicting sets of assumptions about children's 'best interests'. One, operating in court procedures about children's welfare (such as post-divorce settlements), focuses on the need to keep children out of court and not expose them to questioning in such intimidating settings because it is inherently harmful to them. The other is that children can and should be tried for criminal offences and, if they are serious, they should be tried in the adult court: 'Children must be there . . . and they must take responsibility for their actions . . . Well developed abilities to negotiate with adults, to act responsibly and to be held accountable for actions will be expected of the child or young person' (2000: 267).

Abductive inquiry is not designed, nor, indeed, intended to yield 'factual data'. Rather, its purpose to offer insight, sophisticated and in-depth understanding that, its proponents claim, can powerfully inform policy and practice.

Conclusions

Much of the traditional criminology that informs youth justice is based on the modernist assumption that factual, reliable knowledge can be gained about human behaviour and experience; and that, by gathering appropriate evidence, criminologists can identify the key risk factors for criminality, for example. Equally it assumes that it is a relatively simple thing to do to collect valid and reliable evidence about the processes and phenomena that are involved in young people's criminal behaviour – and hence to use this evidence to inform good practice in changing this behaviour.

More recently we have seen the emergence of criminological theory and research informed by postmodern epistemology and ontology, where crime, in itself, is not regarded as some naturally occurring 'thing' but as a product of human meaning-making, that varies from one historical period to another (such as the law on homosexuality) and from one location to another (such as the law about where it is permissible to park a car). From this perspective evidence to inform policy and practice is derived from in-depth, qualitative research, seen to provide insight into why, say, some forms of interventions do not work.

Each of these approaches has real limits on what it can achieve, and it is essential to be aware of them when looking for evidence of what constitutes 'effective practice'. Workers in youth justice need to be wary about the claims made by either group. This chapter is intended to make you more cautious, to persuade you to question the claims sometimes made about 'what works' and more able to scrutinize the empirical basis given for such claims.

References

Blaikie, N. (2000) *Designing Social Research*. Cambridge: Polity Press.

Berger, P.L. and Luckmann, T. (1966) *The Social Construction of Reality*. Harmondsworth: Penguin Books.

Burr, V. (1995) *An Introduction to Social Constructionism*. London: Routledge.

Chalmers, A.F. (1999) *What is this Thing Called Science?* (3rd edn). Buckingham: Open University Press.

Farrington, D.P. (1996) 'The explanation and prevention of youthful offending', in J.D. Hawkins (ed.) *Delinquency and Crime: Current Theories*. New York, NY: Cambridge University Press.

Kuhn, T.S. (1970) *The Structure of Scientific Revolutions* (2nd edn). London: Tavistock.

Pierce, C.S. (1940) 'Abduction and induction', in J. Buchlder (ed.) *The Philosophy of Peirce: Selected Writings*. London: Routledge & Kegan Paul (republished in 1955 as *Philosophical Writings of Pierce*, New York, NY: Dover).

Piper, C. (2000) 'Assumptions about children's best interests', *Journal of Social Welfare and Family Law*, 22 261–76.

Popper, K. (1959) *The Logic of Scientific Discovery*. New York, NY: Basic Books.

Shank, G. (1998) 'The extraordinary powers of abductive reasoning', *Theory and Psychology*, 8: 841–60.

Part III

Policy, Possibilities and Penal Realities in Youth Justice

Introduction

Richard Hester

As noted in the previous part of this Handbook, youth justice practice does not occur in a vacuum. It is influenced by political decisions, which in turn affect the formulation of strategic policy. These decisions and processes are often made far from the youth justice workplace and yet their impact is very much felt at the local practice level. Policy itself is by no means neutral; it is the result of contested ideologies and 'truths' that change over time and space, that can be produced, transformed and interpreted in different ways.

In the following part we attempt to focus down, to make sense, to describe and to contextualize a number of aspects of youth justice policy and practice. We have attempted to do this by examining significant key areas that illustrate the interplay between policy and practice in the current youth justice system in England and Wales.

There are perhaps a number of areas that could have been selected for closer examination in this part, but we have chosen three. First, we have selected the issue of 'parenting' as an example of how certain 'truths' have been used by policy-makers as an attempt to influence practice directly and to prevent offending. This example is located very much at the beginning of what some may see as a 'pathway' to offending. The second area considered is that of 'restorative justice' as a 'competing ideology' within the formal youth justice system. Restorative justice has attracted passionate support and, at the same time, some measured caution as to its ultimate effectiveness. Moreover, its location in the system spans across early prevention to remedial work within the secure estate. Finally, the last two chapters are devoted to the very significant matter of incarceration as a purportedly 'last resort' response to youth crime. The examination of this 'last resort' is taken from two very different perspectives, united by a sense of deep concern as to the use of this particular response.

Amanda Holt takes an in-depth look at one of the recurring themes of New Labour's 'new youth justice' – i.e. the role and influence of parents and the conceptualization of 'parenting'. This chapter provides a brief overview of the historical context of parenting and youth justice before considering current policy. It focuses on the use of parenting orders, and the particular tensions within such policies, including the gendered nature of the orders and the notion that they are a means of making both parent and child criminally responsible. Using the direct experience of the author's own research, the chapter discusses issues relating to involving parents in youth justice practice and explores parents' experiences of parenting orders, reflecting on what this means for practice.

Helen Mahaffey shifts the focus again by looking at how 'community support policies' – particularly restorative justice – could, and should influence youth justice in England and Wales. In 1989, the New Zealand government passed the Children, Young People and their Families Act, which restructured the youth justice system to accommodate and acknowledge traditional Maori practices, such as family group conferences. Subsequent developments in restorative and community approaches to social conflicts and criminalized behaviours owe much to this path-breaking legislation. By looking at the experience of restorative justice practice in New Zealand/Aotearoa, Mahaffey considers the ways in which community support for young people can be developed and how recognition of issues of diversity and cultural sensitivity can contribute to the process of restoration.

Rod Morgan and Rod Earle conclude the part by examining the impact of incarceration by describing the situation of young people in penal custody. Morgan considers three issues using a range of empirical data. First, how many children and young people are there in penal custody, why are they there and what characterizes them? Secondly, what sort of custodial conditions are they in and with what associated problems? Thirdly, what are the prospects for change? The chapter does not provide comforting reading, nor should it do, being an indictment of the current situation with little optimism for immediate amelioration. However it provides a foundation of empirical data that contextualize and explain the multiple problems associated with juvenile incarceration.

Finally, Earle takes a more ethnographic approach and portrays a different perspective to the subject of penal custody by 'telling a story' about life inside a young offender institution with particular reference to the young people's identity who live there. Drawing on his recent research on the lives of young men in prison, he examines the qualities of the carceral experience. Questions of identity and ethnicity are considered in the ways in which young men respond to life behind bars. Using interviews and ethnographic interaction, the chapter seeks understandings of the way young men make sense of their lives as they proceed through a young offenders institution in southeast England. The significance of various forms of identification, through locality, ethnicity and masculinity, is explored to provide insights into how young men from the social margins of London and the south east make life inside, and outside, viable.

It is hoped that this examination of some key examples of the impact of policy on practice will provide practitioners working in both community and custodial settings with 'food for thought', as well as providing an overview of these important issues that can, and do, influence practice.

Parenting and youth justice: policy and practice

Amanda Holt

This chapter considers current policy regarding parenting and youth justice, with a specific focus on the increasing use of parenting orders: court orders which aim to make parents 'responsible' by compelling them to attend parenting programmes to learn new 'parenting skills'.

Parenting and youth justice: policy context

Ever since 'delinquency' was first identified as a social problem, the parents of the supposed delinquents have been identified as part of this problem and, if not part of the solution, then part of the policy response to youth offending. For example, early legislation, such as the Children and Young Persons Act 1933, made parents financially responsible for paying their child's fines or compensation for crimes, while the Children and Young Persons Act 1969 enabled social workers, to whom sentencing power had now shifted, to intervene in families deemed to be 'unsatisfactory'. A more explicit focus on the parent in youth justice policy came with the parental bind over, which was introduced in the Criminal Justice Act 1991 and made parents 'take proper care . . . and exercise proper control over [the child]' (s. 58.2(a)), with a fine of £1,000 for failure to do so.

These differing strands of social interventionism and moral authoritarianism have both found particular expression in the contemporary use of parenting orders, which were introduced in the Crime and Disorder Act 1998. Parenting orders can be issued to parents by magistrates in youth courts and can last for up to 12 months. A concern for welfare is apparent through the parenting order's provision of 'parenting support' for the parents of young people who are involved in, or are at risk of, offending. This support is usually provided through a support programme run by the local youth offending team (YOT) or through an external agency. However, a more punitive thread is also apparent by way of the threat of a £1,000 fine and summary conviction for failure to conform with the terms of the parenting order (notwithstanding the criminalizing arena through which the parenting order is issued in the first place).

Significant concerns have been raised for some time about the use of parenting orders, and it appears that very little has been done to address them. For example, many commentators have suggested that parenting orders are, in effect, 'mothering orders' (Henricson 2003: 58). While the Home Office does not collect data on the sociodemographic characteristics of parents issued with parenting orders, early data from those attending such parenting programmes suggest that they are overwhelmingly attended by mothers, by a factor of 8:2 (Lindfield 2001; Ghate and Ramella 2002). This effect is likely to be the product of both the gendering of family practices in parenting a 'young offender' and the gendering of 'youth justice' practices at an institutional level (Holt 2009). Ghate and Ramella (2002) also found an overwhelming number of attendees to be lone parents (49 per cent) and parents who are unemployed (56 per cent). Clearly, these figures should not be considered in isolation, given the strong and persistent relationship between gender, unemployment and lone parenthood (Pearce 1978). However, while there remain vast possibilities for addressing such profound and related social and economic disadvantage through directed intervention, the relentless focus on individual 'parenting skills' in parenting support provision means that such possibilities remain unrealized.

There is further concern with parenting orders and the practice of justice. Alongside the introduction of parenting orders, the Crime and Disorder Act 1998 also removed the rebuttable presumption of the principle of *doli incapax*: that is, the need for the prosecution to prove that a person under 14 years had formed the necessary criminal intent. This change effectively reinforced the fact that all children in England and Wales over 10 years were criminally responsible. At the same time, the introduction of parenting orders made their parents criminally responsible, meaning that both parent(s) and child(ren) face court orders as a youth justice response to the same offence, and both face criminal sanctions if such orders are breached.

Furthermore, as Goldson points out, the criminalizing interventions which parents experience (and, in cases of anti-social behaviour orders, the child as well) 'are unencumbered by such legal principles as "the burden of proof", "beyond reasonable doubt" and "due legal process"' (2005: 263–4). Consequently, parenting orders present a real violation to parents' civil liberties and human rights, an issue which may be reflected in some magistrates' reluctance to use parenting orders, resulting in (in an inversion to the frequently cited phrase) *injustice by geography*. For example, while some YOT areas have issued over 700 parenting orders in the past ten years, others have yet to issue any (YJB 2008 pers. comm.).

Involving parents in youth justice: some issues for practice

While concerns around equality and justice in parenting orders remain unaddressed, the more mundane realisation of parenting orders raises further, more practice-based issues. As mentioned above, the targeting of particular parents for parenting orders raises concerns that, in the decision-making processes of both the courts and YOTs (who recommend the parenting orders), a division may be constructed between parents who are 'willing' and seen as acting 'responsibly', and those who are 'not bothered', with the latter category issued with parenting orders (Arthur 2005; Koffman 2008). This is despite data from a number of sources which have found that most parents are anything but 'not bothered' in their struggle to cope with their child's behaviour before, during and after their involvement in the youth justice system (see Curtis 1999; Drakeford and McCarthy 2000; Hoskin and Lindfield 2005; Nixon and Parr 2006).

In particular, given the huge sociodemographic disparity between the magistrates who issue parenting orders, particularly in terms of age, occupational and social status (Morgan and Russell 2000) and the parents in receipt of them, magistrates' perceptions may well be based on their own cultural assumptions of what constitutes 'willing parents'. For example, Longstaff (2004) found that it was how parents 'speak and act' in court which determined whether they were issued with a parenting order, a finding which supports Hollingsworth's observation that 'those who parent in the way acceptable to the State, even if their child offends, are not subject to the same intervention as others' (2007: 207).

A further concern involves the use of 'parenting support' to address the assumed support needs of parents whose children are involved in, or are at risk of, offending. The parenting support offered to parents (both voluntarily and compulsorily through the parenting order) generally comprises an eight-week course, usually offered in a group setting but which can also be offered on a one-to-one basis. While the content of such programmes varies between local YOTs, they generally involve the teaching of specific 'parenting skills', covering themes such as 'family conflict', 'boundary-setting and maintenance' and 'supervision and monitoring' (Ghate and Ramella 2002). Lindfield (2002: 75) categorizes such programmes into four 'core elements': *knowledge* (e.g. 'child development'), *skills* (e.g. 'active listening'), *attitudes* (e.g. 'belief and indicators that change is possible') and *experience* (e.g. 'how past impacts on present').

However, while there is some evidence which suggests that parents do find some use in such programmes (e.g. Ghate and Ramella 2002), there remain a number of problems with only presenting 'support' through the prism of individualized psychological 'skills'. Stressed families who face multiple structural disadvantages (e.g. poverty, poor health) will struggle to benefit from parenting support programmes if wider support programmes which address these disadvantages are not also implemented (Moran *et al.* 2004). Certainly, much evidence suggests that such multiple disadvantages are self-reported as impacting negatively on parenting (Drakeford and McCarthy 2000; Ghate and Hazell 2002), and the same families who face these disadvantages are statistically more likely either to refuse to attend or to drop out of parenting support programmes (Moran and Ghate 2005).

Furthermore, despite Ghate and Ramella's reported successes in parenting support, they also note how parents issued with parenting orders (who comprised only 16 per cent of their sample) were initially very resistant to parenting support, with mothers reportedly feeling like 'criminals' in the courtroom (2002). Similarly, Bowers reported that such parents felt that 'they are being chastized or victimized by the courts, rather than assisted' (2002: 56), and such experiences need to be acknowledged by practitioners when working with such 'involuntary' clients. Parents also face a number of practical consequences of attending court with their child, such as the risk of job loss for repeated attendance and the difficulties of attending court when there are other dependants at home (Curtis 1999). The effects of such experiences, including the issuing of the parenting order itself, were the subject of the author's own research study, the findings of which are briefly discussed below.

Findings from the current research

It is very difficult for parents to argue against something which is cloaked as 'support', especially when those parents have been asking for support for a number of years. This was found to be the case in the author's own research, which involved interviewing 17 parents who had been issued with a parenting order, and who found that almost all the parents had been asking various agencies for voluntary support for a number of years. The parents – 15 mothers and 2 fathers – were recruited from four different YOTs and were asked to share their experiences of all aspects of the parenting order process, which included their child's alleged offending, their experiences in court and their experiences of attending the parenting support programme. While it is not possible to discuss their experiences in detail here (but see Holt 2009, forthcoming), some key themes which emerged suggest both advice for best practice and recommendations for change:

- For the parents who were interviewed, the scope of the problems they experienced extended well beyond any individual 'parenting skills deficit' and included structural factors such as unemployment, poverty, lone parenthood (often in large families), domestic violence and mental health problems. Furthermore, many of the children and young people who were involved in offending had been excluded from school and/or were attending special schools for learning and/or behavioural difficulties.

However, in the face of such multiple difficulties, the parents showed huge amounts of resourcefulness, particularly in their management of interactions with a range of state and voluntary agencies, which included social services, housing, education and refuge projects. Rather than *not* taking responsibility, it became clear that parenting a 'young offender' produces additional parenting responsibilities which often go unrecognized: examples include ensuring their child attends YOT appointments and complies with curfews; paying court costs/fines; negotiating with the police and solicitors; and coping with threats of eviction due to their child's behaviour.

In many cases, parents were also the victims of their child's crimes (e.g. assault, theft, criminal damage), an issue which is frequently unrecognized within the dominant political, legal and cultural discourses of 'parent blame' and which needs to be addressed outside the narrow confines of the parenting order/parenting support framework.

- Being issued with a parenting order produced a range of particularly negative experiences for the parents and involuntary clients. These included:

  – *anger* towards their own 'sentences' for their child's actions, which they felt were more severe than their child's sentence in comparison;

  – *humiliation* that they had been publicly branded a 'bad parent' and were being punished accordingly;

  – *confusion* as to why 'support' was being administered through the courts, particularly when they had been voluntarily requesting support for a number of years;

  – *feelings of injustice* that this support was being issued discriminatively by magistrates who appeared to have no idea of their circumstances and who appeared to be letting other parents 'get away with it'; and

  – *frustration* that parents had no involvement in judicial decision-making concerning their child. While the state had supposedly taken responsibility for dealing with their child's behaviour through the courts, parents were still being made responsible for their child's subsequent actions. This exacerbated feelings of powerlessness and blame.

- It is perhaps unsurprising that the negative experiences of court shaped parents' subsequent experiences of the parenting support programmes. In particular, it would appear that the most positive aspect of the support programmes was the opportunity it provided to enable parents to repair the damage done to their own parental identities by the court process. This was achieved by meeting other parents in similar positions which provided them with evidence that they weren't 'bad parents' after all (perhaps divisively so, through the perception that 'there are worse parents out there', as one parent explained).

Parents also reported experiencing support from the practitioners, whom they did not feel held the same negative view of them as they claimed the magistrates did, and some parents found some of the 'conflict management strategies' useful. However, many parents reflected on the lack of material support and the programme's exclusive focus on 'commonsense' parenting skills, which they felt was not needed and/or did not work in practice with their own child(ren).

A few of the parents found the groupwork sessions particularly exposing and overly intimate, as the programme required them to discuss their own family experiences with other parents in the group, which the parents did not necessarily feel comfortable with. It was apparent that each individual YOT organized its parenting support in particular ways and, while all offered one-to-one sessions if it was felt to be more appropriate, some YOTs tended to operate group sessions as the 'default' mode, raising concerns about the suitability of current criteria for judging appropriateness and responsivity to parents' needs.

So, did the parenting order experience make any long-term difference? The parents interviewed had received their parenting orders between two years and two weeks earlier. For one parent, the answer is yes: she found that the parenting support programme enabled her to 'turn my life around' and gave her confidence to work on her personal relationships, her own problems with alcohol and to develop confidence in herself. However, it is telling that this mother's experience of the courtroom differed from all the other parents' experiences in that she *requested* the parenting order as an alternative to the fine which the magistrates were initially offering, perhaps informally shifting the voluntariness of this parent's attendance (this case is discussed in detail in Holt 2008).

For the other parents, whose experiences of criminalization in the courtroom shaped their experiences of subsequent parenting support, the parenting order made little overall difference to their lives. In all cases, none of the parents reported any changes in their child's offending or troublesome behaviour as a result of the parenting support programme and, for most parents, the material and structural problems they were battling with remained long after the parenting order expired.

Discussion and conclusions

This research suggests that attempts to expand the use of parental responsibility laws, as seen in the recently published *Youth Crime Action Plan* (DCSF 2008), will always fail to address the complexities of material and social disadvantage which shape the problem of youth crime, although they clearly perform a politically populist function in showing that the appropriate people are seen to be punished. However, while parenting order policy remains in place (and there is little suggestion of anything changing soon), there are some things which both magistrates and practitioners might do differently. For magistrates, one issue concerns the need to apply practice guidance consistently to *all* parents who come before them (as well as those who do not).

Furthermore, there is a need for consistency across different jurisdictions, which is not the case at present and which would go some way to remedying the experiences of injustice which parents feel. While magistrates are clearly not issuing parenting orders in every case before them where the child is under 16 years (as stipulated by the practice guidance), there is perhaps a greater issue of inconsistency *within* jurisdictions, with parents not being told why they are being issued a parenting order while other parents in seemingly similar situations are seen to be 'getting away with it'. Moreover, magistrates might involve parents in the decision-making processes regarding the sentencing of their child(ren), thus working *with* parents rather than seemingly against them. This involvement should entail an increased recognition of the multiple social and economic difficulties which face such parents, including their own experiences of victimization by their children.

In terms of good practice, many of the parenting practitioners who had to work with such 'involuntary clients' did a very good job: much of their initial work involved convincing parents that they were not 'bad parents' and they could not necessarily control their teenage children. Aside from the messages from elsewhere that they were nevertheless expected to, parents did appreciate the understanding which practitioners showed them, and this early work enabled some degree of engagement which might otherwise have not been possible. In the main, this seems to have been achieved by the practitioners being positioned as distinct from the courts and judiciary: as one parent described her practitioner: 'the people that run them groups aren't even from the courts . . . they're people that are educated through young kids that are naughty.' The practitioners drawing on their own parenting experiences and difficulties enabled parents to construct them as, to use Williams' (2004) phrase, 'quasi-professionals' – that is, professionals who are 'experts-by-experience' and are at once positioned both at a professional distance and as having a shared identity based upon common experiences. However, some parents were unhappy about not being able to discuss their feelings of anger towards the court in the group setting: there was a sense that the parenting programme was put forward as somewhere for parents to 'move on', which meant the closing off of opportunities for parents to explore their negative emotions. This issue did seem particular to parents attending groupwork sessions, where programmes of interaction were perhaps more routinized than one-to-one support programmes.

For practitioners, the kind of support offered could shift from the individualistic model of 'parenting skills' (a model which is based on the psychological theories which underpin our understandings of child development; see Chapter 3 this volume) to an approach that incorporates an understanding of – and a professional response to – the socio-economic pressures they face. This might involve facilitating parents and young people to participate meaningfully in the decisions that affect their lives through their collective involvement in community development initiatives and political action over issues such as housing, local policing, victim support, legal advocacy, poverty, mental health support, education and training, childcare, mobility and transport and local facilities for young people.

Change needs to be focused outwardly, on producing better resourced communities and changing structural inequalities, not inwardly on assumed deficient parenting practices. In facilitating change, the development of informal support networks for parents is vital but, as the author's research demonstrates, such support networks are unlikely to develop by forcing families to meet in a local classroom for two hours a week on a Tuesday evening.

References

Arthur, R. (2005) 'Punishing parents for the crimes of their children', *Howard Journal of Criminal Justice*, 44: 233–53.

Bowers, L. (2002) 'Unrecognised victims: the parents of child and adolescent offenders', *Issues in Forensic Psychology*, 3: 49–58.

Curtis, S. (1999) *Children Who Break the Law – or Everybody Else Does*. Winchester: Waterside Press.

Department for Children, Schools and Families (2008) *Youth Crime Action Plan*. London: DCSF (available online at http://www.homeoffice.gov.uk/documents/youth-crime-action-plan/youth-crime-action-plan-08?view=Binary).

Drakeford, M. and McCarthy, K. (2000) 'Parents, responsibility and the new youth justice', in B. Goldson (ed.) *The New Youth Justice*. Lyme Regis: Russell House Publishing.

Ghate, D. and Hazell, N. (2002) *Parenting in Poor Environments: Stress, Support and Coping*. London: Jessica Kingsley.

Ghate, D. and Ramella, M. (2002) *Positive Parenting: The National Evaluation of the Youth Justice Board's Parenting Programme*. Policy Research Bureau (available online at http://www.youth-justice-board.gov.uk).

Goldson, B. (2005) 'Taking liberties: policy and the punitive turn', in H. Hendrick (ed.) *Child Welfare and Social Policy: An Essential Reader*. Bristol: Policy Press.

Henricson, C. (2003) *Government and Parenting: Is there a Case for a Policy Review and a Parents' Code?* York: Joseph Rowntree Foundation.

Hollingsworth, K. (2007) 'Responsibility and rights: children and their parents in the youth justice system', *International Journal of Law, Policy and the Family*, 21: 190–219.

Holt, A. (2008) 'Room for resistance? Parenting orders, disciplinary power and the construction of the bad parent', in P. Squires (ed.) *ASBO Nation: The Criminalisation of Nuisance*. Bristol: Policy Press.

Holt, A. (2009) '(En)gendering responsibilities: experiences of parenting a "young offender"', *Howard Journal of Criminal Justice*, 48.

Holt, A. (forthcoming) 'Managing spoiled identities: parents' experiences of compulsory parenting support programmes', *Children and Society*.

Hoskin, C. and Lindfield, S. (2005) *Involving Young People in Parenting Programmes.* Brighton: Trust for the Study of Adolescence.

Koffman, L. (2008) 'Holding parents to account: tough on children, tough on the causes of children?', *Journal of Law and Society*, 35: 113–30.

Lindfield, S. (2001) *Responses to Questionnaire: Parenting Work in the Youth Justice Context.* Brighton: Trust for the Study of Adolescence.

Lindfield, S. (2002) 'Parenting orders', *Magistrate*, March: 74–5.

Longstaff, E. (2004) *Good Enough Parenting? Youth Crime and Parental Responsibility.* Cambridge: University of Cambridge Press.

Moran, P. and Ghate, D. (2005) 'The effectiveness of parenting support', *Children and Society* 19: 329–36.

Moran, P., Ghate, D. and ven der Merwe, A. (2004) *What Works in Parenting Support? A Review of the International Evidence.* London: Department of Education and Skills.

Morgan, R. and Russell, N. (2000) *The Judiciary in the Magistrates' Courts.* Home Office (available online at http://www.homeoffice.gov.uk/rds/pdfs/occ-judiciary.pdf).

Nixon, J. and Parr, S. (2006) 'Anti-social behaviour: voices from the front line', in J. Flint (ed.) *Housing and Anti-social Behaviour: Perspectives, Policy and Practice.* Bristol: Policy Press.

Pearce, D. (1978) 'The feminization of poverty: women, work and welfare', *Urban and Social Change Review*, 11: 28–36.

Williams, F. (2004) 'Care, value and support in local self-help groups', *Social Policy and Society*, 3: 431–8.

Restorative justice at the heart of the youth community

Helen Mahaffey

Introduction

Historically, political responses to youth offending have focused on the individual offender. Restorative principles and practices, however, have presented an alternative framework which asserts that responsibility is communal and shared. An examination of the origins of restorative and community approaches and a critical analysis of the ideas and practices that are continuing to develop raise important questions about the directions currently taken in the field of youth justice.

The origins

Restorative justice has its roots in a wide range of community practices, most notably in the indigenous communities in Australia and New Zealand. At a time when the Maori people were successfully reclaiming land and other rights, there was a reclaiming also of responsibility for Maori youth. The community sought ways of responding to offending and the unacceptably high incarceration rates in ways that were more culturally appropriate. What became known as 'Aboriginal justice' and 'Maori justice' addressed problems (not only to do with offending) collectively and informally. The desire to repair social bonds and relationships was at the heart of these processes, which were consensual and inclusive with all parties taking part in the negotiation and shaping of the decision-making. Reflecting back and showing the responsibility that young people had for and to their family and community were an important part of the process. There was a stressing of the young person's power to affect these in a positive manner: not only was it a restoration of the family and the community but it was also a restoration of the individual's dignity, power and freedom.

The practice, which became known more widely as 'family group conferencing' (FGC), developed in New Zealand and Canada with wide political, personal and community implications. While to an extent it was embraced by and expressed in statute with the passing of the Children, Young Persons and their Families Act 1989, to what degree this philosophy was successfully translated into the legislation and policy needs detailed examination.

The new system relied on the Youth Aid division of the police force working with young offenders at the first point of contact. Youth justice co-ordinators prepared for conferences, liaised with the police, courts and the community, some undertaking preparative work in schools and with groups of young people depending on the private sector funding available. The youth courts dealt with monitoring conferences as a form of quality control and dealt with 'not guilty' pleas. Conferencing within youth justice was a comprehensive system of diversion from custodial sentences for young people as well as FGCs for pre-sentence in the case of more serious offences (Maxwell and Morris 2001). This led to the closure of the most of youth detention centres.

The legal framework of the Act did not occur overnight but emerged from a decade of planning and consultation intended to represent a major transfer of power away from the state to community groups. One view is that reform was 'top down and bottom up and embraced child protection as well as youth offending' (Tickell and Akester 2004: 39). The idea was to find family solutions to family problems within the context of the wider community. FGCs became a forum to deal with youth care and protection issues as well as youth crime, and they brought together all members of a young person's family as a means of support (McElrea 1994).

There are questions to be asked about how that was transferred into practice. Who instigated and took the lead in these forums? How were young people supported in fulfilling the plans they made? In practice one early concern was that 'the consensus supporting the goals and aspirations of the system did not produce sufficient government provision of the necessary resources to achieve them' (Tickell and Akester 2004: 42). This translated into a lack of funding to meet the needs of more serious and persistent offenders in particular.

Emerging practice and philosophy

This new language of the direct involvement of ordinary members of the community as well as victims and offenders (Maxwell and Morris 2001) marked a fundamental shift from the formalized, adversarial criminal justice proceedings towards bringing people together face to face to talk about the offence and its effects. The work of Terry O'Connell in New Zealand has been largely drawn upon and has helped move restorative and community practices in a certain direction. His adaptation of the process, which became known as the 'Wagga model', specified essential features: an awareness and acknowledgement of the harm they had caused, an understanding of their responsibility and a need to meet their responsibility with appropriate actions (Barton 2003). O'Connell focused on emotionality (dealing with hurt, anger, fear, etc.) as key to participants reaching a sense of 'closure'.

One of the crucial shifts affected by the Wagga model was that, although there was a strong emphasis on both sides of community involvement, the community was no longer guiding the process: the facilitator became central. Questions about who facilitates these conferences and assumptions about 'appropriate' emotions became central for, rather than the community setting standards and being expert, there was now an externally imposed value base.

An informing criminological theory base suggested that 'shame' directed at offenders was a powerful form of social control (Braithwaite 1989). While an important proviso was the necessity for a context of respect around the process, followed by efforts to reintegrate offenders (reintegrative shaming), it too placed increasing emphasis on facilitation. The obvious risks of alienation and stigmatization and of labelling of the child/young person are apparent – 'the problem' was being placed very firmly back with the young person. The process became more imposed and formalized with set outcomes concerning what individuals *should* feel and when.

After years of debate in the early 1990s the Wagga model was rejected and most of the Australian states adopted statutory schemes. Work on conferencing projects in the South Australia Juvenile Justice Research focused on more violent offences and serious property offences. There have been interesting findings from this on the effects of conferences on individuals (Daley and Hayes 2002). Daley (2003) commented that reduced offending may well emerge as a welcome side effect to conferencing.

The Wagga model (police facilitated and drawing heavily on reintegrative shaming) was adopted and adapted in many countries, including Canada, England and the USA. The fact that it was essentially a police programme may have been attractive for decision-makers at national level since clearly there were huge potential cost savings in employing such practices as alternatives to incarceration.

Developments in England and Wales

In the UK restorative approaches to offending represented a shift in orientation as well as language amid a political debate seeking alternatives to previous demands for toughness and punishment and addressing the causes of crime. The government's growing interest in restorative methods and victims' rights was demonstrated in the Crime and Disorder Act 1998, youth offending teams (YOTs) were introduced to co-ordinate services and a whole raft of orders was put in place, including action plan orders and reparation orders, with the aim of prevention and early intervention. The Youth Justice and Criminal Evidence Act 1999 explicitly endorsed restorative principles for the first time as part of sentencing options for courts within the field of youth justice. Victim–offender mediation (with or without victims present) in which victims might also be collective or corporate in nature moved the practice even further away from those who were personally affected. Restorative conferencing, FGC and youth offender panels became options.

All young offenders pleading guilty for the first time in the youth courts were to be referred to youth offender panels (YOPs), unless they were to be sentenced to custody or absolutely discharged. One representative from the YOT and two selected volunteers with different skills and experience were trained to work out a contract. It was envisaged that every young person would have the opportunity to participate in relatively informal circumstances and parents would be encouraged to attend.

Thames Valley Police, who adopted the Wagga model when it began conferencing, applied a method of delivering police cautions to young offenders: those whose case was deemed appropriate and who faced going to court were given the option of a restorative caution (Paterson and McIvor 1999; Young and Goold 2003). This was police led at every stage of the process and was formulaic and more measurable. Therefore, while good-quality facilitation and getting the process right have been cited as key factors linked to success (Young and Hoyle 2002) the model became an outcome-led and, arguably, managerialist process. Restorative practice moved further from the young person's family and community. It should also be noted that the restorative approach as a voluntary, consensual option was problematic given that alternatives might include further court appearances.

Evidence base: a critique

Leading academics and experts at the Australian National University set up a large-scale field experiment, Reintegrative Shaming Experiments (RISE), which was undertaken to compare the effects of courts and conferences. It was designed to test the effectiveness of conferences and did this mainly by comparing recidivism rates and costs. Research in England and Wales, funded by the Home Office and undertaken by the Metropolitan and the Northumberland Police, drew extensively on the RISE model.

Research has focused mainly on one practice model, yet within the field of youth justice a wide range of models is used, including victim empathy programmes, victim offender mediation, restorative conferencing and cautioning, YOPs, FGC and sentencing circles (Tickell and Akester 2004). All may be introduced at a number of different stages in the criminal justice process.

Overall, the effectiveness of restorative interventions over and above custodial sentences is generally supported (Tickell and Akester 2004), with significant benefits for both young people who have offended and victims in terms of raising awareness and closing the issue (Wilcox et al. 2004).

Sherman and Strang reviewed research on restorative justice (RJ) in the UK and abroad and concluded that it was more effective with serious offences and when personal harm has been caused (Sherman and Strang 2007), although the emphasis to date within youth justice has been to use RJ at earlier stages and for less serious offences. Their conclusions were drawn from a mixed sample of adult and youth studies but only one example featured young people from the UK, relating to property crime by young people under the age of 18 in Northumbria. The review compared conventional justice with RJ at various stages of the criminal justice process for violence and theft, focusing mainly on two forms of RJ: face-to-face meetings with mainly specially trained police officers leading the process and involving all parties connected to an offence, including victims, offenders, families, and friends; and restitution as ordered by the court. RJ with violent crime (as opposed to property crime) was found overall to reduce repeat offending.

Within practice questions also arise about how far victims and offenders are brought together (if at all) in a meaningful way. Low victim rates have been shown across a full range of orders that contain elements of reparation (Newburn *et al*. 2001). Indirect community reparation has been heavily relied on, replacing direct victim involvement in some programmes (Wilcox *et al*. 2004).

General themes emerge here. There is a move away from involving the community towards more individualistic practices – on some occasions even a victim is not present. Furthermore, by searching for such simplistic outcomes as reducing reoffending, Daley's point about a disservice being done to RJ becomes pertinent by raising unrealistic expectations when so many factors are involved. Rather than regarding complete success as reducing reoffending, a reduction in reoffending may emerge as a side-effect (Daley 2003). In restorative and community approaches, the primary aim was not to reduce offending but to repair and build relationships.

The Northumbria findings regarding wider involvement are interesting. Females under the age of 18 whose parents joined in consenting to an RJ conference as part of a final warning for assault were assigned either to the conference or a 'talking to' by a police officer. Within this all-female age group in this area an impressive 71 per cent reduction in recidivism for those who were involved in conferences as opposed to those lectured by a police officer was estimated (Sherman *et al*. 2006). There was, however, no such effect on recidivism when it came to RJ with young white males in the same area and no clear explanation is given for this, but it is does raise interesting questions and is explored further in the schools context below. Daley's (2003) observation of young males who are less integrated and who may have a history of offending provides some useful insights here.

What appears to be a fundamental weakness in the research so far carried out is that it focuses on a comparison between RJ approaches and non-RJ approaches, such as custodial sentences in criminal justice and exclusion when it comes to schools. Scant attention is paid to the specific nature of the RJ process itself and the differences between the various models.

Schools

When restorative approaches were piloted in schools, the National Evaluation of the Restorative Justice in Schools Programme (YJB 2004) focused its research mainly on restorative conferences to identify whether the aims of reducing exclusions, increasing attendance and addressing incidents of bullying, in particular, were being achieved. There exist similar problems to those mentioned above in the field of youth justice. In addition to the many models, such as preventative-type meetings (e.g. restorative circles, circle time, family and restorative conferencing (Mahaffey and Newton 2008)), there are a number of views about how to conduct a restorative conference and many different practices. Some practitioners follow a scripted and structured format while others adopt a more open, semi-structured model; some have used co-facilitation and some single facilitation in conferences; and in some schools pupils (trained mediators) run conferences and in others trained staff.

The results in terms of agreements and apologies made, of repaired relationships and the apparent cessation of behaviours which led to the conference are impressive. However, increasingly the conferences are individualistic and the danger is that the problem becomes once more firmly located within individuals and small groups of pupils. When community members were invited to attend, although the figures were small, the outcomes were positive. Less than one fifth (19 per cent) of the conferences involved parents as parties to the conference. Strikingly, however, when parents (and significant adults) were involved, even more progress was made and relationships, especially between school and parent, were strengthened (YJB 2004).

Discussion

Key questions are raised around the issue of community support and involvement and why more is not being done to ensure parents and significant community members are a more integral part of these RJ processes within both youth justice and a schools contexts. One issue that is often raised concerns the time-consuming nature of such involvement. However this is outweighed by the potential consequences of parents learning to be more restorative and the consequent effect of strengthening agreements made between pupils and the schools (and potentially between families/communities and statutory bodies). This was acknowledged in the research.

There are a great many forms of RJ but, unfortunately, there is a paucity of research which takes that into account, and research relating to one form might wrongly appear to relate to something quite different simply because both bear the title 'restorative'. Furthermore, the choice of measurement may reflect political rather than social needs and may therefore determine the form of RJ that is being preferred and practised. It does appear that the bias appears to be towards individualistic practices which lend themselves to simplistic measurement, with an emerging picture of a narrowing of restorative practices themselves. There is at this stage a need to have clear research into the different models – research which is not measured solely by reoffending rates but which takes into account more general effects.

A current concern is that restorative interventions are being placed within a punitive framework, as illustrated in many of the statutory processes being developed in the domain of youth justice in the UK (Morris and Gelsthorpe 2000). The danger is that retributive and punitive approaches are simply being repackaged as restorative (see also Gray 2005).

RJ and community approaches began as attempts to empower individuals and communities. However, restorative and community practices have moved away from the idea of self-directed community healing towards 'experts' dealing with specific issues and even excluding those who have already been systematically excluded. Restorative approaches in most settings often seem to become restrictive, formalized processes, with concepts of correct procedure and desired outcomes being imposed from without rather than emerging from the individuals and communities concerned. Policy-makers and those involved in the administration of criminal justice can have a very narrow perception of restorative and community approaches. In current practice the facilitator has become fundamental (the author is one such facilitator!), while the parents, the community and even the victim have become optional – often even peripheral. Organizations tend to favour approaches which give them more control and need processes which are easily measurable.

My own experience suggests that, while restorative interventions can have ripple effects in the community, there remains the sense that it is the individual who is dealt with. Providing opportunities to speak out and to express feelings and to have those feelings acknowledged continues to be hugely valued – this is not in question. Yet rarely is there an awareness of the community; when there is that awareness, however, it has been of huge benefit to all concerned.

Conclusion

We need to widen restorative approaches in terms of the range of participants, the issues dealt with and also the depth of involvement. A return to the roots of restorative and community practices could provide us with the orientation we need to view the responsibility as 'ours' and not merely 'his', 'hers' or 'theirs', as community members with a responsibility to recognize, restore and repair from within. We need to return to such concepts as dignity and respect, concepts which informed the original community and restorative approaches – a return to concepts such as *Mana*, an idea embedded in the Maori language which encompasses the individual as an agent, choosing and acting within their life and community.

References

Barton, C.K.B. (2003) *Restorative Justice: The Empowerment Model*. Annandale, NSW: Hawkins Press.

Braithwaite, J. (1989) *Crime, Shame and Reintegration*. Cambridge: Cambridge University Press.

Daley, K. (2003) 'Making variation a virtue: evaluating the potential and limits of restorative justice', in E.G.M. Weitekamp and H.J. Kerner (eds) *Restorative Justice in Context: International Practices and Directions*. Cullompton: Willan Publishing.

Daley, K. and Hayes, H. (2002) 'Restorative justice and conferencing', in A. Graycar and P. Grabosky (eds) *Handbook of Australian Criminology*. Cambridge: Cambridge University Press.

Gray, P. (2005) 'The politics of risk and young offenders' experiences of social exclusion and restorative justice', *British Journal of Criminology*. 45: 938–57.

Mahaffey, H. and Newton, C. (2008) *Restorative Solutions: Making it Work: Improving Challenging Behaviour and Relationships in School*. London: Inclusive Solutions UK Limited.

Masters, G. and Roberts, A. (2000) 'Family group conferencing for victims, offenders and communities', in M. Leibmann (ed.) *Mediation in Context*. London: Jessica Kingsley.

Maxwell, G. and Morris, A. (2001) 'Family group conferences and reoffending', in A. Morris and G. Maxwell, (eds) *Restorative Justice for Juveniles: Conferencing, Mediation and Circles*. Oxford: Hart Publishing.

McElrea, F. (1994) 'Justice in the community: the New Zealand experience', in J. Burnside and N. Baker (eds) *Relational Justice: Repairing the Breach*. Winchester: Waterside Press.

Morris, A. and Gelsthorpe, L. (2000) 'Something old, something borrowed, something blue, but something new? A comment on the prospects for restorative justice under the Crime and Disorder Act 1998', *Criminal Law Review*, 18–30.

Newburn, T., Crawford, A., Earle, R., Goldie, S., Hale, C., Masters, G., Netten, A., Saunders, R., Sharpe, K., Uglow, S. and Campbell, A. (2001) *The Introduction of Referral Orders into the Youth Justice System*. HORS 242. London: Home Office.

Paterson, F. and McIvor, G. (1999). 'Conferencing as a response to youth crime.' Paper presented at the British criminology conference, Liverpool, July.

Sherman, L.W. and Strang, H. (2007) *Restorative Justice: The Evidence*. London: Smith Institute.

Sherman, L., Strang, H., Barnes, G.C. and Newbury-Birch, D. (2006) 'Preliminary analysis of the Northumbria restorative justice experiments.' Unpublished manuscript, Lee Center of Criminology, Philadelphia, PA.

Stephenson, M., Giller, H. and Brown, S. (2007) *Effective Practice in Youth Justice*. Cullompton: Willan Publishing.

Tickell, S. and Akester, K. (2004) *Restorative Justice: The Way Ahead*. London: Justice.

Tutu, D. (1999) *No Future without Forgiveness*. London: Rider.

Wilcox, A., Young, R. and Hoyle, C. (2004) *Two Year Resanctioning Study: A Comparison of Restorative and Traditional Cautions*. Home Office Online Report 57/04. London: Home Office.

Young, R. and Goold, B. (2003) 'Restorative police cautioning in Aylesbury – from degrading to reintegrative shaming ceremonies?', in E. McLaughlin *et al.* (eds) *Restorative Justice: Critical Issues*. London: Sage.

Young, R. and Hoyle, C. (2002) *An Evaluation of the Thames Valley Police Initiative in Restorative Cautioning*. York: Joseph Rowntree Foundation.

Youth Justice Board (2004) *National Evaluation of the Restorative Justice in Schools Programme*. London: YJB.

13

Children and young people in custody

Rod Morgan

Introduction

In this chapter we consider three issues. First, how many children and young people are in penal custody, why are they there and what characterizes them? Secondly, what sort of custodial conditions are they in and with what associated problems? Thirdly, what are the prospects for change given, as practically everyone agrees, it is not desirable that children and young people be in custody and certainly that their custody should be a last resort.

Population trends and characteristics

At any one time there are currently about 3,000 10–17-year-olds in penal custody – that is, remanded to a place of detention prior to trial or sentence, or sentenced to custody on conviction. The number has crept up slightly since the millennium but almost doubled during the 1990s. Why this growth?

There are several reasons. In the early 1990s there was heightened public concern about persistent young offenders and this was hugely exacerbated by the murder by two 10-year-olds of 2-year-old James Bulger in Liverpool in 1992. Both government and opposition politicians responded to the mood of crisis by airing their tough-on-crime credentials, central to which was the use of custody. In 1994 the Conservatives doubled the maximum sentence for 15–17-year-olds in a young offender institution (YOI) and provided for the introduction of secure training orders (STOs) for 12–14-year-olds.

When New Labour came to power in 1997 they took further the Conservative's punitive approach. Their electorally winning mantra was 'tough on crime, tough on the causes of crime', priority being given to the first part of that equation. They combined the STO and youth custody sentences by introducing the detention training order (DTO) for 12–17-year-olds, a sentence of four months to two years' duration, of which the first half is spent in custody. They also replaced the strict criteria for offenders under 15 relating to 'persistence' with the provision that the sentence be available where the court 'is of the opinion that he is a persistent offender', a power which the courts interpreted broadly. New Labour exhibited no embarrassment about the record high number of young offenders in custody. They never maintained it was an achievement but, in 2001, 'arresting, convicting, punishing and rehabilitating persistent young offenders' became a key policy undertaking (Labour Party 2001: 32) and, in 2005, the fact that they had since 1997 built 'over 16,000 more prison places' (which included many for young offenders) was described as an achievement (Labour Party 2005: 3). There were to be, as Labour's key policy statement on youth justice had proclaimed in 1997, *No More Excuses* (Home Office 1997).

These shorter sentences, available to the magistrates' youth court, sit alongside continued provisions whereby serious offences – in the case of murder, mandatorily – are committed to the Crown court and are liable to 'long-term detention' (to distinguish the sentence from a DTO) for which the maximum period is the same as if the child or young person is an adult.

The *proportionate* use of custody for children and young people by the courts has fallen marginally in recent years (Ministry of Justice 2007: Table 1.5). But the number in custody continues to creep upwards because the overall number of children and young people criminalized has significantly increased (YJB 2008: 24), as has the average sentence length (Ministry of Justice 2007: Table 2.5). Yet – and despite current concerns about youth-on-youth gun and knife-related homicides – this more punitive trend is only partly explained by changes in the mix of young offenders' offences or criminal histories (Home Office 2007: para. 6.13 and Table 6.5). Moreover, contrary to what is widely believed, a significant proportion of young offenders committed to custody are not prolific offenders: well over one third (37 per cent) have either none, or only one or two, previous offences, albeit that those offences are often serious.

The children and young people in custody are overwhelmingly 16- and 17-year-olds (78 per cent) and male (93 per cent), though the number of girls has, in recent years, been greater than that for boys (see Figure 13.1).

Of this population, 22 per cent are on remand and, of the sentenced, the overwhelming majority (78 per cent) are serving DTO sentences. However, a disturbing minority of those serving more than two years (116 out of 510) are subject to indeterminate sentences, including those for public protection introduced by the Criminal Justice Act 2003. This parallels the greater-than-anticipated use of such sentences for adults.

Of the sentenced population, robbery (31 per cent), violence against the person (26 per cent), burglary (16 per cent) and vehicle theft or unauthorized taking (6 per cent) are their most common principal offences. This pattern represents a change. A decade ago the proportion of young offenders in

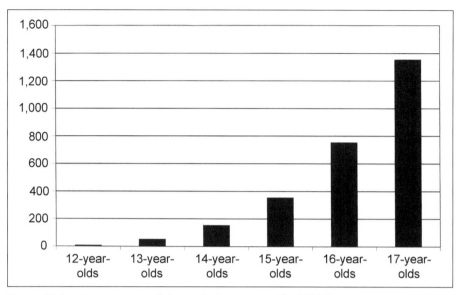

Figure 13.1 Average custodial population age profile 2006–7

custody for violence and robbery offences was significantly lower than today and the contribution of burglary was far greater (Home Office 2003: Table 3.11). Moreover, a growing proportion (currently 18 per cent) of young people have been imprisoned for breach of community orders, a reflection of the increasingly numerous and onerous prohibitions or demands built into community orders and their tighter enforcement (YJB 2008: 38).

Most young people committed to custody are there for a remarkably short time. In 2006–7, if remands are included, the average stay was 76 days. The average stay for DTO prisoners was 114 days or three and a half months. This is very little time to get to know the young people, let alone address what, typically, are their multiple problems. These strains are made worse by the inadequate resourcing of rehabilitative programmes – particularly in hard-pressed YOIs.

Standard recording and epidemiological survey data reveal the following picture of this custodial population, which is overwhelmingly drawn from the most deprived neighbourhoods and socio-economically marginalized sections of the community:

- A disproportionate number (27 per cent in 2006–7) are non-white, with black and mixed race being the largest minority groups (YJB 2008: 38).

- Some 31 per cent have identifiable mental health problems: almost one fifth suffer from depression, a tenth having engaged in an act of self-harm in the preceding month, similar proportions suffering from anxiety and post-traumatic stress symptoms (PTSD), 7 per cent suffering from hyperactivity and 5 per cent suffering from psychotic-like symptoms (Harrington and Bailey 2005).

- Some 40 per cent have been dependent on a substance at some point in their lives; 74 per cent report having drunk alcohol more than once a week with the majority of the drinkers regularly exceeding six units of alcohol on a single drinking occasion; 83 per cent are smokers; 30 per cent report that they have taken drugs not to get high but just to 'feel normal'; 38 per cent say they have taken a drug to 'forget everything' or 'blot everything out' which amounts to a form of self-medication (Galahad SMS Ltd 2004).

- Almost one quarter have learning difficulties (that is, a measured IQ of less than 70), with a further third exhibiting borderline learning difficulties (measured IQ of 70–80) (Galahad SMS Ltd 2004).

- Two thirds have been excluded from education and a high proportion have a literacy and numeracy age some four to five years below their chronological age (HMIP 2005).

- Four in ten have at some stage in their lives been in the care of a local authority and 17 per cent placed on a child protection register (Hazel *et al.* 2002; HMIP 2005).

These multiple problems often serve to reinforce each other (e.g. abuse of drugs and mental health, exclusion from education and illiteracy). The secure estate arguably represents the *least* effective environment in which to address such problems – often exacerbating them by undermining initiatives being taken with the young person in the community (such as college and work placements).

Organization and governance

Custodial provision for children in England and Wales is based on a 'purchaser–provider' split, an arrangement designed to foster competition. Since April 2000 the Youth Justice Board (YJB) has been responsible for commissioning and purchasing the custodial places which the courts, through their individual decisions, demand. In 2008 the board purchased 3,420 beds (YJB 2008: 39) in three categories of establishments:

- Some 2,899 beds in YOIs, two of which are managed by commercial companies and the remainder by the Prison Service. YOI provision is for 15–17-year-olds in the case of boys and 17-year-olds in the case of girls. There are currently 13 institutions or units within institutions for males and 4 units for girls. Of these all but five are split-site establishments – that is, the young offenders are held in more or less discrete sections of institutions which also house prisoners aged 18 or over.

The degree to which there is contact between the young and adult offenders varies according to the nature, layout and facilities in each establishment, though the YJB's aim is to move gradually towards greater separation. Since separation will best be achieved in institutions exclusively for young offenders we can expect, unless the custodial population rises and makes the strategy impossible, the YJB gradually to withdraw from split-site institutions.

• Some 286 beds in four secure training centres (STCs), all managed by commercial companies. The STCs are relatively small compared with most YOIs. They are subdivided into small living units of six–eight beds and generally accommodate adolescents in the middle age range (14–16 years). However, they also house older young people considered too vulnerable to be housed in the YOIs and, on occasion, younger children for whom there are no spaces available in secure care homes.

• Some 226 beds in 15 secure care homes (SCHs), all of which were until recently managed by local authorities but one of which was, in 2005, sold to a commercial operator. SCHs vary in size, but are mostly very small and, like the STCs, are subdivided into small living units of six–eight beds. Children under the age of 15 are invariably housed in the SCHs, but these homes also accommodate the occasional older adolescent considered too vulnerable to place in a YOI or an STC.

Placement of all children and young people remanded or sentenced to custody is initially undertaken by the YJB, which operates something akin to a call centre. It is notified by the local youth offending teams (YOTs) of court decisions and the age and characteristics of the young people concerned. This means that the YJB's allocational decisions are dependent on the quality of the risk assessments undertaken by YOTs.

The average number of children and young people held in the beds purchased by the YJB in recent years is shown in Table 13.1. These figures suggest that there is currently about 15 per cent spare capacity, which is not the case. Quite apart from seasonal fluctuations, the YOIs normally accommodate several hundred 18 or even 19-year-olds. These are mostly young offenders serving DTOs who have attained the age of 18 during the course of their sentence and who, it is agreed, should not be transferred to an adult establishment prior to the custodial part of their sentence expiring. To transfer them, it is argued, would be inhumane and counterproductive in terms of continuity in offender or educational programme participation. The consequence, however, is that YJB-commissioned accommodation is typically close to full. The YJB has little room for operational manoeuvre, and there are many more young people being held distant from their community roots than is considered desirable. In 2005–6 approximately one third of all boys and half of all girls were being held in institutions more than 50 miles from home (YJB 2007: 36), an aspect of system overcrowding about which the prisons inspectorate is increasingly critical (HMIP 2007: 43).

Table 13.1 Children and young persons in penal custody

	1997	1999	2001	2003	2005	2007
Secure homes	95	90	258	292	238	226
Secure training centres		55	118	185	248	257
Young offender institutions	2,479	2,422	2,415	2,267	2,339	2,431
Total	*2,574*	*2,567*	*2,791*	*2,744*	*2,825*	*2,914*

The prisons inspectorate also takes the view that most YOI living units are too large. This, however, is the estate which the YJB inherited and which will not easily be changed without either a substantial reduction in the custodial population or a significant increase in the YJB's budget, the prospects for both of which seem unlikely. The YJB's budget, 70 per cent of which is already spent on purchasing custodial places, is severely constrained. Further, though the board had a target of reducing, by influencing sentencers, the number of children in custody, it was failing in that objective (Solomon and Garside 2008: 47–8) and in 2008 dropped it. Were YOIs less intensively used and the size of YOI living units reduced (allowing for the more effective but intensive interventions undertaken in SCHs and STCs), then custodial unit costs would inevitably rise. It already costs on average £53,112 per annum to keep a young offender in a YOI, £172,260 in an STC and £185,532 in an SCH (information from YJB). These substantial differences are largely accounted for by the very different staffing ratios.

All establishments for young offenders are regularly, independently inspected, and each of the YOIs has attached to them an independent monitoring board of lay persons. Further, the YJB has provided child advocates and social workers in every institution to assist the young inmates find their voice and to safeguard them from a child protection standpoint. The YJB also employs field staff to monitor compliance with the legal contracts they have with the STCs and SCHs and the service-level agreement they have with the Prison Service. These contracts and agreements have been backed by significant investment to raise the standards of education, health and other provision required. Successive inspectorate reports testify to the progress that has been made but also confirm the YJB's own assessment that 'there is still a long way to go' (YJB 2005: para. 2).

All the current custodial provision for children and young offenders involves operational shortcomings and dilemmas. In relation to YOIs, the Prison Service represents an 'organizational tanker', difficult to turn round, with staff insufficiently child-centred (despite the minimal training for working with children which the YJB is funding) and housed in premises many of which are clearly 'unfit for purpose'. STC staff, most of whom have little or no prior experience of, or qualifications for, working with children, let alone the most difficult job in the land, arguably also have insufficient training to develop the skills they need. There is at present no central, strategic management or funding of the SCHs by central government and thus the aggregate supply of places remains uncertain. The local authorities may not seek profits in the Marxist sense as, objectionably in the eyes of some, the commercial companies which run the STCs do, but they do not aim to make a loss either and their costs vary.

The problems endemic to the secure estate are reflected in the deaths which have blighted the youth custody system. Fifteen children and young persons have died in custody since 1997 (see Coles and Goldson 2005), 14 by suicide and one while being restrained. Two of these deaths occurred in STCs, the remainder in YOIs. Several of these cases have attracted considerable media attention. This scrutiny has identified what has been held to be scandalously inappropriate sentencing and placement decisions (a key example being the death of Joseph Scholes, aged 16, at Stoke Heath YOI in 2002, a case in which the inquest coroner called for a public inquiry subsequently denied by the government) or inappropriate behaviour of staff (as in the case of Gareth Myatt, aged 15 and weighing seven stone, who died while being restrained by three members of staff at Rainsbrook STC in 2004). No member of staff was prosecuted in the case of Gareth Myatt but a subsequent Howard League inquiry report (Carlile Report 2006) was scathing about the culture of physical restraint existing in the STCs and the shortcomings of the youth custody system more generally.

Young offenders with multiple previous convictions (seven or more) are virtually certain to be reconvicted (96 per cent) and returned to custody (83 per cent) within two years (Home Office 2003: Table 9.10). Effectiveness thus measured is not improving, which is scarcely surprising given the inadequacies inherent within the current system of resettlement and aftercare. For example, if a young person is still of school age it is at present very difficult to get them back on a school roll or if, for whatever reason, they cannot return to their parental homes, resource limitations mean that many end up in unsupervised bed-and-breakfast accommodation, both of which conditions are recipes for disaster.

There is a serious debate to be had about the proportion of young children in custody who might be dealt with through family as opposed to criminal proceedings, and alternatives, such as intensive fostering, which might be employed as an alternative to custody. However, few commentators would doubt that those very few young children whose behaviour, which sometimes includes murder or other acts of serious violence including arson and rape, means detention in a secure environment, with specialist and other staff-intensive child-centred provision, is anything but a necessity. Whether such provision goes under the label of 'welfare', 'penal' or 'psychiatric' treatment, it is always going to be very expensive.

Possible futures

In summer 2005 the YJB (2005) published its strategy for the future of the secure estate for children and young persons. The document is both principled and pragmatic and concedes that the realization of the board's objectives depends on two factors: 'the sentencing trend' and the 'availability of resources'. With respect to the first the board is clearly failing. To what extent the board's objectives are shared by the government and their prospects of being successfully achieved remain moot.

From a positive perspective, the board has set out aspirational principles with which few would disagree. All secure institutions for children and young people should have a child and young person-centred culture; be run by staff committed and trained adequately to engage with children and young people in this area of work; have regimes geared to the individual educational, training, recreational, cultural and personal developmental needs of children and young people and should not be disrupted by unnecessary transfers; should employ behaviour management practices which emphasize positive encouragement and reward rather than physical restraint or negative sanctions; and, finally, should be located as close to young offenders' community ties as possible (YJB 2005: para. 10).

Unfortunately the principal arguments do not lie here. They lie rather in the degree to which children are held fully accountable for their behaviour in criminal law and, to the extent that they are held accountable, are dealt with effectively by means of penal custody. What are the prospects for positive change in these regards?

The evidence suggests that, at present, the prospects are poor. There is now so little political support for change in the direction adopted in many other European jurisdictions – for instance, raising from 10 the age of criminal responsibility and merging once again aspects of criminal and welfare legal proceedings so that fewer children are dealt with by penal means – that critical commentators in the UK have almost given up expressing their aspirations. It is left largely to international observers, from the United Nations or the Council of Europe (see Chapters 19 and 20 this volume), to express the views held by many leading members of the various groups campaigning for children's interests but seldom now pressed by them. Significantly, when the Council of Europe's Commissioner for Human Rights recently criticized the low age of criminal responsibility in England and Wales, the government, in its response, did not even think it necessary to comment on either his observations or his recommendation that the age of criminal responsibility be raised 'in line with norms prevailing across Europe' (European Commissioner for Human Rights 2005: paras 105–7).

With the formation, in 2007, of the Department for Children, Families and Schools (DCFS) and the announcement that, henceforward, the DCFS would be co-sponsor of the YJB, hopes were raised that a less criminal justice-oriented approach to youth crime was heralded. However, the long-awaited, jointly published, *Youth Crime Action Plan* (HM Government 2008) made no reference to youth custody numbers or conditions and offered no immediate prospect that numbers might be reduced or conditions improved. At about the same time, the YJB dropped from its business plan its numerical target for reductions in the use of youth custody.

The operational pressures resulting from the rising numbers in custody are undeniable. The smaller the degree of headroom within the system, the greater the likelihood that children will have to be placed either at an unacceptable distance from home or in institutions less than ideal for them. To the extent that this happens the greater the stresses on all concerned – the children, their families and the staff who work with them – and the greater the likelihood of self-harm and disorder. The more the system is overcrowded the greater the operational risks that things will continue to go badly wrong.

Implications of the use of custody for the practitioner

The fact that youth custody institutions are often physically distant from the community roots of their charges undermines the ability of YOT supervisors to maintain regular, good-quality contact with their custodial caseload and to prepare them for resettlement. By the same token the penal institutions are inhibited from developing a genuine community orientation by involving local services and voluntary sector groups in delivering some of their programmes. Further, though there is no evidence that the fact that the direct costs of penal custody are borne by central government serves as an *incentive* for local practitioners to recommend resort to custody, it is a fact that the arrangement provides no *disincentive* to local authority services.

It is partly for this reason that the government has decided that the provision of education and training services in custody should in future be paid for by the local authorities, and active consideration is being given to the proposition that the local authorities pay for the cost of any use of custody for their young people (HM Government 2008: para. 5.7). Given the current impetus generally in favour of devolving service delivery responsibilities, it seems at least possible that a progressive way forward might be to make the local authorities, as regional consortia, responsible for both youth penal provision and custody. One implication would be that they would then have a vested interest in providing effective early-prevention programmes and community-based supervision.

References

Carlile Report (Lord Carlile of Berriew) (2006) *The Carlile Inquiry: An Independent Inquiry into the Use of Physical Restraint, Solitary Confinement and Forcible Strip Searching of*

Children in Prisons, Secure Training Centres and Local Authority Secure Children's Homes. London: Howard League.

Coles, D. and Goldson, B. (2005) *In the Care of the State? Child Deaths in Penal Custody.* London: Inquest.

East Potential (2008) *Young Offenders in East London: A New Approach.* London: East Potential.

European Commissioner for Human Rights (2005) *Report by Mr Alvaro Gil-Robles, Commissioner for Human Rights, on his Visit to the United Kingdom, 4–12 November 2004.* Strasbourg: Council of Europe.

Galahad SMS Ltd (2004) *Substance Misuse and the Juvenile Secure Estate.* London: YJB.

Harrington, R. and Bailey, S. (2005) *Mental Health Needs and Effectiveness of Provision for Young Offenders in Custody and in the Community.*, London: YJB.

Hazel, N., Hagell, A., Liddle, M., Archer, D., Grimshaw, R. and King, J. (2002) *Detention and Training: Assessment of the Detention and Training Order and its Impact on the Secure Estate across England and Wales.* London: YJB.

Her Majesty's Inspectorate of Prisons (1997) *Young Prisoners: A Thematic Review by HM Chief Inspector of Prisons for England and Wales.* London: HMIP.

Her Majesty's Inspectorate of Prisons (2005) *Annual Report 2004/5.* London: HMIP.

Her Majesty's Inspectorate of Prisons (2007) *Annual Report 2005/6.* London: HMIP.

Her Majesty's Inspectorate of Prisons and Youth Justice Board (2005) *Juveniles in Custody 2003–2004: An Analysis of Children's Experiences of Prison.* London: HMIP/YJB.

HM Government (2008) *Youth Crime Action Plan.* London: CPI.

Home Office (1997) *No More Excuses: A New Approach to Tackling Youth Crime in England and Wales* (Cm 3809). London: Home Office.

Home Office (2003) *Prison Statistics, England and Wales 2002* (Cm 5996). London: National Statistics.

Home Office (2007) *Sentencing Statistics, 2005, England and Wales. Home Office Statistical Bulletin 3/7.* London: Home Office.

Labour Party (2001) *Ambitions for Britain: Labour's Manifesto, 2001.* London: Labour Party.

Labour Party (2005) *Britain Forward not Back: The Labour Party Manifesto, 2005.* London: Labour Party.

Ministry of Justice (2007) *Sentencing Statistics, 2006. Statistical Bulletin.* London: RDS NOMS.

Solomon, E. and Garside, R. (2008) *Ten Years of Labour's Youth Justice Reforms: An Independent Audit.* London: Centre for Crime and Justice Studies.

Youth Justice Board (2005) *Strategy for the Secure Estate for Children and Young People.* London: YJB.

Youth Justice Board (2007) *Youth Justice Annual Statistics, 2005/6.* London: YJB.

Youth Justice Board (2008) *Youth Justice Annual Workload Data, 2006/7.* London: YJB.

14

Living in a box: ethnicity and identity inside a young men's prison

Rod Earle

That's what makes this age group so difficult. Some are just so ... so difficult. Especially the eighteen year olds. They are the worst I think. Still, emotionally, children really. But in a man's body. I think it's after 21, about 24 I reckon, that you notice change, a bit of sense emerging. (HMYOI Rochester officer, unrecorded conversation, fieldnotes, 2 August 2006)

Introduction

As the evening association period draws to a close there is a Tannoy announcement, 'Last ten minutes!', followed by lots of calls and shouts, then further Tannoy announcements, 'One minute'; '30 seconds – behind your doors' then a countdown through the Tannoy speakers – 'ten', 'nine', 'eight', 'seven' 'six' etc. – and suddenly, as doors slam shut, the wing is quiet. The transformation of the noisy 'ragged edged vitality' (Irwin 1980) of dozens of young men to still, almost clinical, silence is eerie. The procedure is repeated five or six times a day as prisoners are locked back in their cells after meals, activities and association and, finally, at 7 p.m., for the night. Each day of a custodial sentence, the same rhythm of 'banging up', and the same dull routine of unlocking, is repeated, day, after day, after day.

This chapter offers an account of life inside a young offender institution (HMYOI Rochester in Kent) that houses nearly 400 young men aged between 18 and 21 years. It draws from a study of the ways in which ethnicity and masculinity are understood and experienced by the young men and how ideas about gender, race and racism shape daily interactions between them (Phillips 2008; Earle and Phillips 2009; Phillips and Earle 2009). As the preceding chapter made clear, the prison population of children and young people includes a statistically disproportionate number of minority ethnic youth. Despite this there are relatively few studies that focus on how conditions inside prison are experienced in relation to ethnicity. This is all the more surprising given the duty placed on public institutions, such as prisons, by the Race Relations (Amendment) Act 2000 (s. 2(1)a), to 'promote equality of opportunity and good relations between persons of different racial groups'.

It was the murder of Zahid Mubarek by a white racist cell-mate in HMYOI Feltham in March 2000, as well as the preceding Macpherson Report into police mishandling of the murder of Stephen Lawrence, that placed the issue of 'race relations' in the criminal justice system under fuller public scrutiny (Bowling and Phillips 2002). In the Prison Service the investigation by the Commission for Racial Equality (2003), prompted by Zahid's murder, identified 17 incidents of unlawful racial discrimination, including widespread acts of racist abuse and the circulation of racist material among prisoners and staff. As a result of this report, considerable investment and effort has been made to improve relations between officers and prisoners and to address other inadequacies within the secure estate. However, there continues to be a dearth of research into the influence of ethnicity on social relations between prisoners. What research has been done on prisoner/prisoner relations is now rather dated, tends to neglect ethnicity and is heavily influenced by American experiences (see Phillips 2007).

HMYOI Rochester is situated on the Thames estuary just beyond the M25 London orbital. It lies at the eastern edge of the largest, most cosmopolitan city in England while also being adjacent to one of its most famous rural idylls: Kent, the 'garden of England'. It was the site of the original Borstal institution established by the Children Act 1908, and much of the accommodation dates from that time. Its presence as a thriving, full-to-the-brim, custodial institution, with two new neighbours in the form of the Medway Secure Training Centre and Cookham Wood Women's Prison,[1] speaks volumes about the trajectories of crime and punishment over the last 100 years.

The prison's catchment area includes the massive and diverse population of London where, notwithstanding their higher-than-average general presence, black and minority ethnic youth are heavily over-represented in the criminal justice system. Prisoners are also likely to be sent to HMYOI Rochester from courts in the counties of Kent, Essex and East Sussex where white ethnicities predominate, and from other YOIs in southeast England.

The inmate population of HMYOI Rochester at the time of the research was composed of:

- 56 per cent white British, white European, white other;
- 30 per cent black/black Caribbean/black African;
- 7 per cent mixed heritage; and
- 6 per cent Asian.

This chapter draws on the findings of two researchers, Earle and Phillips, who attended the prison for three to four days each week over a period of eight-months during the latter half of 2006. A relatively long-term period of access to the prison was felt to be necessary to secure understandings of the depth and range of prisoners' experience. The eight month period of fieldwork gave the research team the opportunity to appreciate the flux and flow of prison life over a reasonably sustained period of time. During the course of the fieldwork, 60 semi-structured interviews were conducted with a sample selected to reflect the composition of the prison population, in terms of religion, nationality and ethnicity. Part of the sample was made up of informal contacts established during the fieldwork but, to avoid selection bias (i.e. talking only to talkative or confident prisoners), just under half the sample was drawn at random from the prison roll, stratified by ethnicity.

This research was influenced by an interest in the daily negotiation of ethnic difference and the micro-politics of everyday social contact (Amin 2002), but within the closed world of the prison. Insight into this was gained by adopting an ethnographic style of research and spending as much time as possible with inmates in conversation and social interaction.

Negotiating ethnic difference

When asked directly about inter-ethnic interaction, many of the inmates described a process of informal separation, although it was usually emphasized that this loose gathering was not marked (as in many American prisons) by aggravation and stress. For instance, a common first reaction to the research project's interest in ethnicity and social relations between prisoners was: 'That is simple man. The Asians keep to themselves, the blacks to themselves and the whites too. Just simple. I don't know why but that is how it is' (RE fieldnotes, August 2006). Conversely, however, another inmate commented as follows:

> What can I say? Well, I get along with everyone, I get along with everyone. This will make me sound . . . but I have more in common with the black people . . . You see he is Asian, and me and him are cool, I'm not prejudiced at all. Some of the [white] people who rap, I get along with them as well, but a lot of them tend to be black, it's just the way it is. (black, foreign national, Christian – R2[2])

Although prisoners initially referred to the existence of loose ethnic separation, involving 'black', 'white', 'Asian', Muslim and foreign national groupings, the fieldwork and in-depth interviews indicated that these groupings and associations between prisoners were not rigidly fixed and were only rarely actively exclusive. Hence, while prisoner groupings appeared to have a low-key ethnic component, this was just part of the story, a part that receded when it was discussed more extensively in interview.

Conjuring with racism: now you see it, now you don't

A notable finding of this fieldwork was the extent to which overt or explicit racism was suppressed within the YOI. While there appeared to be a general acceptance of the simple facts of ethnic diversity and grouping, the opposite was the case in respect of overt racism. Racism of this kind was widely regarded as totally unacceptable, and inmates acting in an explicitly racist manner risked considerably more than disapproval from other inmates, both black and white. Interestingly, many prisoners referred to the existence of an informal code in which racist behaviour would be met with violent retaliation.

For example, the researchers were told of some specific examples where such action had been taken, usually, but not always, by black prisoners and there appeared to be widespread acceptance of the legitimacy of this kind of behaviour among inmates. This suggested a consensus against explicit racism, and condemnation of any inmate identified as 'being a racist'. This consensus went so far as to be included and exploited, instrumentally, in the informal sanctions inmates used against each other: 'Say I wanted you kicked in. I'd say to a black feller, "Look he's a racist, him, he's telling me you're a monkey and all that", and you'd get your head kicked in' (white, British national, Christian – R30). The stigmatization of racism seems to have acquired a kind of dual currency within the prison, part of both its informal and formal structures of social control. Hence, the prisoner's self-policing of racism co-existed with the high-profile diversity policy of the prison but was quite distinct from it.

However, this did not mean that the prison was free of tension, fear or anxiety around the questions of race and ethnicity. For example, there was a tendency, in the privacy of interviews with the white researcher, for white inmates to invoke traditional narratives of white superiority. Some, for example, expressed irritation with the linguistic styles and expressive vernacular of minority ethnic inmates, objecting to the use of words and phrases such as 'Wha' Gwaan', 'Hey Blood', 'Fam' and 'Wasteman', or the habit of wearing trousers low down off the hips. The research team (composed of a white man and a mixed-race woman) were struck by the extent to which their own ethnic identities tended to elicit and/or obscure aspects of these racialized narratives (Phillips and Earle 2008).

For white prisoners, it appears that racism remained a potent resource, although the sanctions against it (both informal and formal) meant that it was activated mainly in private. Public expressions of racist sentiments or slang were used sparingly and rarely in 'mixed company'. Nevertheless, the fieldwork provides further evidence of the common use of racist language and of the existence of racist hostility (see Wilson 2003) expressed in interview through terms such as 'the niggers', 'black pricks', 'Pakis'.

Moreover, the comments of some white foreign nationals were particularly illuminating, reflecting perhaps how their own ambiguous white status offered them insights into the hidden dynamics of racialized antagonism. As one white foreign national commented:

> There are a few prisoners, there are some English that live around Kent around here, they saying they don't like refugee, like black people, stuff like that. They don't really like us. I am white and when I'm with them I can see they say like 'Oh fuck the black fucking . . .', you know, 'look at the niggers', stuff like that. (white, foreign national, Muslim – R22)

Thus, although there appeared to be a remarkably durable, consensual and stable 'surface' equanimity among an ethnically diverse prisoner population, this was relatively thin, concealing the persistence of submerged racialized tensions.

One of the most common ways white prisoners vented these tensions and anxieties was through the vocabulary of racialized victimization, arguing that they suffered as a consequence of both the prejudice of black inmates and the existence of double standards in the recognition of what constituted 'racism'. A typical comment was:

> it's just the way they talk, like, 'That little white ting, and that little white prick,' you know and 'white this and white that' . . . But if we're sitting there going, 'Yeah that little Paki cunt,' or 'Big black prick', then all of a sudden, we're, we're labelled as a racist. (white, British national, nil religion – R53)

The anxiety and resentment expressed in the accounts of some white prisoners can be seen as testimony to the difficult terrain that race and ethnicity occupy in late modernity (Phillips 2008). The comments reveal an uncertainty among these white prisoners about how to navigate everyday contacts with black prisoners. Clearly, some white prisoners experienced this more acutely than others, and their bewildered and resentful withdrawal seems to reproduce the phenomenon of 'white flight' from some urban areas in open society (Frey 1979).

Postcode pride

Many of the informal exchanges with the young men, and the more structured interviews exploring aspects of their identity, revealed that a sense of ethnic identity was superseded by a locality-based identification. Although most white English prisoners frequently regarded ethnicity as something suspiciously prescriptive, a label attached by others and for 'others', many of the minority ethnic young men also expressed similar sentiments, conveying an impression that ethnicity was a dormant, low-profile aspect of their identity. The disavowal, by white prisoners, of ethnicity in general, and whiteness in particular, is consistent with much of the empirical and theoretical work on the perceived normative, naturalized, character of whiteness. White ethnicities are invisible, denied or regarded as devoid of ethnic content (Nayak 2003; Garner 2007). A white prisoner, for instance (R6), put it like this:

> No, I don't feel white, I don't feel white, you know. I know I'm white and all that, but the thing is, though, I'm still the same person as a black and Asian, Chinese people, you know, I'm still, they're still the same person as me. You know, we all growed up from the apes and everything you know.

While an Asian Muslim prisoner (R51) remarked: 'Ethnicity is not really a big thing. Obviously it is a big thing but nobody takes it as a main mark. It's more on the lines of who you are personally. Not your race as an individual, exactly.'

The fieldwork firmly suggested, however, the experiential significance of local neighbourhood identities among both London, Kent and Essex-based prisoners. It is, of course, possible that, because of the geographical concentration of ethnic groups within Britain, a local or neighbourhood identification could also be largely synonymous with an ethnic identification (Simpson 2007), but what was notable was that a sense of belonging was primarily articulated by the young men through locality rather than ethnicity. In other words, many inmates frequently chose to talk about themselves primarily in terms of place and territory rather than race (Phillips 2008).

We found frequent reference to a London differentiated by the compass points, North, South, East, West and, more specifically still, the use of postcodes to situate selves and anchor belonging. For example, one foreign national prisoner described how, in the evenings while locked in their cells, some prisoners would 'shout where they're from, you know, they shout out their postcode'. In one of the prison workshops postcodes or other area identifiers, like 'E3', 'Roman Rd' or 'Eastside', were often painted, graffiti style, on to the storage boxes prisoners could make for themselves.

Significantly, local identification appeared to operate as a mode through which new contacts were forged at Rochester or old ones re-established. It enabled the young men to retain a sense of ontological connection with their local communities despite the prison severing their physical connection to them. Asserting local identities operated as a way of anchoring belonging to somewhere external to the prison, helping them to resist the 're-coding of their existence' that Foucault (1979) argued is a key feature of carceral regimes.

'Postcode pride' can be thought of as a means of resisting the punitive attempts at dislocation, displacement and exclusion that accompany imprisonment. The young men's assertion of postcode pride might be read as a 'transcript of resistance' (Scott 1998). Their territorial claims assert how they want to know themselves as opposed to how they might be known by others in authority. The young men's accounts of local identification can be taken as a form of resistance to other ways of knowing them and their lives, particularly a knowledge that seeks to rule them. In their frequent references and claims to a postcode and local area the young men in prison deploy a short-hand for obscure, illicit and potent social networks. In de Certeau's (1984) terms they use the convivial tactics of the weak in the face of the ordering strategies of the powerful (see Earle and Phillips 2009).

Local affiliations also created obligations among prisoners to support and assist each other in disputes involving fellow prisoners or even prison officers. As one young man put it: 'if you're from someone's ends [neighbourhood] then, yeah, they are, they got a certain amount of liability to look out for you, innit . . . you have to look out for each other' (R13 – white, British national, nil religion).

These narratives of locality echo what Robins and Cohen (1978) long ago claimed was an integral part of masculine, working-class cultures: the participation in the symbolic process of 'owning' a territory. Their effacement of ethnicity also recalls Back's (1996) study of south London urban youth cultures, where neighbourhood nationalism attempts to banish the racial referent and replace it with a simple commitment to a local territory. According to recent research conducted by the Joseph Rowntree Foundation, these localized, territorial identities are assuming greater significance for marginalized young people throughout Britain. They represent 'a sense of inalienable belonging . . . something that no one could, and could be allowed to, take away' (Kintrea *et al.* 2008: 32).

Implications for youth justice policy and practice: new understandings of race, ethnicity and social relations

The study in HMYOI Rochester was followed by further similar research (Phillips and Earle 2009) at an adult men's prison (HMP Maidstone). It suggests that, while a certain level of convivial equanimity remains, the strength of local identification declines, and there is, particularly among older white men, an increasing level of racialized resentment expressed through frustration and incomprehension of formal diversity policies.

The young men in HMYOI Rochester are, as the quotation from the prison officer at the start of this chapter indicates, often regarded as being on the cusp of transition from childhood to adulthood (see Chapter 2 this volume). The 'young adult' categorization of the YOI formally institutionalizes this understanding of a linear progression towards an adult identity. If male adulthood is becoming increasingly recognized as both elusive and complex (Frosh *et al.* 2002; McDowell 2003), the struggle to understand how young men cope with 'maturing' and adversity becomes all the more urgent. The 'senses' they come to in prison, and elsewhere, are shaped by social dynamics of class, gender and ethnicity, personal biography and unique experiences. This new research finds that the 'ragged edged vitality' (Irwin 1980) of imprisoned young men sustains a variety of lived understandings of masculinity, 'race' and ethnicity. While the new conviviality of multiculture (Gilroy 2004) was in evidence in HMYOI Rochester, so also were more traditional working-class assertions of local identity. Emergent among these there are problematic articulations of 'whiteness' organized loosely around feelings of victimhood, loss and disorientation. These have significant implications for people working in public institutions governed by the Race Relations (Amendment) Act 2000, such as YOIs and other elements of youth justice system.

The concept of white resentment takes shape in the YOI as incomprehension of diversity policies, hostility towards minorities who are accused of 'playing the ''race'' card' and dispirited retreat into white ethnic enclosure. White resentment is increasingly identified as a reaction to deeply felt perceptions of unfairness that key into the wider public discussion of the so-called 'failure of multiculturalism' (Ware 2008: 1.1). It fosters and justifies identification with a myth of white decline and the embrace of embattled, resentful, victim identities (Hage 2003; Sveinsson 2009). These reactions pose a considerable threat to the fragile, but remarkably convivial, multicultures we found in the prisons, that are themselves sourced in the vibrant, unruly, cosmopolitanism of modern urban Britain (Gilroy 2004). Youth justice practitioners in these areas can find ways of engaging with multiculture, but everyone must also develop resources to challenge a white retreat into racialized resentment that recasts hard-won progress as mere political correctness.

Acknowledgements

The author gratefully acknowledges the support of Dr Coretta Phillips of the London School of Economics in developing this chapter. None of it would have been possible without the generous support of the Governor and staff of HMYOI Rochester. The author is equally grateful to all the young men serving sentences there who made the research team welcome and who freely shared their thoughts and experiences.

Notes

1 In July 2007, after the research was completed, Cookham Wood was re-roled as a YOI for 15–17-year-old young men.
2 Responders are referred to in this fashion to protect their anonymity and to indicate their ethnicity, nationality and faith as recorded in HMPS data.

References

Amin, A. (2002) 'Ethnicity and the multicultural city: living with diversity', *Environment and Planning A* 34: 959–80.

Back, L. (1996) *New Ethnicities and Urban Culture: Racisms and Multiculture in Young Lives.* London: UCL Press.

Bowling, B. and Phillips, C. (2002) *Racism, Crime and Justice.* Harlow: Pearson Education.

Commission for Racial Equality (2003) *A Formal Investigation by the Commission for Racial Equality into HM Prison Service of England and Wales. Part 1. The Murder of Zahid Mubarek.* London: CRE.

Crewe, B. (2006) 'Prison drug dealing and the ethnographic lens', *The Howard Journal*, 45: 347–68.

de Certeau, M. (1984) *The Practice of Everyday Life.* London: University of California Press.

Earle, R. and Phillips, C. (2009) 'Con-viviality and beyond: identity dynamics in a young men's prison', in M. Wetherall (ed.) *Liveable Lives.* Basingstoke: Palgrave.

Foucault, M. (1979) *Discipline and Punish: The Birth of the Prison.* Harmondsworth: Penguin Books.

Frey, W.H. (1979) 'Central city white flight: racial and nonracial causes', *American Sociological Review*, 425–48.

Frosh, S., Phoenix, A. and Pattman, R. (2002) *Young Masculinties.* Basingstoke: Palgrave.

Garner, S. (2007) *Whiteness: an Introduction.* London: Routledge.

Gilroy, P. (2004) *After Empire: Melancholia or Convivial Culture?* London: Routledge.

Hage, G. (2003) *Against Paranoid Nationalism: Searching for Hope in a Shrinking Society.* London: Merlin Press.

Hallsworth, S. and Young, T. (2008) 'Gang talk and gang talkers: a critique', *Crime, Media, Culture*, 4: 175–95.

Irwin, J. (1980) *Prisons in Turmoil.* Chicago, IL: Little Brown.

Kintrea, K., Bannister, J., Pickering, J., Reid, M. and Suzuki, N. (2008) *Young People and Territoriality in British Cities.* York: Joseph Rowntree Foundation.

McDowell, L. (2003) *Redundant Masculinities.* Oxford: Blackwell.

Nayak, A. (2003) *Race, Place and Globalization: Youth Cultures in a Changing World.* Oxford: Berg.

Phillips, C. (2007) 'Ethnicity, identity and community cohesion in prison', in M. Wertherall *et al.* (eds) *Identity, Ethnic Diversity and Community Cohesion.* London: Sage.

Phillips, C. (2008) 'Negotiating identities: ethnicity and social relations in a young offender's institution', *Theoretical Criminology*, 12: 313–32.

Phillips, C. and Earle, R. (2008) 'Unsettling moments – racialised, gendered and classed dynamics of prison ethnography.' Paper presented at the annual meeting of the American Society of Criminology, St Louis, MO.

Phillips, C. and Earle, R. (2009) *Ethnicity, Identity and Social Relations in Prison: Full Report. End of Award Report* (RES. 1 48-25-0053). Swindon: ESRC.

Pitts, J. (2008) *Reluctant Gangsters: The Changing Face of Youth Crime.* Cullompton: Willan Publishing.

Robins, D. and Cohen, P. (1978) *Knuckle Sandwich: Growing up in the Working-class City.* Harmondsworth: Penguin Books.

Scott, J. (1998) *Seeing Like a State: How Certain Schemes to Improve the Human Condition have Failed.* New Haven, CT: Yale University Press.

Simpson, L. (2007) 'Ghettos of the mind: the empirical behaviour of indices of segregation and diversity', *Journal of the Royal Statistical Society A*, 170: 405–24.

Sveinsson, K. (2009) *Who Cares about the White Working Class?* Runnymede Trust (available online at www.runnymedetrust.org).

Ware, V. (2008) 'Towards a sociology of resentment: a debate on class and whiteness', *Sociological Research Online*, 13 (available online at http://www.socresonline.org.uk/13/5/9.html).

Wilson. D. (2003) '"Keeping quiet" or "going nuts": some emerging strategies used by black young people in custody at a time of childhood being re-constructed', *Howard Journal of Criminal Justice*, 45: 411–25.

Part IV

Reflective Practice

Introduction

Wayne Taylor

Offending by young people can be seen as a natural part of growing up, a component of the experiential process of taking risks – and making mistakes – that young people employ in response to the challenges of achieving adulthood. As Monica Barry explains in the opening chapter of this part, the correlation between age and offending is pronounced. Although there are important caveats to be aware of when considering the nature of this correlation (such as its variability in relation to types of offending and offender), the significance of the 'age–crime curve' is confirmed by the fact that the age distribution of offending behaviour takes on a similar shape and follows a similar trajectory in most American and European jurisdictions.

Any theory of criminal behaviour should be capable of providing an explanation in terms of individual development and maturation. Such explanations, however, are complicated by the range of factors that can be seen as exerting an influence, including constitution, personality, cognition, social interaction, experiences as offender and victim, processes such as labelling and stigma and the level of social standing. The primacy given to each of these factors will depend on the perspective of the observer, the assumptions they use in judging causality and the explanations they bring to bear in describing the underlying processes at work. As a consequence, research on human behaviour such as offending is fundamentally different from the 'closed systems' experiments of natural science, where the link between two or more variables can be isolated and 'tested'. Recognition of this provides a key lesson for practice, warning that 'age' should not be taken as a personal characteristic but, rather, as a rough indicator of where young people are *likely* to be in relation to each of these factors.

Broadly speaking, the age–crime curve rises in the early teens but then (for most) 'naturally' (and rapidly) declines as young people complete their transitions to adulthood. Interestingly, policy-makers in youth justice have been preoccupied with different points on the curve at different times. Youth justice policy since the early 1990s, for instance, has primarily focused on preventing offending or, at least, in reducing the gradient of the curve as it climbs upwards. In the past it could be argued that the emphasis was more on diversion from formal classification as 'offenders' (keeping them away from the curve) or, where offending persisted, in concentrating on the process of young people becoming ex-offenders (the downward curve). More recently, there has been a resurgence in interest in this part of the curve, an interest that has been heightened by evidence pointing to the benefits of an approach centred on 'desistance'.

The idea of desistance is one of the central themes of this part. In examining this component of transition, it considers what lessons this might hold for youth justice, both in the way it informs (or should inform) the interventions of professionals working with children and young people in trouble, and in terms of its compatibility – as a way of working – with the principles of a humane and value-based practice.

As the chapters of this Handbook have persistently argued, the way we think about both children and young people and crime is dependent on the ideological lens we bring to bear. The nature of this lens will influence what we see as well as where we will look for solutions. Do we look to the individual, to psychology and the relationship between the professional and young person? Or do we focus on the external factors that shape, support and provide the social capital that offers opportunities for some young people but limits hope for others? In fact, as Barry suggests, there are aspects of both these 'ways of seeing' that are of value. Seeing the young person in isolation from the contexts of their behaviour is both ineffective and – as Yates argues in the opening chapter – politically and morally indefensible. However, when looking at the actual work of youth justice, it is undeniable that much of this necessitates an understanding of the processes involved in the building of relationships between individuals. Here psychology, and shared or disparate life histories, gender, race, sexuality, etc., are all likely to play a role in the interaction between individuals. The concept of a 'relationship' between those engaged in offending and the professional committed to the traditional role of 'advising, assisting and *befriending*' them has always been recognized as a crucial factor in the rehabilitative process. The idea that this relationship might prove useful in helping young people move beyond the barrier of offending is also central to formulations of the professional responsibilities – and associated sense of professional worth – of practitioners.

The adoption of an 'integrative' approach has been presented by writers such as Barry as effective in combining the benefits of an individual and structural focus. For instance, from her own discussions with young people, Barry discovered both 'push' and 'pull' factors involved in the process of desistance. These represent the negative influences (both individual and environmental) undermining this process and the positive ones (also incorporating individual and environmental factors) promoting it.

Like Barry, Jean Hine argues that theorizing youth justice interventions as relationships highlights the importance of responsivity. Put simply, this suggests that interventions imposed on young people without their consent or active collaboration are unlikely to prove successful. Hine takes this further, suggesting that without an integrated understanding, the limitations in the tools of analysis are likely to exclude the meanings that young people attach to their actions, promoting a perception of them as passive and lacking the sense of agency, capability, competence and responsibility necessary for maturation.

Reflecting earlier chapters, the 'voices' of young people themselves are here presented as an essential source of evidence that should be of greater influence in shaping policy and practice than is currently the case. Drawing on her research with young people, Hine offers several examples of how these voices might steer policy on to a more progressive course. Adopting an integrative approach, she queries the lack of sophistication (and critical reflection) associated with some ways of working within a risk-based paradigm. Instead, she suggests that advances in the new sociology of childhood (see Part I this volume) offer better insights into what can be done to assist young people in the process of desistance and transition to adulthood.

Of course, we should not accept uncritically what children and young people tell us. As every practitioner – and everyone who has done something they regret – will attest, we all put a 'spin' on the stories we use to explain our actions. Often these narratives are employed to show us in a more favourable light, justifying our misconduct and minimizing its harmful features. At other times we may struggle to acknowledge the 'problem' itself, operating in a state of denial or 'pre-comprehension'. Consequently, self-perception and 'reality' are likely to be quite distinct, yet this does not mean that children's and young people's views – reflectively considered – are not of immense value.

Hine points to the savvy nature of young people's perceptions and their sensitivity regarding the 'fairness' of both the 'system' as a whole and the relationships they have with youth justice professionals. A common complaint heard here is that of dissatisfaction with the type of relationships possible within the current system. In part, this appears to have arisen as a consequence of the case management model, with its emphasis on short-term interventions involving a variety of specialist professionals and groupwork programmes. The result – especially when combined with inadequate staffing – can be a woefully impersonal experience for the young person, as they are shunted from one worker to another with little time or opportunity for forming meaningful relationships.

Because the factors impeding desistance are varied and multifaceted, it might seem sensible to think of these as posing a 'joined up' problem and, as such, as representing an ideal candidate for partnership working. Accepting Hine's warnings about the way ineffective partnership arrangements can damage the relationship at the heart of rehabilitative endeavours, it is nevertheless clear that partnership can offer benefits in both the range and types of help it can provide. However, as Mo Barratt explains in the third chapter of this part, there remains a good deal of confusion about what 'true partnership' working should involve. This is true at both the micro-level of practice, with competing ideas of what constitutes effective work with young people, and at the macro-level, where the policy environment is muddied by competing theories of what works and how.

One aspect of this confusion revolves around the differing professional ideologies partnership throws together, some of which are closer to, or more compatible with, contemporary youth justice practice than others. Interestingly, one feature of the evaluations undertaken on progress in youth justice since 1997 has been a recognition of the need to focus more on the achievement of improved outcomes for children and their families, a finding that echoes the views of those calling for an integrated, desistance-based approach. This approach is also likely to appeal to practitioners because, as Barratt observes, 'for many working in the youth justice system, the primary purpose of practice – preceding and superseding that of preventing offending – is the provision of better futures for young offenders'.

In considering partnerships, Barratt returns to the themes of responsivity and user involvement raised by Barry, Hine and others, suggesting that the success of such work is dependent on the extent to which these are taken seriously. Where involvement is more rhetorical than real, the benefits tend to be minimal. Conversely, the development of a radical model of desistance – stressing 'joined up' thinking and a more holistic model of 'true partnership' between professionals, young people, their families and their communities – can provide the basis for a shared vision practitioners can use to work effectively across professional boundaries.

Effective partnerships stressing an integrated approach to desistance necessitates a process of continual learning and a conscious commitment to professional development. How this might be sustained and developed in the current environment – where practitioners are subject to the dictates of agency accountability – is the topic of the final chapter in this part.

In this final chapter, Wayne Taylor looks at the idea of 'reflective' practice as both a tool to enhance practice competencies and as a means of critically evaluating the wider issues that impact on the youth justice practitioner. Taylor suggests that the process of 'experiential learning' that reflective practice entails is useful in both instances, allowing the practitioner some anchorage in the choppy waters of youth justice, where political and public opinion can encourage an overly punitive response to youth offending. Interestingly, the account of reflective practice Taylor advocates is one that also sits well with the other themes in this part. It is integrative – incorporating an understanding of the individual and structural factors influencing youthful offending. It is also inherently multidisciplinary, drawing on research in areas such as criminology, developmental psychology and the full range of professional work with children and young people and is, as such, compatible with a partnership working. At the same time, its critical stance towards the way knowledge is constructed and its concern with relationships also point to a desistance approach.

Looking at earlier research around reflective practice in youth justice, Taylor explores the dilemma of the practitioner who must both follow agency policy *and* their own consciences. This can be a problem when policy is at odds with the professional judgement or ethical values of the practitioner. This tension between accountability and the use of professional discretion has been a perennial one in criminal justice work. Drawing on recent work in this area, Taylor accepts there has been an erosion of professional discretion but argues that there is still space to operate reflectively.

Taylor's chapter concludes the part by drawing on the themes of the preceding chapters and pointing forward to Part V, in which attention turns to the various 'visions' of a future youth justice – shaped by developments in legislation around the idea of 'rights' and illustrated by examples from other jurisdictions both within and outside the UK. Interestingly, the idea of a rights-based youth justice sits well alongside an emphasis on desistance, with both advocating future-orientated interventions that stress relationship building and which offer encouragement, motivation and a listening ear.

15

Promoting desistance among young people

Monica Barry

Introduction

'Youthful' offending is a common and, many would say, natural aspect of growing up, despite the differing theories – biological, social, cultural and political – that attempt to understand its causes in more specific terms. Across the developed world, crime and age have a strong correlation, depicted by the 'age–crime curve' which sees offending start in the early teens, peak between 16 and 18 years, and then decline rapidly into the early twenties (Blumstein *et al*. 1988; Farrington 1997). But while the literature on youth offending has all but exhausted the reasons why young people *start* offending, there has been a dearth of literature until recently on why young people *stop* offending. This chapter focuses on that latter phenomenon, known as desistance, and in particular desistance among young people as they reach their late teens and early twenties. It is argued here that only in understanding young people's attempts to stop offending can practitioners help those who are willing to adopt alternative and more constructive lifestyles.

Theories of desistance are briefly described, as are the views of young offenders themselves about what helps and hinders them in that process. The chapter concludes by drawing together theoretical and practical aspects of the desistance process which may help practitioners and others working with young people to encourage an earlier and lasting shift from offending to law-abiding behaviour.

Theories of desistance

'Desistance', like the term 'persistence' and even 'offending' itself, is a contentious term, meaning different things to different people in different contexts. Farrington (1997) suggests that one can never know that desistance has occurred in an individual until that individual dies. Other commentators are more optimistic in suggesting that desistance can be assumed when serious criminal activity ends (Shover 1996) or when criminal activity ceases for prolonged periods of time (Matza 1964; Maruna 2001). The two most commonly used means of gauging desistance, however defined, are through official reconviction data and through self-reported data. Both of these have their disadvantages, including the fact that only a minority of offenders come to the attention of the police, let alone statisticians, and that perceptions of offending by offenders themselves can often be unreliable. Thus, measuring desistance is problematic, not least when it is unclear when and for how long offending behaviour has been avoided.

Theories of desistance tend to come under one of three headings, defined here as 'individual', 'structural' and 'integrative', and these are described briefly below before exploring the views and experiences of young people who offend.

Individual theories of desistance

Two sets of theories in particular focus on the age, attitudes and characteristics of offenders. The first set emphasizes the inevitability of maturation in reducing or stopping offending behaviour in youth (Glueck and Glueck 1940; Rutherford 1986), but such theories tend to operate in a vacuum, devoid of external influences such as schooling, employment, relationships and the social status of young people in transition. Theories of maturational reform also imply that interventions to reduce offending may be counterproductive, given that young people will naturally grow out of crime. This argument poses difficulties not only for policy-makers but also for practitioners who wish to work constructively with young people who offend, and will be discussed later in this chapter.

The second set of theories, rational choice theories (Cornish and Clarke 1986), stress the decision-making capacities of individuals not only to start, but also to stop offending, the latter because of possible 'burn out' the deterrence effect of the youth and criminal justice systems and/or a rational reassessment of the costs and benefits of crime, not least in the transition to adulthood. Rational choice theories are not, however, so appropriate in explaining youthful criminal activity, which is arguably more impulsive and spontaneous at a younger age – often committed as an end in itself rather than a means to an end – although it would seem from much of the research evidence that young people make more rational choices in deciding to stop offending than in deciding to start (see, for example, Barry 2006).

Structural theories of desistance

The structural factors which may influence desistance mainly include social bonds, employment and marriage. Hirschi (1969) defined social bonds as involving emotional ties to others, an investment in relationships, access to legitimate activities and a commitment to the rule of law. Structural theories relating to relationships and other social bonds have proved relatively successful in understanding gender differences in the desistance process, in that young women with commitments to partners and children are more likely to desist from crime than young men. Graham and Bowling (1995) found that young women were more likely to make a successful and speedier transition to adulthood, with more opportunities for independent living and less peer pressure to offend. Young women may also have greater access to social and other forms of capital which may enable an earlier progress towards desistance (Barry 2006, 2007a).

Several theorists suggest that conventional opportunities, such as marriage and employment, are crucial influences in the desistance process for young people in their late teens and early twenties (Sampson and Laub 1993; Shover 1996), which is the most common age at which desistance occurs, but it is often stressed that it is the *quality* of such opportunities that is important in encouraging desistance, rather than the event itself (Sampson and Laub 1995; Rutter 1996). Relationships and employment *per se* will affect different young people in differing ways, depending on their commitment to, for example, settling down, leaving home or working for a living. Young people are also at a disadvantage in the transition to adulthood because of the instability of, for example, youth labour market opportunities, the seeming transience of peer-group relationships and limited access to social and other forms of capital at that age (Barry 2006, 2007a).

Integrative theories of desistance

A combination of individual and structural theories into what could be termed 'integrative' theories of desistance is receiving increasing attention, not least given the limitations of the theories outlined above which focus on individual or structural factors in isolation. Integrative theories increasingly draw on offender narratives about reasons for starting and stopping offending, since the 'phenomenology of desistance' (Maruna 2001: 32), from an offender perspective, can offer valuable insights into subjective interpretations of, and reactions to, events both individual and structural which may, or may not, encourage desistance.

Several theories emphasize events in the life course (Sampson and Laub 1993; Shover 1996; Farrall and Bowling 1999; Maruna 2001) or, more specifically, in the transition from childhood to adulthood (Barry 2006), as having an impact on one's likelihood of choosing to continue offending into adulthood. A combination of conventional social bonds/opportunities and strengthened resolve/motivation is key to the desistance process, as are power differentials in youth, individual agency and changing perceptions of self within a social context. Indeed, young offenders themselves often cite self-motivation as the critical factor in the desistance process, although this focus on the self can often lead to the 'epistemological fallacy' described by Furlong and Cartmel (1997), where an overemphasis on individual responsibility and self-determination without taking into account the powerful impact of existing social barriers may result in young people taking sole responsibility for their predicament. The implications of this are discussed in greater detail towards the end of this chapter.

Young people's views of desistance

The views and advice of young people who offend are crucial in better understanding both individual and structural theories of desistance. Thus, using the above brief summary of the desistance literature as a backdrop, two recent research studies undertaken by the author of young people's views and experiences (Barry 2006; Cruickshank and Barry 2008) are drawn on here to illustrate how they understand the process of desistance both for themselves and for other young offenders. These two Scottish studies explored the views of young people currently or previously involved in offending, asking them what helps or hinders both themselves and other young people in the process of desistance.

The first study (Barry 2006) involved in-depth interviews with 20 male and 20 female current and ex-offenders, aged 18–33, who had previously been subject to probation supervision. The second study (Cruickshank and Barry 2008) involved interviews and focus group discussions with 21 young men and 14 young women aged 13–21 who were currently, or were recently, looked after in residential and secure care. The focus here is confined to their perceived reasons for their own desistance and to their views about how to promote desistance in other young people.

Personal reasons for desistance

The young people in these two studies suggested several factors which they felt were influential in at least discouraging them from continuing offending (push factors – the negative connotations of offending *per se*), if not positively encouraging them to stop offending (pull factors – the positive influences of alternative lifestyles/opportunities). Interestingly, the vast majority of respondents cited 'push' factors when describing why they themselves stopped offending, and 'pull' factors as potential reasons why other young people might stop offending. Most push factors could be subsumed under 'individual' theories of desistance and pull factors under 'structural' theories of desistance, as described below.

The main push factors for these young people were the 'hassle' of offending (being caught and losing their liberty), concerns about their declining health and wellbeing (resulting from drug use) and, for the older women in particular, feeling no longer able to look after their children as a result of their offending lifestyle. These were all seen as individual factors to these young people, changed only through their own resolve, agency and motivation. For those younger people in the care system, being caught had seemingly fewer repercussions than for those older people in the community (since in Scotland, those under the age of 16 are dealt with by a more welfare-oriented children's hearings system known as a 'panel', whereas those aged 16 and over are dealt with in the adult criminal justice system):

> I knew I would get away with it because I was in a children's unit, they would take me to a panel and [I] wouldn't have to go up in front of a judge or anything. (15-year-old female, Cruickshank and Barry 2008)

> You could get away with it when you're under fifteen, sixteen. You can get away with crime and that. But after that, you can't get away . . . it's not worth going to all the hassle of being in 'jail'. (22-year-old male, Barry 2006)

Hill *et al.* (2005) suggest that there is a greater escalation of offending for young people who are accommodated by dint of their living situation. Equally, for such young people, whether in residential units or secure care, the excessive and often painful use of restraint procedures by staff as a controlling mechanism can result in retaliation by young people, and there is also a tendency among residential care staff to resort to police involvement for often minor disturbances within the residential establishment.

Thus, young people who are looked after in residential care and who pose a risk to themselves or others through their behaviour can inadvertently escalate through the youth justice system because of staff responses to such behaviour rather than be enabled to reduce their offending:

> When I was out in the streets, I didn't have people trying to hold me. It leads [you] to assault them, if they're trying to hold me then they're pushing buttons. I don't like it. I don't like getting held, so obviously I assault them. (14-year-old male, Cruickshank and Barry 2008)

> Me and other young people get hurt in restraints all the time. People who are claustrophobic getting into a safe hold would make them worse. (15-year-old male, Cruickshank and Barry 2008)

Few respondents in both studies mentioned pull factors which encouraged them to desist from crime and while some of the older women may have suggested current commitments to a partner or child as a pull factor, the young men tended to talk more hypothetically about potential pull factors, such as hoping to gain employment or to have more constructive things to do in their leisure time:

[My fiancé] brought a really different side out on me. He makes me relaxed, more calmer, and it's like as if I found someone who really cares and actually is interested in me, for who I really was. (25-year-old woman, Barry 2006)

A lot more to do, a lot of activities in the community, a job maybe, that would take your mind off these sort of things ... I never played on a swing or nothing when I was young, never had that experience. (17-year-old male, Cruickshank and Barry 2008)

For the young men, reasons for desistance tended to be not only hypothetical but also more practical (alternative leisure or employment opportunities), whereas the young women's reasons were more relational, in terms of having responsibilities and opportunities to care for others, whether that be family members, their own children or law-abiding partners. The younger – and predominantly male – respondents were more likely to talk of constructive leisure opportunities rather than employment opportunities, or of having supportive relationships (with parents, peers or professionals), although relationships tended to be more important to the younger women than the younger men.

Promoting desistance in others

Respondents in both studies spoke of how they would help other young people to stop offending, and three key approaches emerged. The most popular approach to reducing crime and problematic behaviour in young people, mentioned equally by male and female respondents, was to offer constructive activities to reduce boredom and to give young people a stake in society, whether through leisure, education or employment:

Give them something to do. Let people wake up in the morning and the first thing they don't think about is getting wasted. They need something to keep their mind off it, you know. They need opportunities. (24-year-old man, Barry 2006)

There was nothing to do but hang about street corners ... If you put in more football parks and youth clubs in your areas, that would help you sort out offending. (15-year-old male, Cruickshank and Barry 2008)

As has been seen in other critiques of young people's views of the youth justice and criminal justice system (see, for example, Webster *et al.* 2004; Gray 2005; Barry 2007b; Barry and Moodie 2008), interventions of a practical nature (for example, advice about housing, employment, education or state benefits) were preferred to those interventions that focused on surveillance or addressing offending behaviour in a vacuum. In this respect, respondents commented on the need for information and advice in respect of alcohol or drug-awareness training and treatment, since much offending was seen as a consequence of, or associated with, substance misuse.

Secondly, the majority of respondents stressed the importance of social workers talking and listening to their clients about the problems, fears and consequences of offending. As one 27-year-old woman said: 'I think a lot of young people really just need somebody to listen to them' (Barry 2006). However, this important facet of the worker-client relationship was often not in evidence, not least for many young people who are looked after and accommodated, and who are subject to a myriad of professional interventions, as one 14-year-old male respondent explained:

> Anger management, counselling, therapy and weekly meetings with somebody I can't remember . . . they just looked at you as their work, there was a paycheque at the end of it. They weren't listening to what you were saying . . . In therapy, that psychotherapist asks you questions and doesn't give you any advice back. It's a waste of an hour. (Cruickshank and Barry 2008)

Finally, many inferred that youth and criminal justice interventions could only be effective if they were tailor-made to suit the needs and circumstances of individual young people and were 'hands-on' rather than undertaken in a vacuum divorced from the reality of everyday life in the community. This suggests a need for interventions which can motivate young people to change through positive reinforcement, rather than for interventions which focus solely on the impact of their offending on others (Farrall 2002, 2004). Farrall suggests that motivation to desist from crime (through encouraging and non-judgemental relationships with significant others) is more likely to aid desistance than supervision which focuses on offending behaviour and its consequences in a vacuum.

McNeill (2006), among others, also argues that the relationship between worker and client is a central part of any intervention, not least because of the importance of that relationship to the client. The 'neo-correctionalist', punishment-oriented approach (Cavadino and Dignan 2006), which increasingly and prematurely draws young people into the youth justice system, can all too often undermine the capacity and discretion of youth justice professionals to build a meaningful and proactive relationship with their clients.

Conclusions

Given that young people tend to view their own attempts at desistance as individually negotiated and yet suggest that other young people need structural opportunities to stop offending, it is important to understand the process as combining modifications in attitude and behaviour with alternative opportunities for integration and status, based on the third set of 'integrated' theories of desistance cited earlier in this chapter.

In terms of the individually negotiated process of desistance, young people in these studies, as elsewhere, imply that workers can offer three crucial elements in reinforcing behavioural change among young offenders. These elements are a 'listening ear', motivation and encouragement. McNeill (2006) and others have stressed the importance of returning to a welfare-oriented approach to offender rehabilitation, where a meaningful relationship between worker and client is the basis of good listening, strengthened motivation and encouragement to change. Such a relationship needs to be built on trust and reciprocity, since young people's perceptions of authoritarianism or perceived injustice by workers can often result in defensiveness or even retaliation. Such a relationship also needs to be attuned to the differing approaches of young women versus young men: the former tend to relate better to emotional or relational support, whereas young men often prefer practical support.

In terms of the structurally negotiated process of desistance, practitioners will need to work beyond the confines of the youth justice system to access opportunities (whether education, employment, leisure or family oriented) which are meaningful to young people, in order to help them to access social and other forms of capital which can give them the motivation and incentive to replace offending behaviour with more meaningful and integrative main-stream activities in the longer term. Young women's seemingly easier and earlier access to such capital has been equated with their greater likelihood of desistance from crime, compared with young men (Barry 2006).

Although the age–crime curve suggests that young people tend to stop offending in their early to mid-twenties irrespective of any obvious outside intervention, I have argued elsewhere (Barry 2006, 2007a, 2007b) that the point in time at which young people stop offending is closely associated with the opportunities they are afforded in the transition to adulthood. Such opportunities are equated with being trusted, being given responsibilities and being recognized as key players in mainstream (i.e. 'adult') society. It is likely that the 'limbo' effect that many young people experience in the transitional period between childhood and adulthood will be closely associated with their propensity to offend in youth, and this is the period when practitioners are perhaps best able to create constructive opportunities for change and integration.

However, the youth justice system on its own cannot address all the needs of young people who have offended, since it tends to focus on individual deficits in a vacuum rather than on structural constraints. Youth justice practitioners and others can only be proactive in the process of changing lives if they can work in a multidisciplinary environment, as much as possible devoid of criminalizing, stigmatizing and marginalizing notions of youth crime as 'problematic' and young people as 'deficient'.

References

Barry, M. (2006) *Youth Offending in Transition: The Search for Social Recognition*. Abingdon: Routledge.

Barry, M. (2007a) 'Youth offending and youth transitions: the power of capital in influencing change', *Critical Criminology*, 15: 185–98.

Barry, M. (2007b) 'Listening and learning: the reciprocal relationship between worker and client', *Probation Journal*, 54: 407–22.

Barry, M. and Moodie, K. (2008) *'This isn't the Road I Want to Go Down': Young People's Perceptions and Experiences of Secure Care*. Glasgow: Who Cares? Scotland.

Blumstein, A., Cohen, J. and Farrington, D.P. (1988) 'Criminal career research: its value for criminology', *Criminology*, 26: 1–35.

Cavadino, M. and Dignan, J. (2006) *Penal Systems: A Comparative Approach*. London: Sage.

Cornish, D. and Clarke, R.V. (1986) *The Reasoning Criminal*. New York, NY: Springer-Verlag.

Cruickshank, C.-A. and Barry, M. (2008) *'Nothing Has Convinced Me to Stop': Young People's Perceptions and Experiences of Persistent Offending*. Glasgow: Who Cares? Scotland.

Farrall, S. (2002) *Rethinking What Works with Offenders*. Cullompton: Willan Publishing.

Farrall, S. (2004) 'Social capital and offender reintegration: making probation desistance focused', in S. Maruna and R. Immarigeon (eds) *After Crime and Punishment: Pathways to Offender Reintegration*. Cullompton: Willan Publishing.

Farrall, S. and Bowling, B. (1999) 'Structuration, human development and desistance from crime', *British Journal of Criminology*, 39: 253–68.

Farrington, D. (1997) 'Human development and criminal careers', in M. Maguire *et al.* (eds) *The Oxford Handbook of Criminology* (2nd edn). Oxford: Oxford University Press.

Furlong, A. and Cartmel, F. (1997) *Young People and Social Change: Individualization and Risk in Late Modernity*. Milton Keynes: Open University Press.

Glueck, S. and Glueck, E. (1940) *Unraveling Juvenile Delinquency*. New York, NY: Commonwealth Fund.

Graham, J. and Bowling, B. (1995) *Young People and Crime*. London: Home Office.

Gray, P. (2005) 'The politics of risk and young offenders' experiences of social exclusion and restorative justice', *British Journal of Criminology*, 45: 938–57.

Hill, M., Walker, M., Moodie, K., Wallace, B., Bannister, J., Khan, F., McIvor, G. and Kendrick, A. (2005) *Fast Track Children's Hearings Pilot: Final Report*. Edinburgh: Scottish Executive.

Hirschi, T. (1969) *Causes of Delinquency*. Berkeley, CA: University of California Press.

Maruna, S. (2001) *Making Good: How Ex-convicts Reform and Rebuild their Lives*. Washington DC: American Psychological Association.

Matza, D. (1964) *Delinquency and Drift*. New York, NY: Wiley.

McNeill, F. (2006) 'A desistance paradigm for offender management', *Criminology and Criminal Justice*, 6: 39–62.

Rutherford, A. (1986) *Growing Out of Crime: The New Era*. Winchester: Waterside Press.

Rutter, M. (1996) 'Transitions and turning points in developmental psycho-pathology: as applied to the age span between childhood and mid-adulthood', *Journal of Behavioural Development*, 19: 603–26.

Sampson, R.J. and Laub, J. (1993) *Crime in the Making: Pathways and Turning Points through Life*. Cambridge, MA: Harvard University Press.

Sampson, R.J. and Laub, J. (1995) 'Understanding variability in lives through time: contributions of life-course criminology', *Studies on Crime and Crime Prevention*, 4: 143–58.

Shover, N. (1996) *Great Pretenders: Pursuits and Careers of Persistent Thieves*. Boulder, CO: Westview Press.

Webster, C., Simpson, D., MacDonald, R., Abbas, A., Cieslik, M., Shildrick, T. and Simpson, M. (2004) *Poor Transitions: Social Exclusion and Young Adults*. Bristol: Policy Press.

Young people's 'voices' as evidence

Jean Hine

Introduction

Policies for responding to the criminal and anti-social behaviour of children and young people, whether actual or potential behaviour, are promoted as 'evidence based'. But what does this mean? These policies are determined by adults using 'evidence' collected and interpreted by adults and containing implicit adult beliefs and assumptions about the nature of childhood/youth. These assumptions include ideas about the appropriate behaviour of children and young people, about the likely future course of their behaviours and, crucially, about the most 'effective' ways of responding to those behaviours. However, as several of the chapters in this Handbook indicate, there is another body of 'evidence' which seeks to problematize these assumptions by considering the behaviour from the perspective and understandings of the children and young people themselves. The research discussed in this chapter adopts this more critical approach and, in doing so, calls aspects of the current 'orthodoxy' into question, suggesting alternative approaches that are likely to be more fruitful and less damaging for the young people involved. The chapter concludes by outlining ways in which practitioners can use this alternative understanding to work in ways that can be more meaningful and useful for children and young people, and ultimately more effective for practice.

Underlying beliefs and assumptions

The beliefs and assumptions underpinning current policy and practice are rooted in a variable history which has played host to different discourses about, and understandings of, young people's behaviour at different times. Vestiges of most of these understandings are still discernible today (France 2009). Hence, childhood is seen as a distinctive stage in the life course, in which children gradually develop physically and mentally from dependent childhood to independent adulthood. The 'normal' journey is relatively straightforward, with common stages along the way leading to a satisfactory, rational, responsible and prudent adulthood. Youth, or adolescence, represents the most critical stage of 'transition' to adulthood, where things are most likely to go wrong and, if not corrected, can result in an unsatisfactory adulthood. The motors for this transition are theorized as being primarily internal to the individual, with a 'smooth transition' identified more by what it is not (e.g. an absence of problems) than by what it is. Structural factors, such as relative deprivation and disadvantage, are downplayed. Social policy is designed to support this 'normal' and desirable development, and deviations from that desired pattern provide a trigger for a range of interventions to get the young person 'back on course'.

Involvement in criminal and anti-social behaviour is, of course, one such trigger. A key belief/assumption of youth justice policy since 1998 is that without targeted intervention to 'nip it in the bud' such inappropriate behaviour is likely to continue and to worsen (Home Office 1997).

The 'risk factor model' of assessment – utilizing predictive tools such as Asset and Onset – has been lauded as an effective means of identifying the 'risk factors' that impede 'normal' development and portend continued involvement in offending. These 'risk factors' are the targets for interventions that the 'what works' evaluations have proven to be effective in reducing offending. This model is not without its critics (see, for example, Chapters 9 and 15 this volume). Of particular concern is the way that, under New Labour, this concern to rehabilitate has coalesced with an imperative that young people must also be punished for their behaviour. This is a very different approach from that practised in the 1980s and early 1990s. That policy – which stressed a minimal or non-intervention approach – was underpinned by the belief that a high proportion of young people would have some passing involvement in crime or anti-social behaviour, that this was fairly normal and that most children would grow out of it without professional intervention (Rutherford 1986), and there is some evidence that this approach was effective (Soothill *et al.* 2008).

Challenges to the assumptions

The new sociology of childhood presents challenges to many commonly held views about the nature of childhood (James *et al.* 1998; Lavallette and Cunningham 2002; Brown 2005), and a range of research is shedding a new and different light on the nature of transitions through adolescence and youth to adulthood (see, for example, Chapter 15 this volume). At the same time, research looking into risk factors is throwing doubt on their efficacy as either predictors or identifiers for appropriate intervention (Case and Haines 2009).

One key set of assumptions under challenge has to do with the notion of 'normal' childhood and the trajectories taken in the 'transitions' to adulthood.

Aitken, for instance, argues that this idea of normal progression is an artefact of western, white, middle-class ideals rather than a reflection of the real lives of most children, and that 'young people's public and private rights are assaulted by moral panics over seemingly unchildlike behaviours' (2001: 23). This is important because, while the concept of normality is fundamental to the creation of 'good citizens' and the management of their behaviour, the search for normality and its concomitant risk factors is one that tends to 'homogenize' normality (Armstrong 2006), by which he means that the wide-ranging and different routes to a satisfactory adulthood are blended into a narrow conception of what is 'normal'. The creation of the good, active citizens of the future involves both protection and control through the wide range of professionals and organizations that impinge upon the lives of children and young people (Rose 1989).

However, as noted earlier, the assumption of 'normality' underpinning this work relies more on beliefs about what it is not than on what it is. Hence, the 'criteria of normality are elaborated by experts on the basis of their claims to scientific knowledge of childhood and its vicissitudes. [Yet] this knowledge of normality has not, in the main, resulted from studying normal children' (Rose 1989: 131). In fact, research has shown that young people's transitions vary substantially both geographically and temporally (Furlong and Cartmel 2007), as well as being shaped by gender, race and social class (Bynner 2005). These differences and changes are to some extent acknowledged by policy-makers, although this acknowledgement has done little to undermine the continuing attachment to the idea of normality itself.

Indeed, the increasingly harsh and prescriptive approaches to dealing with young people are premised on this ahistorical and uncontextualized model of individual transition. The result is an often counterproductive attempt to hammer the square pegs of young people's lives into conceptually round holes. Moreover, the idea: 'of childhood dependency, based as it is on conceptions of children as developing objects, and therefore as incompetent and irresponsible, precludes us from acknowledging the extent to which children are capable, competent, and have agency and responsibility in their own lives' (Morrow 2005: 260).

Much of the research concerned to identify delinquent 'trajectories' and 'risk factors' associated with offending behaviour is based on the retrospective study of serious or prolific offenders (see, for example, Loeber and Farrington 2000). This suggests that young people begin their offending 'careers' with relatively minor and infrequent offending but will, if left unchecked, escalate into more frequent and more serious offending. However, there is growing evidence from wider studies of children and young people (see, for example, Armstrong *et al.* 2005) that challenges this, indicating that for a majority of young people their problem behaviour remains relatively minor in terms of seriousness, does not escalate and, irrespective of professional intervention, is relatively short lived (Francis *et al.* 2007).

Farrington *et al.* show that, of the 409 10-year-olds recruited to the Cambridge study, the largest number of convicted offenders at any age was 46 boys aged 17 years. This quickly declined to just 11 men offending at the age of 23, and two of them were first offenders (2006: 20). Of the 167 people in the study who were convicted of an offence at some time, more than half of them were convicted three or fewer times in their life (2006: 24). Findings such as these highlight the problem of focusing on the statistical 'link' between individual risk factors and offending while neglecting the evidence that there are more young people with identified risk factors who do *not* offend than there are who do.

The existence of these large numbers of 'false positives' raises obvious concerns about 'net widening' and the labelling processes arising from unnecessary criminalization. Equally worrying, the risk factor paradigm causes practitioners to focus on the negative aspects of young people and to give limited credence to the positive aspects of young people's lives (Smith 2007). This focus on individual deficits also diverts attention from the more important environmental and structural factors that impact negatively on young people's lives, such as poverty (Duncan *et al.* 1998).

Another fallacy within the policy model is that offenders and victims are two separate and mutually exclusive groups. In reality this is far from the case. Surveys (Smith 2004; Armstrong *et al.* 2005) show a high degree of overlap, with a high proportion of offenders having been victims at some point. The majority of serious young offenders have been disproportionately vulnerable to victimization (Boswell 1998).

Young people's perspectives

Increasingly, research with young people is challenging the idea that youthful misconduct and deviancy are 'irrational' or the result of cognitive dysfunction associated with 'abnormal' development. Ungar (2004, 2005), for instance, argues that young people's behaviour is generally purposeful and should be seen as an attempt to produce an outcome they consider desirable. Apparently irrational and problematic behaviour, in this reading, is usually about children and young people doing the best they can given their circumstances. Understanding the *meanings* which children and young people attach to their behaviours gives a different perspective, and actions which (from the outside) appear negative or self-destructive are revealed as having positive functions: 'the most vulnerable youth . . . found through their delinquent and disordered behaviors the same health resources (self-esteem, competence, meaningful involvement with their communities, and attachment to others) as their more stereotypically resilient peers' (Ungar 2004: 354).

A good illustration of this is disengagement from education. Although this can be viewed as 'irrational' behaviour on the part of the individual – limiting their prospects in later life – it can also be seen as more reasoned and purposeful when viewed through the wider lenses of environment and social class (Berridge *et al.* 2001). MacDonald and Marsh, for example, reported that some young people disengaged from school because 'being a swot was an identity to be avoided' and that '*any* display of educational engagement was treated as signalling conformist acceptance of the school deal' (2005: 55, emphasis in original), findings that are similar to educational ethnographies of the past (see, for example, Willis 1977; Brown 1987). Again, truanting is not always about 'bunking off' for fun: it can be thought of as a 'rational' response to conflict with teachers or bullying by other students or as a means for struggling students to avoid the social embarrassment of academic under-achievement (Gleeson 1994). Doubt has been cast on the predictive power of a lack of engagement with education, as MacDonald and Marsh (2005) found little difference in the employment prospects and careers of those who were not engaged with education and those who were.

The outcomes that young people are seeking are often related to their self-perception or identity and are concerned with maximising what Cote (1996) calls their 'identity capital'. As Goffman (1969) demonstrated, everyone has a range of 'identities' which they use in various circumstances, and young people are no different. A 'problematic' identity may play a limited role in the young person's life and, in most circumstances, be transitory. However policies and practices that give primacy to this identity are – contrary to intentions – likely to reinforce and sustain that identity by labelling the young person as an 'offender'.

In my own research I have found that children have been criminalized for behaviour that had no criminal intent (Hine 2007), particularly for relatively trivial incidents. One example is children playing in an abandoned vehicle: the two 12-year-olds were arrested for taking a lighter out of the stolen car. This was at the time when there was concern that individual police officer targets for 'offences brought to justice' were leading to inappropriate arrests and convictions, particularly of young people (Flanaghan 2008). Such actions call into question the notion of 'crime' and who decides what is and what isn't one. Young people who live in disadvantaged areas are more likely to receive a criminal record because of the way in which their behaviour is identified and formalized (McAra and McVie 2005). These children and young people are more likely to be in public areas in their neighbourhoods; these neighbour-hoods have more crime and are more heavily policed; and thus the behaviour of the young people is more likely to be seen by the police and more likely to be construed as criminal.

Young people display an acute sense of fairness (Hine 2004) and see the unfairness in these actions by the criminal justice system but are sometimes willing to accept unfair responses, again paradoxically given the potentially serious ramifications, for a range of reasons (Hine 2007). Adults, particularly those in positions of authority, are able to exercise power over young people that ignores or trivializes their own accounts of events because of competing objectives and priorities.

Implications for practice

Offending is, for the vast majority, usually only a very small part of the life of young offenders. The majority hold prosocial values and their aspirations are conventional – having a job that generates reasonable income, being able to pursue leisure pursuits, the prospects of settling down to family life. Assessment tools such as Asset and Onset, by focusing on the young person as an offender, neglects these positive aspirations and may even weaken the young person's attachment to them by a process of labelling. Individualized risk assessment also fails to locate offending adequately in its wider context. For writers such as Smith, this means 'positive practice needs to reframe the problems of young people to recognize that these largely stem from processes of discrimination, disadvantage and exclusion' (2008: 8). Young people in my own research described the frustration of being viewed as 'guilty by association', when they feel an agency or professional responded to them on the basis of being a member of a particular family, living in a particular area or having certain friends. They have little opportunity or power to challenge these views and negative labels, and attempts to do so can reinforce those labels by identifying the young person as 'aggressive' or 'unco-operative'. Some young people, however, have a more sophisticated understanding of the processes that are applied to them by the professionals with authority over their lives, and find more subtle ways of maintaining some semblance of control – for instance, by providing only information that they feel will have a positive impact for them.

A key theme of this chapter is that, like all of us, young people have strengths as well as weaknesses or 'deficits'. Contrary to the assumptions in the current risk factor model, young offenders do not always want to be involved with crime and often find ways to avoid being drawn into offending. Young people can be easily prompted to provide a range of reasons for not wanting to be involved in crime, such as not upsetting a member of their family (usually their mother), being concerned for the potential victim, fear of the consequences of being caught or wanting to be 'normal'. Such an approach also highlights the strategies they use to avoid being involved in offending (Hine 2006), such as staying away from particular places or people. Contemporary theories around desistance (see Chapter 15 this volume) suggest an understanding of these points acknowledges the strength and viability of such strategies and can help professionals to identify ways in which they can support positive attempts to steer clear of crime, such as cultivating new pastimes and more law-abiding friends, and drawing on the support of family and community. Listen to what young people have to say (Coleman *et al.* 2004): look for the strengths and build on them.

Risk factors, generally perceived as criminogenic, can, in some circumstances, perform a protective function for young people, so it is important to check out the possible 'hidden benefits' of behaviours when contemplating an intervention to change them. For instance, although a young person's peer group may indeed be one of the reasons they are involved in criminal activity, those same friends may also be providing the young person with substantial support in dealing with problems in their life (Walker and McCarthy 2005).

The current position of standardized risk assessment as the primary tool shaping professional decision-making is being called into question, in part from an acceptance that the predictive power of risk-based assessment is limited. Longitudinal research reveals that many young people have had positive and satisfactory adult futures despite assessments made to the contrary (Laub and Sampson 2003; Williamson 2004). This is also the case for the classic Cambridge study (West and Farrington 1973) which underpins much of the UK research about risk factors as a predictive tool (Farrington 1996), where follow-up work has revealed similar satisfactory outcomes for most of the young offenders (Farrington *et al.* 2006).

A common theme emerging from all of this research is the importance of serendipity and unexpected and unpredictable events in determining the futures of young offenders. The nature of their involvement with the youth justice system could be that event, for both good and ill. It has also been proposed that this increasing technicization of assessment and the management of young offenders has more to do with the protection of the worker and the organization (defensibility) than the wellbeing of young people (Kemshall 2002). This uncertainty around risk-based assessment adds weight to the view that the best way to understand young people is through a professional assessment in which the practitioner uses their reflexive knowledge and consults closely with the young person and their family to supplement the risk-based analysis.

Interventions and programmes can have a negative impact on young people, sometimes because insufficient account has been taken of the broad context of young people's lives, and sometimes because of labelling. Little is published about unsuccessful or harmful intervention, though some work has been done (McCord 2003), and a growing literature is revealing how contact with the criminal justice system can have a negative impact (e.g. Hazel *et al.* 2002; McAra and McVie 2005).

The lives of young offenders are frequently complex and chaotic, with many having been a victim of abuse by adults. Too narrow a focus on offending can mean that past victimization unrelated to current offending is not dealt with, and this too can have harmful consequences. Lack of trust means they are often reticent to discuss such issues and thus the resultant problems may be unresolved despite a range of agencies and professionals being involved in their lives (Whyte 2004). Young people can feel let down by adults who could have cared for them or helped them but did not (Lyon *et al.* 2000). This is not to argue for non-intervention but that account should be taken of the context and understandings of young people, their lives and behaviours and the possibility that intervention may impact negatively as well as positively.

Young people are often concerned about the ways in which data held about them are used and shared, and this can lead to a reluctance to share important information with professional adults until they feel they can be trusted. Even then this trust is tenuous and can easily be damaged should they feel that information has been shared inappropriately (Munro 2001). This reinforces the importance of being honest with young people about who has access to what and the limits of confidentiality.

What young people value the most about intervention by professionals is a good relationship with an adult who, they feel, cares about them as an individual and who offers help (Yates 2009). A respectful, listening and consistent adult can help a young person cope with the often numerous difficulties in their lives. The 'how' of intervention and practice is perceived by young people as more important for effective work with them than the 'what' of 'what works' programmes. The old adage of 'start where the client is at' should not be dismissed lightly.

Conclusion

Although the current approach tends to concentrate on 'risk' as a negative construct, 'problem' behaviour is in fact multifaceted (Kemshall 2002), with many positive attributes, such as self-improvement, emotional engagement (pleasure) and feelings of control (empowerment) (Lupton 2006). Exposure to risk can build resilience (Ungar 2004). Conversely young offenders can, in some ways, be 'risk averse' (Boeck et al. 2006), and this can reduce their opportunities for a satisfactory transition to adulthood. Behaviour that is categorized as problematic or an indicator of risk can be a rational and reasonable response to what young people perceive to be a more problematic situation (Ungar 2004). And importantly, young people are not merely passive recipients of risk. They are very aware of and actively negotiate the risks that they perceive and confront on a day-to-day basis, though these may not be risks as identified by the professionals they work with (France 2000; Miles 2002).

Children and young people should be acknowledged as competent active participants in their interventions and should be encouraged to be involved in the framing of their problems and dealing with them. Look for the positives in young people (Perkins 2009) and support them in their here and now rather than focus primarily on their possible and unpredictable futures.

References

Aitken, S.C. (2001) *Geographies of Young People: The Morally Contested Spaces of Identity*. London: Routledge.

Armstrong, D. (2006) 'Becoming criminal: the cultural politics of risk', *International Journal of Inclusive Education*, 10: 265–78.

Armstrong, D., Hine, J., Hacking, S., Armaos, R., Jones, R., Klessinger, N. and France, A. (2005) *Children, Risk and Crime: The On Track Youth Lifestyles Survey. Home Office Research Study* 278. London: Home Office.

Berridge, D., Brodie I., Pitts J., Porteous, D. and Tarling, R. (2001) *The Independent Effects of Permanent Exclusion from School on the Offending Careers of Young People. RDS Occasional Paper* 71. London: Home Office.

Boeck, T., Fleming, J. and Kemshall, H. (2006) 'The context of risk decisions: does social capital make a difference?', *Forum Qualitative Sozialforschung* (available online at http://nbn-resolving.de/urn:nbn:de:0114-fqs0601170).

Boswell, G.R. (1998). 'Criminal justice and violent young offenders', *Howard Journal*, 37: 148–60.

Brown, P. (1987) *Schooling Ordinary Kids*. London: Tavistock.

Brown, S. (2005) *Understanding Youth and Crime: Listening to Youth?* (2nd edn). Maidenhead: Open University Press.

Bynner, J. (2005) 'Rethinking the youth phase of the life course: the case for emerging adulthood?', *Journal of Youth Studies*, 8: 367–84.

Case, S. and Haines, K. (2009). *Understanding Youth Offending: Risk Factor Research, Policy and Practice*. Cullompton: Willan Publishing.

Coleman, J., Catan, L. and Dennison, C. (2004) 'You're the last person I'd talk to', in J. Roche *et al.* (eds) *Youth in Society* (2nd edn). London: Sage.

Cote, J.E. (1996) 'Sociological perspectives on identity formation: the culture–identity link and identity capital', *Journal of Adolescence*, 19: 417–28.

Duncan, G.J., Brooks-Gunn, J., Yeung, W.J., Smith, J.R. (1998) 'How much does childhood poverty affect the life chances of children?', *American Sociological Review*, 63: 406–23.

Farrington, D. (1996) *Understanding and Preventing Youth Crime*. York: Joseph Rowntree Foundation.

Farrington, D.P., Coid, J.W., Harnett, L., Jolliffe, D., Soteriou, N., Turner, R. and West, D.J. (2006) *Criminal Careers and Life Success: New Findings from the Cambridge Study in Delinquent Development. Home Office Findings* 281. London: Home Office.

Flanaghan, R. (2008) *The Review of Policing: Final Report*. London: Home Office.

France, A. (2000) 'Towards a sociological understanding of youth and their risk taking', *Journal of Youth Studies*, 3: 317–31.

France, A. (2009) 'Changing conceptions of youth in late modernity', in J. Wood and J. Hine (eds) *Work with Young People: Theory and Policy for Practice*. London: Sage.

Francis, B., Soothill, K. and Piquero, A.R. (2007) 'Criminal career length estimation issues and generational changes in modeling', *Crime Delinquency*, 53: 84–105.

Furlong, A. and Cartmel, F. (2007) *Young People and Social Change: New Perspectives* (2nd edn). London: Sage.

Gleeson, D. (1994) 'Wagging, bobbing and bunking off: an alternative view', *Educational Review*, 46: 15–19.

Goffman, E. (1969) *The Presentation of Self in Everyday Life*. London: Allen Lane.

Hazel, N., Hagell, A. and Brazier, L. (2002) *Young Offenders' Perceptions of their Experiences in the Criminal Justice System. End of Award Report to ESRC*. Swindon: ESRC.

Hine, J. (2004) *Children and Citizenship. RDS On Line Report* 08/04. London: HMSO.

Hine, J. (2006) 'Risky business', *Safer Society*, Summer: 25–7.

Hine, J. (2007) 'Young people's perspectives on final warnings', *Web Journal of Current Legal Issues*, 2 (special issue: 'Diverting juveniles, diverting justice') (available online at http://webjcli.ncl.ac.uk/2007/issue2/hine2.html).

Home Office (1997) *No More Excuses: A New Approach to Tackling Youth Crime in England and Wales.* London: Home Office.

James, A., Jenks, C. and Prout, A. (1998) *Theorising Childhood.* Cambridge: Polity Press.

Kemshall, H. (2002) *Risk, Social Policy and Welfare.* Buckingham: Open University Press.

Laub, J.H. and Sampson, R.J. (2003). *Shared Beginnings, Divergent Lives: Delinquent Boys to age 70.* Cambridge, MA: Harvard University Press.

Lavallette, M. and Cunningham, S. (2002) 'The sociology of childhood', in B. Goldson *et al.* (eds) *Children, Welfare and the State.* London: Sage.

Loeber, R. and Farrington, D.J. (2000) 'Young people who commit crime: epidemiology, developmental origins, risk factors, early interventions, and policy implications', *Development and Psychopathology*, 12: 737–62.

Lupton, D. (2006) 'Sociology and Risk', in G. Mythen and S. Walklate (eds) *Beyond the Risk Society: Critical Reflections on Risk and Human Security.* Milton Keynes: Open University Press.

Lyon, J., Dennison, C. and Wilson, A. (2000) *'Tell Them So They Listen': Messages from Young People in Custody. Home Office Research Study* 201. London: Home Office.

MacDonald, R. and Marsh, J. (2005) *Disconnected Youth? Growing Up in Britain's Poor Neighbourhoods.* Basingstoke: Palgrave Macmillan.

McAra, L. and McVie, S. (2005) 'The usual suspects? Street-life, young people and the police', *Criminal Justice*, 5: 5–36.

McCord, J. (2003) 'Cures that harm: unanticipated outcomes of crime prevention programs', *Annals of the American Academy of Political and Social Science*, 587: 16–30.

Miles, S. (2002) 'Victims of risk? Young people and the construction of lifestyles', in M. Cieslick and G. Pollock (eds) *Young People in Risk Society: The Restructuring of Youth Identities and Transitions in Later Modernity.* Aldershot: Ashgate.

Morrow, V. (2005) 'Invisible children? Towards a reconceptualization of childhood dependency and responsibility', in C. Jenks (ed.) *Childhood: Critical Concepts in Sociology.* Abingdon: Routledge.

Munro, E. (2001) 'Empowering looked-after children', *Child and Family Social Work*, 6: 129–37.

Perkins, D. (2009) 'Community youth development', in J. Wood and J. Hine (eds) *Work with Young People: Theory and Policy for Practice.* London: Sage.

Rose, N. (1989) *Governing the Soul: The Shaping of the Private Self.* London: Routledge.

Rutherford, A. (1986) *Growing Out of Crime.* Harmondsworth: Penguin Books.

Smith, D. (2004) *The Links between Victimisation and Offending. Edinburgh Study of Youth Transitions and Crime Report* 5. Edinburgh: University of Edinburgh.

Smith, R. (2007) *Youth Justice: Ideas, Policy, Practice* (2nd edn). Cullompton: Willan Publishing.

Smith, R. (2008) *Social Work with Young People.* Cambridge: Polity Press.

Soothill, K., Ackerley, E. and Francis, B. (2008) 'Criminal convictions among children and young adults: changes over time', *Criminology and Criminal Justice*, 8: 297–315.

Ungar, M. (2004) 'A constructionist discourse on resilience: multiple contexts, multiple realities among at-risk children and youth', *Youth and Society*, 35: 341–65.

Ungar, M. (2005) 'Pathways to resilience among children in child welfare, corrections, mental health and educational settings: navigation and negotiation', *Child and Youth Care Forum*, 34: 423–44.

Walker, J. and McCarthy, P. (2005) 'Parents in prison: the impact on children', in G. Preston (ed.) *At Greatest Risk: The Children Most Likely to be Poor.* London: Child Poverty Action Group.

West, D.J. and Farrington, D.P. (1973) *Who Becomes Delinquent?* London: Heinemann.

Whyte, B. (2004) 'Responding to youth crime in Scotland', *British Journal of Social Work,* 34: 395–411.

Williamson, H. (2004) *Milltown Boys Revisited.* Oxford: Berg.

Willis, P. (1977) *Learning to Labour: How Working Class Kids get Working Class Jobs.* London: Saxon House.

Yates, S. (2009) 'Good practice in guidance: lessons from connexions', in J. Wood and J. Hine (eds) *Work with Young People: Theory and Policy for Practice.* London: Sage.

17

Partnership: putting relationships to work

Mo Barratt

Introduction

The concept of partnership is one of the strongest themes in the current government's policy agenda. The commitment to partnership can be seen in the frequent reiteration of this theme in governmental rhetoric and in the fact that it runs through legislation and policy rather like the lettering through a stick of Blackpool rock. It is central to both the government's modernization agenda and the more general rhetorical aim to find 'joined-up solutions to joined-up problems'. Hence, 'true partnership working is' seen as the 'the only way to address some of the Government's most challenging long-term social and economic objectives' (HM Treasury 2002: 4).

Exactly what 'true partnership' means and how it might best be achieved, however, remain less than clear. While the stated aspiration is of 'some perfect, seamless robe of shared endeavour', in respect of daily practice working, partnership can prove challenging to different people, from different organizations, who act in different ways according to different knowledge bases, cultural traditions and objectives (Payne 2000: 5). In these circumstances, the task of continually seeking new ways of working together, in what can sometimes seem like a very confused and unjoined-up policy environment, can prove more of a problem than the rhetoric suggests.

Forms of partnership

The forms of partnership working in health, welfare and criminal justice contexts are numerous: multi-agency, multi-professional or multidisciplinary teamwork; collaboration between agencies; co-ordination of services; joined-up policy and practice; strategic partnerships; organizational mergers; and integration are but a few. To confuse matters further, the language of partnership is amorphous and ill-defined, with many of the descriptive terms used interchangeably even within the same document or report. What partnership means, as well as what it is intended to achieve, is also subject to ambiguity and is likely to be characterized in different ways by those involved in the process. There are many possible (and often competing) perspectives: those of politicians, policy-makers, managers, front-line staff, communities, service users and the families and carers of service users (Payne 2000). The potential benefits of the approach, and expectations of what might be achieved, must therefore be viewed through multiple lenses.

The rhetoric of joining up appeals to common sense. It is widely assumed that working in partnership should result in the more effective provision of services, with overall efficiency gains and some cost savings thrown in for good measure. Early work by Trevillion (1992) identified many of the benefits of partnership working for each of the stakeholders involved, enabling:

- better interpersonal relationships that can increase caring and trust, and that can develop people's self-image and the identity of their network as a set of important links. Here the idea is that the youth justice network enhances practitioners' capability and enjoyment of the job rather than it being peripheral to it;

- a sense of community identity that can enhance mutual support and make wider choices of lifestyle and services available. Practitioners are therefore an important part of their community and their community network through their contributing to it;

- joint work and the collective ownership of tasks, which helps to overcome mutual suspicion and also helps to promote multi-professional partnership working;

- better communication through a variety of means, which improves information and links between people and contributes to the development of holistic and seamless service responses;

- action learning, which allows people to put groups together to help achieve both community and personal/professional outcomes (see also Payne 2000: 19).

Overall, the potential appeal of the approach for service users is that it should facilitate access to more consistent, co-ordinated and comprehensive services in which needs are assessed and addressed in a more holistic and 'seamless' way. To ensure this happens, service providers need to make the best use of the available resources by managing services in a more co-ordinated and cost-effective way, recognizing and utilizing the strengths and areas of expertise of all the agencies involved. They also need to have an effective strategy for developing the wider skills base of staff to meet the diverse needs of individual service users. When these objectives are achieved, partnership has the potential to tackle those complex problems that transcend traditional professional boundaries (Tate and Shah 2007).

Theory and practice

This is the aspiration but what is the theory? Social welfare research on partnership, or joined-up thinking, is underpinned by two schools of thought. The first of these, termed the 'systematic thesis', suggests that joined-up thinking is needed to fill gaps in welfare service provision that have arisen from a *lack of co-ordination* between organizations (Allen 2003) and the failure of successive administrations to join up thinking at a strategic, governmental level (Blagg *et al.* 1988; Loxley 1997; Irvine *et al.* 2002). Viewed from this perspective, the new youth justice system created by the Crime and Disorder Act 1998 emerged as a response to the (perceived) failure of existing services. This was, of course, the view behind the critique of the Audit Commission (1996), which argued that previous administrations had consistently failed to co-ordinate youth offending services or clarify the aims of the youth justice system as a whole. The second school of thought – the 'epistemological move thesis' – proposes that joined-up thinking is needed to overcome deficiencies in the institutional division and distribution of welfare knowledge (Allen 2003). This position, which is related to and compatible with the systematic thesis, responds to public disillusionment with (and declining deference towards) professional expertise, a deepening dislike of bureaucracy and 'state interference' (Payne 2000).

Both systematic and epistemological positions blame the wider socio-political system for a failure to improve services, and both present joined-up thinking as a progressive solution that is capable of creating more effective and therefore less fallible systems of service provision (Allen 2003). However, the ascendancy of partnership working has also attracted criticism, with some seeing it as a means to extend the state's ability to discipline and control into every aspect of service recipients' lives (Allen 2003).

Pitts, for instance, famously described the specific form of 'joined up' working in youth justice as constituting a form of 'korrectional karaoke'. Here the notion of 'effective practice' involves both the problem of youth offending and its solutions being determined by the political elite and enacted by multiple agencies who are compelled by legislation and funding mechanisms to work together within narrowly confined parameters (Pitts 2001). In effect, this means that the 'rich repertoire of responses to the complex problem of youth crime is reduced to a narrow range of correctional techniques' (Pitts 2001: 11), delivered by an increasingly homogeneous and deprofessionalized workforce trained to comply with nationally accredited practice routines. In this account, partnership working generally, and the joining up of youth justice in particular, is underpinned by ideological assumptions and politicized ways of working.

Are we there yet?

So how useful has partnership been in producing savings in terms of the efficient use of resources? In 2008 the Audit Commission published an analysis of partnership working in services for children following the Laming Inquiry (2003) into the death of Victoria Climbié and the implementation of the Children Act 2004, specifically examining progress in the development of children's trusts in England. The commission's view was that there was little evidence that children's trusts had improved outcomes for children and young people in England or delivered additional value for money, not least because there was confusion about how the trusts were intended to bring agencies together to work in partnership and what they were meant to achieve: 'continuing uncertainty about the purpose of the new arrangements may be a barrier to their success in the eyes of many participants', it concluded (Audit Commission 2008: 66).

Partnership arrangements in the youth justice system fared little better in an analysis of progress after ten years of reform (Solomon and Garside 2008). Solomon and Garside concluded that, after a decade of intensive reconfiguration and massive injection of funding (since 2000–1 spending on youth justice has increased by 45 per cent in real terms rising to £648.5 million in 2006–7), the youth justice system in England and Wales was still struggling to meet the needs of some of the nation's most vulnerable, and challenging, children and young people. Success had been far more elusive than the government had hoped, with the record on youth justice reform being 'at best mixed'. The Youth Justice Board, the body set up by government to lead the new joined-up way of working, strongly refutes this assessment, pointing out successes in areas such as improving the secure estate, involving volunteers in youth justice work and reducing the numbers of first-time entrants to the system. The board, however, appears unable to dismiss two of Solomon and Garside's main findings: that the category of spending with the largest increase in the area of youth justice was in the operation of the board itself, and that overall levels of self-reported offending by children and young people have remained remarkably stable since 1997. More generally, there appears little evidence to suggest that the model of practice introduced since 1998 has been more effective than that of the previous decades and, in relation to some key indicators (such as custodial admissions and 'net widening'), it has been far less effective.

In the case of English children's trusts, the overly intrusive micromanagement of partnership initiatives by central government appeared to be a primary culprit standing in the way of progress. The Audit Commission's view was that agencies would do well to focus less on creating joined-up structures and processes and concentrate more on how these might contribute to the achievement of improved outcomes for children and their families. In youth justice, Solomon and Garside's observation was that there was also a confusion at the level of strategic objectives, and that fundamental questions needed to be asked about how youth justice agencies and their partners can best address the complex social and economic factors that are a root cause of youth offending. The view of these authors was that government expectations have been unrealistically high in terms of what the youth justice system can achieve and that it needs to be clearer about these limitations. It is possible that more effective solutions to youth offending might reside in the delivery of more effective co-ordinated services through mainstream local authority children and young people's provision.

Irrespective of the perspective taken then, there appears to be some consensus about the need for policy-makers to think closely about the potential of joined-up structures and processes. The exhortation to 'Join Up!' and form partnerships may not be the panacea for achieving more effective and therefore less fallible systems of welfare and justice that it was hoped (see Allen 2003). However, instead of accepting this, there is evidence of a tendency to cast blame for failed policy streams and unsuccessful partnership initiatives down towards those agency staff who have the least power to influence them. Moreover, partnership working generates a secondary joined-up power which also acts to cascade blame to individuals for the failures of the system supposedly designed to help them (Allen 2003). Young offenders and their parents who are unable to engage with the interventions offered to them through a lack of social, educational or economic reasons, or who are in receipt of interventions poorly delivered or designed, can be brought to the Courts for further legal action and face further exclusion for their lack of participation or ability to achieve targeted outcomes. In some respects this punitive outcome itself seems to indicate the failure of partnership, where 'joined up' thinking might have addressed some of the problems leading to non-compliance.

Joining up practice for better futures

For many working in the youth justice system, the primary purpose of practice – preceding and superseding that of preventing offending – is the provision of better futures for young offenders. This is important because this aim can provide a unifying objective for practitioners working across their personal, professional and organizational boundaries. The view taken here is that the development of such a shared vision at a practice level is likely to be central to effective partnership. Frost (2005) suggests that, however partnership is described, it is intended to provide added value for service users, beyond the capability of one single organization or profession to offer. Partnership, then, offers the prospect that 'we can perhaps perceive a continuum through co-operation, to collaboration through co-ordination, or to merger, with joined-up working acting as a rhetorical device to connect these, and with partnership acting as an underlying theme' (Frost 2005: 13).

The partnership literature has identified a number of key themes for effective practice. It is suggested that, to be successful, partnerships need to:

- be trustworthy;

- communicate with one another effectively;

- have the right representation (people who can make decisions and represent their organization effectively);

- provide motivation towards a common vision;

- have mechanisms to deal with conflict resolution;

- have clarity of objectives and responsibility; and

- incorporate room for manoeuvre (flexibility) (Markwell 2003).

These attributes reinforce the notion that working in partnership can be built on the development of dynamic relationships between people: between service users and service providers, between the practitioners of various agencies, between organizations, communities, societies and governments via the people who represent them. Norlin and Vogel (2004) suggest that when people choose to be partners they are choosing to put their relationship to work, and that their achievements will be the result both of their willingness to see their relationship as key to their potential to be effective and of their ability to use it as such. In this respect, working in partnership generally might be characterized as a successful relationship in service to specific tasks. In youth justice the specific task is to create strong working relationships between the myriad of professionals and organizations that might be involved, or should be involved, with a young person and to contribute jointly to a plan that results in improved outcomes for young people (which is likely to be effective and therefore compatible with the objective of the Youth Justice Board to prevent offending).

Focusing on the specific tasks that can improve outcomes for service users challenges practitioners to consider how the boundaries between their teams and organizations will need to change, becoming more porous and fluid to create networks of practice around service user need. Youth offending teams have the potential to exemplify an effective partnership approach in a very demanding area of practice. For Payne, teamwork, networking and partnership are indistinguishable, 'so professionals must foster close, positive relationships within their own work groups so that they may build them into co-operative multiprofessional networks and empowering, participative service networks' (2000: 4).

The idea that partnership involves a process of continual learning and sharing through the conscious development of working relationships is further developed by the social theorist, Wenger, who coined the concept of 'communities of practice' (1998). The interesting aspect of communities of practice for this discussion is that they can be developed in any setting and therefore transcend traditional ideas about professions, teams and organizations. A community of practice develops through its members sharing knowledge, involving meaning, practice, community and identity, which are created in the context of practice through the processes of participation and reification. Participation derives from how practitioners contribute to identifying new joined-up ways of working together and, through the process of reification, knowledge and practice, these ways of working are turned into solid representations such as procedures, protocols and policies via mutual engagement (motivation/relationship), joint enterprise (shared goals) and shared repertoire (communication). Each of these attributes relates to core success factors of working in partnership, but the essential ingredient here is that joined-up communities of practice are developed from the ground upwards and are shaped by the delivery of an end product at the place of delivery, returning us to the idea that any changes in practice, for example closer partnership working, should result in improved outcomes for service users – or why do it at all? Crucially, although Wenger's 'communities of practice' operate in a necessarily imperfect wider political social system with organizational culture as a pervasive influence, they are never fully defined by that external mandate. Youth justice practitioners had considerable success in shaping their practice environment prior to the launch of the new youth justice system in 2000 and they have the opportunity to do so again by demonstrating how working in partnership can be realised in daily practice for the benefit of service users.

Conclusion

Partnership is a dynamic process that is never fully realised but has to be worked at, redefined and renegotiated continually, not least because the context of partnership working is always changing (Frost 2005). Managing change in ways that efficiently join up policy and practice is far from easy. The government is itself a large and complex organization, which has to find ways to co-ordinate very disparate activities. It pursues complicated policy objectives which are inevitably driven by external political agendas and expediencies, or are the result of compromises between disputed and confused aims (Payne 2000). Different agencies have different and sometimes conflicting aims and priorities, while service provision develops as a result of both the intended and unintended consequences of Acts of Parliament, which are passed at different times to meet different political demands and socio-economic needs. At the local level these create a wide range of challenges of co-ordination and collaboration in respect of the implementation of the government's objectives. Criminal justice agencies, the police, health and social services, education and the voluntary sector each pursues its own objectives and priorities, and each employs different occupational and professional groups within which power struggles and uncertainties about roles, responsibilities and the distribution of scarce resources create inevitable tensions. There is therefore no one-size-fits-all solution to working in partnership and little to suggest that, after more than a decade of sustained effort, the approach is capable of achieving all that is expected of it.

However, it is to practitioners that service users turn to 'get it right' and provide the most effective response to their needs – whatever the organizational or political climate, theoretical or philosophical uncertainties and in this respect, practitioners need to develop their own networks, or communities of practice, to support joint working. It has become increasingly important for practitioners and managers to understand the policy and professional context of the current emphasis on partnership because they have to help others understand it. Youth justice workers, probation officers, education and health workers need to understand how their colleagues from other domains of practice see the job in hand, how policy and legal requirements impact upon their practice, and to find out what each can reasonably expect of the other. Crucially, joined-up youth justice is about working together with others in the right way, at the right time, for the right reasons in ways that generates *additional* value and better outcomes for service users. Failing to work effectively in partnership fails service users and damages their trust both in frontline workers and their agencies. If practitioners cannot sort out their working relationships with other professionals how can they truly work in partnership with the key stakeholders in the youth justice system – children and young people and their families?

References

Allen, C. (2003) 'Desperately seeking fusion: on "joined-up thinking", "holistic practice" and the economy of welfare professional power', *British Journal of Sociology*, 54: 287–306.

Audit Commission (1996) *Misspent Youth: Young People and Crime*. London: Audit Commission.

Audit Commission (2008) *Are We There Yet? Improving Governance and Resource Management in Children's Trusts*. Local Government National Report, October (available online at www.audit-commission.gov.uk).

Blagg, H., Pearson, G., Sampson, A., Smith, D. and Stubbs, P. (1988) 'Inter-agency co-operation: rhetoric and reality', in T. Hope and M. Shaw (eds) *Communities and Crime Reduction* (Home Office Research and Planning Unit). London: HMSO.

Done, F. (2008) 'Letter to Richard Garside: response to *Ten Years of Labours' Youth Justice Reforms: An Independent Audit*.' Youth Justice Board, June (available online at http://www.crimeandjustice.org.uk/opus792/YJBdoneletter010808annex.pdf).

Frost, N. (2005) *Professionalism, Partnership and Joined-up Thinking: A Research Review of Front-line Working with Children and Families*. Dartington: Research in Practice.

HM Treasury (2002) *Effective Partnership Working*. London: Public Enquiry Unit, HM Treasury (available online at http://www.hm-treasury.gov.uk/d/PSPP_partnerships_report.pdf).

Irvine, R., Kerridge, I., McPhee, J. and Freeman, S. (2002) 'Interprofessionalism and ethics: consensus or clash of cultures?', *Journal of Interprofessional Care*, 16: 199–210.

Loxley, A. (1997) *Collaboration in Health and Welfare: Working with Difference*. London: Jessica Kingsley.

Markwell, S. (2003) *Partnership Working: A Consumer Guide to Resources*. NHS Health Development Agency, May (available online at http://www.nice.org.uk/niceMedia/documents/partnership_working.pdf).

Norlin, P. and Vogel, J. (2004) 'An inner blueprint for successful partnership development: putting a relationship to work', *OD Practitioner*, 36: 22–7.

Payne, M. (2000) *Teamwork in Multiprofessional Care*. Basingstoke: Palgrave.

Pitts, J. (2001) 'Korrectional Karaoke: New Labour and the zombification of youth justice', *Youth Justice*, 2: 3–16.

Solomon, E. and Garside, R. (2008) *Ten Years of Labours Youth Justice Reforms: An Independent Audit*. London: Centre for Crime and Justice Studies, King's College.

Tate, R. and Shah, S. (2007) 'Partnership working: a policy with promise for mental healthcare', *Advances in Psychiatric Treatment*, 13: 261–71.

Trevillion, S. (1992) *Caring in the Community: A Networking Approach to Community Partnership*. London: Longman.

Wenger, E. (1998) *Communities of Practice: Learning, Meaning and Identity*. Cambridge: Cambridge University Press.

18

Reflective practice in youth justice

Wayne Taylor

Introduction

This chapter considers how a 'reflective' approach to youth justice practice might help practitioners in resolving some, if not all, of the dilemmas arising from an ambivalent political and occupational climate. It asks how practitioners might legitimately exercise discretionary judgement within the constraints of professional accountability by examining the key components and principles of 'reflective practice' (Schön 1983, 1987, 1991). Beginning with a brief overview of reflective practice within the wider 'helping professions', it explores the value of this approach to professional development in youth justice. Following this, the chapter continues by drawing on the work of Eadie and Canton (2002) to delineate the ways in which reflective practice might – or might not – operate as a positive force within youth justice, given the specific challenges of this multidisciplinary and multi-agency sector. It aims to look at the way the process of critical reflection impacts on the day-to-day work of the practitioner, developing and shaping their professional competencies.

Equally, however, it is also concerned to examine the implications of a more radical version of reflection, in which some of the underlying theoretical assumptions for criminal justice interventions might themselves be subjected to scrutiny by the 'reflexive' practitioner (Whyte 2009). How might such an approach enhance the ability of practitioners to intervene in the policy debate to foster a model of practice that uses a form of 'counter-hegemonic' (Cohn 2003: 131) engagement and struggle with contemporary policy to resist the corrosive influence of the 'punitive turn' and help practitioners organize themselves against the political imperatives to reject 'excuses' and 'get tough' on youth offending?

The tools of reflective practice

There is a considerable literature covering the concept of 'reflective practice' and its application in a range of occupational settings. The theoretical debate it has generated is substantial and well documented (see, for example, Redmond 2004: ch. 2). Yet at its core it is a deceptively simple concept. Reflective practice – developed in many professions in the 1980s – can be thought of as a model for how practitioners make sense of their day-to-day work by adopting a straightforward technique for learning. This involves a three-stage process in which practitioners actively analyze their practice experiences; extract lessons from these experiences; and, finally; use this learning to analyze and respond to similar (although not identical) experiences in different contexts.

This process of experience followed by reflection followed by informed action (ERA) draws on Kolb's idea of the *ongoing* cycle of 'experiential learning'. Hence:

> The cyclical nature of reflective practice is the key to moving forward as practitioners, in that we rarely stop at just the one cycle. If we complete the first cycle, i.e. we consciously take action as a result of the reflective processes we have undertaken, then the next time we have that experience, or one similar to it, we will encounter it in a different way. Thus the experience itself has been transformed, making it into a different experience. So, if we go through the cycle again, we are building our knowledge and understanding of it each time. (Jasper 2003: 3)

The idea of the 'reflective practitioner' is usually credited to Donald Schön (1983, 1987, 1991), who developed the term to think about the ways practitioners negotiate the complex realities of practice in the 'real world'. In Schön's reckoning, the reflective practitioner rightly recognizes and reflects on the complexity of practice and the way this can involve not just practical dilemmas but also conflicting values, goals, purposes and interests. Referring to the terrain of practice as the 'swampy lowlands', he cautioned against the adoption of techical, 'quick fix' solutions and formulaic responses. Rather – accepting that complexity, variability, uncertainty and difficulty will be inevitable in any work involving people – the reflective practitioner is encouraged to adopt a flexible, questioning approach to practice, accepting these difficulties and responding to obstacles in the ERA cycle as positive challenges.

Theory and practice

The reflective practice model values the practical experiences (and professional expertise) of the practitioner and relies on their ability to exercise professional discretion to find creative solutions to the issues they encounter. For Thompson (2005), there are no 'off the peg' solutions to rely on, although this does not mean that evidence or academic work are not important in identifying key components of 'effective practice'. In fact, while empirical evidence (gathered during the process of practice and considered reflectively) can inform subsequent practice, the 'high ground' of theory is also very useful in providing a framework and overview for informing practice on the ground. Reflective practice, then, involves working within a complex assembly of commonsense, research evidence and abstract ideas. To maximize the benefits of this multifaceted approach, the practitioner should consistently engage in a process of gathering (and actively testing) both empirical and theoretical 'evidence'.

Looking in detail at this process, Thompson (2005) suggests that this involves six elements: reading, questioning, watching, feeling, talking and, crucially, thinking. By continuing the practice of reading they started as students, practitioners engage more constructively and critically with what is presented as 'evidence based' practice. This has wider organizational benefits by fostering greater potential for job satisfaction, and hence commitment and retention. Similar benefits accrue from a critical questioning of both the literature and its 'fit' with practice. Applying this in a collaborative manner – involving discussion with colleagues – is a fundamental feature of the 'learning organization'. Watching how others work or, more specifically, developing improved observational skills, is also a useful means of comparing evidential experience (what is actually happening) with theory. By looking out for the unique features of each situation, practitioners guard against a drift into routinization of practice through the unthinking application of generalized assumptions.

Recognizing the emotional dimension of work with people and the importance of the feelings this engenders is equally important (not least given the relational basis of much youth justice work). In a similar way to questioning, talking about practice with colleagues (particularly in a multi-agency environment) creates a broader perspective and opens up the prospect of learning from others and 'modelling excellence'. Finally, the process of actively and critically thinking through the 'evidence' enables practitioners to shape their practice in a way that accords more fully with their professional values.

Reflective practice in youth justice

Given the benefits of a reflective approach outlined above, it might seem that its adoption within the youth justice system would be anything other than contentious. In fact, while there is strong support for the adoption of a reflective approach among both critical writers in the field (see, for instance, Whyte 2009: 200–4) and those more closely associated with government policy (see, for example, Stephenson *et al.* 2007: 34–8), views about whether the policy environment makes this possible are varied and conflicting.

For instance, it can been argued that reflective practice sits well alongside the 'what works' model of practice developed from the late 1990s, in which criminal justice interventions are informed by a substantial body of international research which draws on empirical observations of practice. This sanguine view, which suggests a strong coincidence between the 'effective practice' of policy-makers and that of reflective practitioners, however, has not been without challenge. Set against it are the views of a range of critical commentators who have suggested that there is a disingenuousness within 'what works' research (Case 2007). This means it serves primarily as 'a smokescreen for the implementation of routinized forms of control, which require very little professional imagination, but rely rather on standardized processes to deliver fixed and measurable levels of compliance' (Smith 2003: 96). In this reading, the problem with a lack of real reflection at a theoretical level have serious implications at a practice level in that 'theory' operates as a constraint on practitioners, negating the possibility of truly reflective practice and imposing instead a form of deprofessionalized, mechanistic and task-focused practice – what has been referred to as 'korrectional karaoke' (Pitts 2001).

Eadie and Canton (2002), in a thoughtful and practitioner-focused account of working effectively and humanely in a sector characterized by political and policy ambivalence, ask how a reflective approach to practice can survive in the face of diminished professional discretion. A key problem they identify is that in youth (and adult) offending there is no coherent vision or agreed set of objectives. Indeed, they suggest that there can be no such coherence in youth justice, given that it 'acts out' the inherent ambivalence of a sector charged both to punish young people (as offenders) and, at the same time (often incompatibly), to have regards to their interests and vulnerabilities. Although there is nothing necessarily new about this ambivalence – when combined with diminished professional discretion and an ill-defined value base – it risks a profound and deleterious effect at both the individual level (undermining the efficacy of the relationship between the practitioner and young person) and at the level of occupational culture.

Although Eadie and Canton accept that practice is (rightly) constrained by organizational discipline and accountability, they argue for a model that balances accountability with a sufficient degree of discretion and judgement to operate effectively – that is, reflectively. Their point is that discretion and accountability should not be understood as opposite ends of the same spectrum and that confusion has led to an unnecessary narrowing of discretion on the pretext of enhancing accountability. Discretion and accountability are not things to be 'balanced' against each other. Instead, the balance might be between, on the one hand, following agency instructions (such as national standards) and, on the other, using professional judgement case by case. They provide the diagram shown in Figure 18.1 which operates as both an account of historical practice and as a indicator of effectiveness.

It is their view that, prior to 1998, the youth justice practitioner operated in quadrant B, enjoying wide discretion and low accountability to the organization but has subsequently moved to a position of higher accountability. Crucially, whether this is within quandrant A or D 'is dependent upon

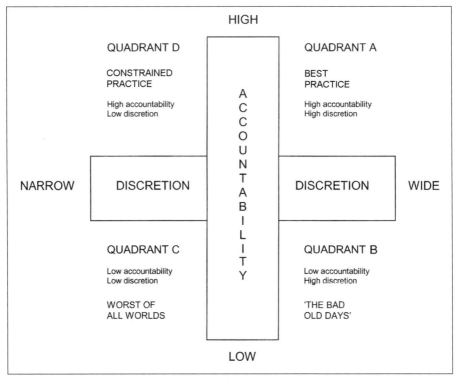

Figure 18.1 Managing accountability and discretion in youth justice practice
Source: Eadie and Canton (2002)

practitioners' ability to withstand managerial insistences on *sameness* as opposed to professional workers' recognition of *relevant difference*' (Eadie and Canton 2002: 18, emphasis in original). Signfianctly for the discussion here, they conclude that:

> There is no inconsistency in authorising practitioners to exercise their discretion *and* holding them to account for the manner in which this is done. To be aware of the need to work as a member of an organization, while also affirming the professional discretion to engage with each young offender on an individual basis, is precisely what characterizes Schön's (1991) concept of the 'reflective practitioner'. (2002: 18, emphasis in original)

Towards a reflexive, criminologically informed practice?

In a related manner to Eadie and Canton, Nelkin reflects on the impasse reached within criminology following the attempt to take social constructionist views of crime and apply them to practice. While acknowledging the benefits of this approach, he cautions that it is inevitably vulnerable to the charge of 'theoretical incoherence and practical impotence' (1994: 7). Explaining that crime – and the response to it – are socially contingent does little, in itself, to further the debate or to provide a solution for either the policy-maker or practitioner faced with the dilemma of how to address the harm caused to people by this 'social construction'.

In recent years criminology has been driven by attempts to resolve this dilemma with a variety of models proffered by, for example, 'left realism', restorative justice, human rights theory and cultural criminology (see Walklate 2007). Each of these approaches has its advantages (and there are a number of commonalities that 'speak' strongly to the practitioner) although – within the confines of this chapter – the most important feature is perhaps the way each highlights the complexities of the contemporary relationship between theory, politics and policy, and the actualities of practice. In addition to the well documented tensions between 'welfare' and 'justice', the ambivalence surrounding youth justice interventions is further exacerbated by the existence and interplay of a number of wider 'discourses' (Muncie and Hughes 2002; Fergusson 2007) that influence the policy processes shaping the nature of the work undertaken by practitioners. This has implications for 'value based' practitioners who will be concerned, for example, to challenge populist demands for more punitive responses to youth offending with a coherent and realistic model of professional practice. They also need to be aware of, and able to respond to, powerful countervailing 'discourses', such as managerialism (with its emphasis on efficiency), 'remoralization' (with its reductive simplification of ethical choices) and 'responsibilization' (with its insistence on making individuals accountable). In the real world of youth justice these competing influences can lead to inconsistencies and contradictions within practice. How might practitioners negotiate this effectively without placing themselves in an untenable position *vis-à-vis* the obligations to, and disciplines of, the agency for which they work? This returns us to the concerns of Eadie and Canton.

Taking oppression seriously?

Interestingly, Thompson (2000) identifies six advantages at the macro-level of reflective practice that are relevant to this discussion. The first of these is the positive impact it can have in terms of anti-discriminatory practice. This is because theories of discrimination and oppression point to the inequitable nature of society and alert the practitioner to the operation of both structural and other factors in consolidating disadvantage and social exclusion for their clients. The second advantage is that a radical model of reflection avoids the 'fallacy of theory-less practice', in which an apparently neutral approach to practice conceals a number of (often untested) assumptions and 'theories', through the explicit, deliberate and critical interrogation of all ideas relevant to practice. This leads on to the third benefit in which the application of a critical and questioning approach to the theories underpinning practice helps in the process of evaluating particular interventions. This both enhances professional accountability (advantage four) by opening up practice to scrutiny and guards against the inappropriate and often counterproductive responses that may arise from 'common sense' responses to problems (advantage five). The final benefit in Thompson's list is the way reflective practice encourages continuing professional development by requiring the practitioner to reflect consciously and self-critically on their own practice and the ideas informing this.

Reflective and 'reflexive' practice both require an approach to interventions that is critically informed by – equally – the raw data we gather with our senses and the conceptual and theoretical frameworks we use to place and make sense of these. Reflecting on Nelkin's proposition of reflexive criminology leads to a critical model of practice in which youth justice practitioners are not only aware of the range of theories concerning punishment, criminal justice interventions, social justice, etc., but are also able to position themselves within these. This suggests that a *standpoint epistemology* is central to reflective practice. Thinking about the structures of youth justice from the level of policy management, there is a sense in which these constitute 'contested terrain' in which rival meanings compete and conflict. Interestingly – taken together – these echo older concerns about practice, articulated in the vocabulary of 'radical social' work, the community development projects of the 1970s and (associated) neo-Marxist ideas. It is worth reflecting that, as long ago as 1971, Habermas identified the importance of recognizing the unjust ideologies (often uncritically accepted) that underscore and are embedded in everyday practice. The Italian revolutionary, Antonio Gramsci, famously suggested a response to these in terms of 'counter-hegemonic struggle' (Habermas 1971: 316; Cohn 2003).

The notion of youth justice workers enaged in 'counter-hegemonic struggle' might appear alarming to some and – at first glance – a clear breach of Eadie and Canton's sympathetic concern for the strictures of professional accountability. Yet need this be the case? In fact, most practitioners are probably involved in some level of counter-hegemonic struggle as a regular component of their day-to-day practice. These small acts of rebellion might include 'turning a blind eye' to minor indiscretions in terms of time-keeping, behaviour and language, refusal to prioritize administrative over client-related tasks, perhaps even the use of subversive humour! Similar transgressions are also likely to be practised on a regular basis by the more effective organizations and teams within the youth justice system! Interestingly, in these heinous crimes against official orthodoxy, it is likely that both the 'reflective' practitioner and the 'learning organization' will find some justification for using their discretion in the burgeoning 'alternative' literature around effective practice and will find considerable support from within the literature on reflective practice.

Conclusion

Ironically, sometimes the inexperienced or hard-pressed practitioner might be keen for a 'toolkit' of practice, feeling comforted by the details of a prescriptive manual of 'how to' practice. This desire often arisies from a lack of confidence – and a desire to do the job well. This – although understandable – is unhelpful to effective practice, as are the more prescriptive versions of national standards in criminal justice work with both adults and young people. A hidden aspect of this approach is that it involves an *inappropriate* model of professional development: 'The workers should be seen not as a receptacle or storehouse to be "stocked up" with methods and techniques, but rather as a generator of ideas and potential solutions' (Thompson 2005: 201). This distinction between the practitioner as passive receptacle and active agent is central to the conundrum of youth justice practice. All too often highly skilled and innovative workers are grossly under-utilized and undervalued as a result of a narrow managerialism that prioritizes a crude mechanistic competence at the expense of the development of professional judgement.

Reflective practice is about using theory to understand commonalities across situations but, crucially, it is also about recognizing the unique features of each situation faced and responding to this with the nuanced use of discretion. This is the crux of 'responsivity' – responding to the person or situation as given by 'thinking on our feet'. Interestingly, Thompson cites populist practical philosopher, Edward De Bono approvingly, suggesting that his famous concept of 'lateral thinking' is also a central component of 'reflective practice'. He goes on to suggest that this can be encouraged in practitioners by the adoption of five strategies:

1. Making a habit of looking at situations from a different angle – allowing fresh insight and purposefully developing empathy for both clients and our work colleagues and partners.

2. Developing a vision of the future – asking where do you want to be and how we might get there?

3. Stepping back – to allow a more panoramic view of an issue in its wider context, minimizing the entrenchment of 'blinkered' practice.

4. Letting go – where creative 'blue sky' thinking is used to challenge conventional paradigms or ways of working.

5. Provocation – asking the 'what if' or 'so what' questions.

Thinking about each of these strategies for even a short time should convince us that reflective practice, used in this way, is inimical to the idea of youth justice as 'korrectional karaoke'.

195

References

Case, S. (2007) 'Questioning the "evidence" of risk that underpins evidence-led youth justice interventions', *Youth Justice: An International Journal*, 7: 91–105.

Cohen, S. (1985) *Visions of Social Control*. Cambridge: Polity Press.

Cohn, T.H. (2003) *Global Political Economy: Theory and Practice*. London: Longman.

Eadie, T. and Canton, R. (2002) 'Practising in a context of ambivalence: the challenge for youth justice workers', *Youth Justice*, 2: 15–26.

Fergusson, R. (2007) 'Making sense of the melting pot: multiple discourses in youth justice policy', *Youth Justice: An International Journal*, 7: 197–4.

Goldson, B. (ed.) (2000) *The New Youth Justice*. Lyme Regis: Russell House.

Habermas, J. (1971) *Towards a Rational Society*. London: Heinemann.

Haines, K. and Drakeford, M. (1999) *Young People and Youth Justice*. London: Macmillan.

Jasper, M. (2003) *Beginning Reflective Practice*. Cheltenham: Nelson Thornes.

Muncie, J. (1999) *Youth and Crime: A Critical Introduction*; London: Sage.

Muncie, J. and Hughes, G. (2002) 'Modes of youth governance: political rationalities, criminalization and resistance', in J. Muncie *et al.* (eds) *Youth Justice: Critical Readings*. London: Sage.

Muncie, J. and McLaughlin, E. (eds) (1996) *The Problem of Crime*. London: Sage.

Nelken, D. (1994) 'Reflexive criminology', in D. Nelken (ed.) *The Futures of Criminology*. London: Sage.

Pitts, J. (2001) 'Korrectional karaoke: New Labour and the zombification of youth justice', *Youth Justice*, 1: 3–16.

Redmond, B. (2004) *Reflection in Action: Developing Reflective Practice in Health and Social Services*. Aldershot: Ashgate.

Schön, D.A. (1983) *The Reflective Practitioner*. New York, NY: Basic Books.

Schön, D.A. (1987) *Educating the Reflective Practitioner*. San Francisco, CA: Jossy Bass.

Schön, D.A. (1991) *The Reflective Practitioner: How Professionals Think in Action*. Aldershot: Arena.

Smith, R. (2003) *Youth Justice: Ideas, Policy, Practice*. Cullompton: Willan Publishing.

Smith, R. (2005) 'Welfare verses justrice – again!', *Youth Justice*, 5: 3–16.

Stephenson, M., Giller, H. and Brown, S. (2007) *Effective Practice in Youth Justice*. Cullompton: Willan Publishing.

Taylor, C. and White, S. (2004) 'Practising reflexivity', in M. Robb *et al.* (eds) *Communication, Relationships and Care: A Reader*. London: Routledge.

Thompson, N. (2000) *Theory and Practice in Human Services*. Buckingham: Open University Press.

Thompson, N. (2005) 'Reflective practice', in R. Harrison and C. Wise (eds) *Working with Young People*. London: Sage.

Walklate, S. (2007) *Understanding Criminology: Current Theoretical Debates*. Maidenhead: Open University Press.

Whyte, B. (2009) *Youth Justice in Practice: Making a Difference*. Bristol: Policy Press.

Part V

Widening Contexts

Introduction

Rod Earle

The importance of guiding principles anchored in an understanding of children's rights is the focus of the final five chapters. Children make up a substantial proportion of the UK population and, though only a minority ever become embroiled in the youth justice system, this is arguably the time when their rights most urgently need defending. Asserting these rights and embedding them in youth justice is not simply a matter of preference or predilection, but neither is it simple or straightforward.

For John Muncie the priority is to raise the profile of these principles and build concrete commitments to children's rights. He goes so far as to list in his chapter nine key principles of the United Nations' Convention on the Rights of the Child that he sees as absolutely central to a policy and practice that is child-centred and rights compliant. He identifies in the UK a mixed picture of 'compliance, ambivalence and violation' and his chapter is particularly helpful in distilling the latest report of the United Nations' Committee on the Rights of the Child that monitors signatory nations' compliance. It does not make for happy reading. An instrumental and calculating approach to children's rights may not characterize completely the UK's responses but it is certainly a part of it. Muncie is sanguine about the potential for the 'rights' discourse to transform and transcend the deeply embedded ambiguities of the youth justice system in England and Wales. By presenting – in typically clear and forthright terms – the significance of children's rights in youth justice systems, he offers strategic possibilities for advancing along the path towards a genuinely 'ambitious civilizing project' (first outlined in Goldson and Muncie 2006).

The pursuit of a public identity for youth justice may be a part of this project, and Rob Canton turns to this by focusing not so much on the familiar rhetoric of 'what works' in youth justice but on 'what is right' in youth justice. Canton asks searching questions about how youth justice thinks of itself, and how it might want to be known, both publicly and professionally. In the murky soup of multi-agency policies, interdisciplinary perspectives and plural professional identities, Canton finds potential nourishment in 'framing youth justice values in the language of human rights'. It is the outward-looking universalism of human rights that is attractive here. By explicitly fostering an international vision, a human rights perspective draws the practitioner towards an awareness of 'how other countries respond differently to youth crime' while, at the same time, offering a yardstick against which comparisons can be made. A model of international collaborative oversight is offered in the working of the Council of Europe. Readers who are also practitioners are invited to begin the task of giving greater effect to agreed European rules for juvenile offenders by conducting a mapping exercise of their own 'agency, team or unit' to see how it measures up. It is an invitation to start developing greater fluency in the language and practice of human rights that Canton persuasively argues is 'the most promising discourse within which to affirm the wellbeing of children and to defend the rights of young people'.

While appreciating that both the diversity and tentative 'standardization' of youth justice practice within Europe are important, the final three chapters turn their attention to the much misunderstood and frequently overlooked diversity of systems within the UK. Bill Whyte begins by exploring the peculiar 'lack of social consensus' within the UK as to what youth justice systems should be about and what they are intended to achieve. By examining the most notable and well-known contrast of the Scottish children's hearings system, Whyte lays out the complex patterns of divergence and convergence that are occurring both within the UK and in response to the gathering momentum of European harmonization and human rights discourse. The presence of competing 'dominant value frames', operating in different but intersecting jurisdictions, poses unique ethical challenges for practitioners who may feel more 'locked into' them than a part of them. The decision, in March 2009, of the Scottish Parliament to raise the age of criminal responsibility to 12 in the forthcoming Criminal Justice and Licensing Bill represents an endorsement of the hearing system and brings it closer in line with mainland Europe than with its insular neighbour to the south. The comments of the Scottish Justice Secretary, Kenny MacAscill, allude to the increasing salience of this context: 'There is no good reason for Scotland to continue to have the lowest age of criminal responsibility in Europe. Most importantly, the evidence shows prosecution at an early age increases the chance of re-offending – so this change is about preventing crime' (quoted in *The Journal* 2009).

The tendency towards internal divergence within the UK is developed by Kevin Haines through the evocative use of the term 'dragonization'. Haines uses this to encompass the efforts of Welsh practitioners and the Welsh Assembly to consolidate distinctive patterns of provision for young people in trouble with the law. Haines sketches the historical sources of this divergence that have left Scotland with a recently reconstituted Parliament and Wales and Northern Ireland with newly established 'assemblies'. Neither Wales nor Northern Ireland can bring forth legislation on the age of criminal responsibility but both are forging innovative approaches which draw more explicitly and assertively on international conventions of human rights. In assessing the implications of 'dragonization', Haines is quick to note that, though deeply imbued with historical significance, the institutions and processes referred to draw from less than a decade of devolution.

A similar starting point forms the focus of the final chapter in this collection which considers developments in youth justice across the Irish Sea. Perhaps the most persistently and deeply contested of the constituent elements of the UK, 'Northern Ireland' draws the inspiration for youth justice reform from the wider well-springs of the Peace Process. Kelvin Doherty's chapter encapsulates the themes of this final, forward-looking part. His concerns are simultaneously intensely local and profoundly international. In emerging from bitter and bloody armed conflict, the challenges facing young people in Northern Ireland are unlike those faced elsewhere in the UK, and thus it is perhaps no surprise that the novel and idealistic principles of restorative justice have come to the fore. Doherty explores how these principles are synthesized with the equally novel institutionalization of human rights perspectives in the Belfast Agreement, and how both draw on the experience of reconciliation and reconstruction in post-apartheid South Africa. Although noting the absence of a specific truth and reconciliation commission, the changes in youth justice in Northern Ireland are situated in transitional processes that draw more freely from both non-western and human rights discourse than elsewhere in the UK.

Taken together these five chapters offer the reader unique insights into the unusual landscapes of youth justice in the British Isles and beyond. They afford inspiration on the possibilities of the future.

References

Goldson, B. and Muncie, J. (2006) 'Critical anatomy: towards a principled youth justice', in B. Goldson and J. Muncie (eds) *Youth Crime and Justice*. London: Sage.

The Journal (2009) 'The journalonline – the members' magazine of the Law Society of Scotland' (available online at http://www.journalonline.co.uk/News/1006274.aspx).

19

The United Nations, children's rights and juvenile justice

John Muncie

In 1989 the United Nations resolved to recognize specific children's rights worldwide. The 1989 Convention on the Rights of the Child (CRC) came into force in September 1990 and was ratified by the UK, for example, in 1991. The child is defined as anyone under the age of 18 years. The CRC (Article 2) entitles every child, 'without regard to race, sex, language, religion, political or other opinion, national, ethnic or social origin, property, disability, birth or other status', to have resort to 40 specific rights. In particular it advocates special protection for 'children in conflict with the law'. The most pertinent articles of the CRC (United Nations 1989), specifically for juvenile justice policy and practice, are as follows:

- In all actions concerning children . . . the best interests of the child shall be a primary consideration (Article 3).

- State Parties recognize the rights of the child to freedom of association and to freedom of peaceful assembly (Article 15).

- No child shall be subjected to arbitrary or unlawful interference with his or her privacy, family, home or correspondence (Article 16).

- No child shall be subjected to torture or other cruel, inhuman or degrading treatment or punishment (Article 37a).

- No child shall be deprived of his or her liberty unlawfully or arbitrarily. The arrest, detention or imprisonment of a child shall be in conformity with the law and shall be used only as a measure of last resort and for the shortest appropriate period of time (Article 37b).

- Every child deprived of liberty shall be treated with humanity and respect for the inherent dignity of the human person, and in a manner which takes into account the needs of persons of his or her age. In particular, every child deprived of liberty shall be separated from adults unless it is considered in the child's best interest not to do so (Article 37c).

- Every child deprived of his or her liberty shall have the right to prompt access to legal and other appropriate assistance, as well as the right to challenge the legality of the deprivation of his or her liberty before a court or other competent, independent and impartial authority, and to a prompt decision on any such action (Article 37d).

- States Parties recognize the right of every child alleged as, accused of, or recognized as having infringed the penal law to be treated in a manner consistent with the promotion of the child's sense of dignity and worth, which reinforces the child's respect for the human rights and fundamental freedoms of others and which takes into account the child's age and the desirability of promoting the child's reintegration and the child's assuming a constructive role in society (Article 40(1)).

- States Parties shall seek to promote the establishment of laws, procedures, authorities and institutions specifically applicable to children alleged as, accused of, or recognized as having infringed the penal law, and, in particular: (a) The establishment of a minimum age below which children shall be presumed not to have the capacity to infringe the penal law; (b) Whenever appropriate and desirable, measures for dealing with such children without resorting to judicial proceedings, providing that human rights and legal safeguards are fully respected (Article 40(3)).

Consistently restating, promoting and defending these principles is a vital first step for governments (States Parties) if they are to move towards child-centred and rights-compliant systems of youth and juvenile justice (see, for example, United Nations Committee on the Rights of the Child 2007). To date the CRC had been ratified by 193 countries, making it the most recognized international human rights convention in history. The only countries not to have ratified are the USA (which claims it would interfere with parental rights) and Somalia (which has no internationally recognized government).

After a government has ratified the CRC, it must report to the United Nations Committee on the Rights of the Child at five-year intervals outlining how it is applying the convention's provisions within domestic law, policy and practice. The committee then issues a series of 'concluding observations' detailing each country's record of compliance (or violation). It is through the study of such reports that we can begin to make some assessment of the disjuncture between rights rhetoric and children's rights in policy and practice in various jurisdictions.

The UN committee: assessing implementation

In 2007 the committee focused its attention specifically on juvenile justice and concluded that:

> many States Parties still have a long way to go in achieving full compliance with the CRC, e.g. in the areas of procedural rights, the development and implementation of measures for dealing with children in conflict with the law without resorting to judicial proceedings, and the use of deprivation of liberty only as a measure of last resort. (United Nations Committee on the Rights of the Child 2007: 1)

The CRC is binding under international law and carries a clear obligation for nation states to ensure its full implementation. However the CRC holds no sanctioning powers and the committee has to rely on persuasion and admonishment rather than enforcement. Most worryingly, various pressure groups (see, for example, Abramson 2000, 2006) have concluded that, even within the 'children's rights movement' itself, juvenile justice reform is the most marginalized, disregarded and 'unwanted' issue. The reasons are probably not too hard to find. While most governments are keen to see themselves aligned against child abuse and exploitation, this logic disappears when those same children are deemed to be 'offenders'.

Ironically, the rolling out of the CRC has been alongside a growing politicization of the 'youth problem' and of 'problem youth' in particular. A punitive mentality evident in many western societies – albeit differentially expressed – has shifted juvenile justice agendas away from protecting 'best interests' and towards criminalization and retribution (Muncie 2008). For example in the UK, when the Secretary of State for Justice was asked what he might do to reduce the trend of demonizing children and young people, his response was unequivocal: 'these are not children; they are often large unpleasant thugs' (Hansard 10 June 2008).

Abramson's (2000) analysis of committee observations on the implementation of juvenile justice in 141 countries noted a widespread lack of 'sympathetic understanding' necessary for compliance with the CRC. He argued that a complete overhaul of juvenile justice was required in 21 countries and that, in others, torture, inhumane treatment, lack of separation from adults, police brutality, poor conditions in detention facilities, overcrowding, lack of rehabilitation, failure to develop alternatives to incarceration, inadequate contact between minors and their families, lack of training of judges, police and prison authorities, lack of speedy trial, no legal assistance, disproportionate sentences, insufficient respect for the rule of law and the improper use of the juvenile justice system to tackle other social problems, were rife. In addition, the committee has long complained that there is a notable lack of reliable statistics or documentation as to who is held in juvenile justice systems and where they are. Disproportionate sentences, insufficient respect for the rule of law, excessive use of custody and a general failure to take children's rights seriously appear widespread.

The recurring issues raised by the committee focus in particular on ss. 37 and 40 of the CRC. Analysis of the 'concluding observations' for 15 western European countries (Muncie 2008) found that every state (except Norway) had been asked to give more consideration to implementing the CRC's core principles. Despite almost 20 years in which to put the CRC into effect, most of these European states appear to have failed to recognize the centrality of such issues as distinctive needs, dignity, humane treatment and so on as core to the realization of children's rights. Eight states (Finland, Denmark, Switzerland, Austria, Ireland, the UK, Germany and Portugal) were specifically criticized for failing to separate children from adults in custody or because they were beginning to break down distinctions between adult and juvenile systems, allowing for easier movement between the two (as is characteristic of the widely used juvenile transfer to adult court in the USA).

In 2004 the committee's report on Germany condemned the increasing number of children placed in detention, especially affecting children of foreign origin, and the fact that children in detention or custody are placed with persons up to the age of 25 years. The report on the Netherlands in the same year expressed concern that custody was no longer being used as a last resort. In its report on France the committee reiterated its concern about legislation and practice which tend to favour repressive over educational measures. It expressed concern about increases in the numbers of children in prison and the resulting worsening of conditions (Muncie 2008: 112).

Just as significantly, most of these European jurisdictions were criticized for discriminating against minorities/asylum seekers and for having over-representations of immigrant and minority groups under arrest or in detention, particularly the Roma and traveller communities (in Italy, Switzerland, Finland, Germany, Greece, the UK, Ireland, France, Spain and Portugal), Moroccans and Surinamese (in the Netherlands), and North Africans (in Belgium and Denmark). Some of the most punitive elements of juvenile justice do appear to be increasingly used/reserved for the punitive control of primarily immigrant populations (Muncie 2008: 113).

In 2006, the United Nations Secretary-General's study on violence against children revealed the existence of widespread global violence. While some forms – such as the trafficking of children, the excesses of child labour and the impact of war – appeared to be relatively high on international agendas, the report concluded that 'attention to violence against children *in general* continues to be fragmented and very limited – different forms of violence in the home, schools, institutions and the community are largely ignored in current debates in the international community'. Moreover, 'much violence against children remains legal, state authorized and socially approved' (Pinheiro 2006: 3).

The UK: compliance, ambivalence and violation

The UK has been far from immune from such critique. The committee (rather confusingly) chooses to report on Great Britain and Northern Ireland as if one entity, even though there are significant differences in youth justice, particularly between England and Scotland (and, to a lesser extent, between England and Wales). In all three UK jurisdictions, though, the CRC has not been incorporated into domestic legislation. As a result children's rights issues are typically heard legally with recourse to European rather than United Nations' conventions. The UK Human Rights Act 1998, which placed the European Convention on Human Rights (ECHR) into UK law, is the chief mechanism though which CRC principles can be articulated. The most notable case was the European Court of Human Rights ruling that hearing the case of 11-year-olds in adult courts was in violation of their right to a fair trial (*V* v. *United Kingdom*; *T* v. *United Kingdom*).

The UK's record has been scrutinized by the committee on three occasions (1995, 2002, 2008). In 1995 the UN committee was particularly critical of the low age of criminal responsibility. Set at the age of 8 in Scotland and at the age of 10 in England, Northern Ireland and Wales, the UK has to date the lowest ages of criminal responsibility in Europe. The low age of 8 in Scotland was placed under review in 2009 and it was proposed that under 12-year-olds be given immunity from prosecution. However if an offence is admitted then this can be considered a conviction and, in these circumstances, the possibility remains that 8–12-year-olds can be deemed as fully criminal as an adult. The UN committee has consistently advocated an age of criminal responsibility of 14 or 16 and considers a minimum below the age of 12 'not to be internationally acceptable' (United Nations Committee on the Rights of the Child 2007: 8). The UN committee report of 1995 also condemned the (then proposed) introduction of secure training centres for 12–15-year-olds in England and Wales (for which there are no European equivalents) and a general failure to use custody as a measure of last resort.

In 2002 these concerns were reiterated alongside critical comment on increasing numbers of children held in custody (despite decreases in the crime rate); at earlier ages for lesser offences and for longer periods (not as a 'last resort'); custodial conditions that do not adequately protect children from violence, bullying and self-harm (failure to accord with 'best interests'); as well as failure to move on the low age of criminal responsibility (indeed the Crime and Disorder Act 1998 had moved in the opposite direction by abolishing the principle of *doli incapax* for 10–14-year-olds). The committee concluded that the UK's record on compliance was 'worsening'. At that time, the Children's Rights Alliance for England (2005) declared that England and Wales had effectively 'torn up' the CRC.

As part of the consultation prior to the 2008 report, the four children's commissioners for England, Scotland, Wales and Northern Ireland submitted a joint report to the committee in which they made clear their concerns that the UK was continuing with some 'serious violations' of the convention, including excessive criminalization, a failure to distinguish adequately between adult and child offenders and the promotion of a general punitive ethos of 'offender first, child second' (UK Children's Commissioners 2008: 32). The committee's 'concluding observations' in 2008 commended some recent developments, such as the lifting of a reservation against detaining children with adults, but its overall tone, as regards juvenile justice, remained negative (Nacro 2008). In general: 'The Committee regrets that the principle of the best interests of the child is still not reflected as a primary consideration in all legislative and policy matters affecting children, especially in the area of juvenile justice, immigration and freedom of movement and peaceful assembly' (UN Committee 2008: 7).

Their assessment focused in particular on five core issues.

I. Intolerance and criminalization

Successive UK governments have not only resisted CRC demands that the age of criminal responsibility be raised but have also introduced a range of civil powers and statutory orders (curfews, child safety orders, anti-social behaviour orders (ASBOs) and so on) that have targeted, or have been used disproportionately against, under 18-year-olds, including in some cases those below the age of 10. Because such interventions are 'pre-emptive' or 'preventive' they can be applied without either the prosecution or commission of a criminal offence. The committee reported that it was:

> concerned at the application to children of the Anti-Social Behaviour Orders (ASBOs), which are civil orders posing restrictions on children's gathering, which may convert into criminal offences in case of their breach. The Committee is further concerned:
>
> (a) At the ease of issuing such orders, the broad range of prohibited behaviour and the fact that the breach of an order is a criminal offence with potentially serious consequences;
>
> (b) That ASBOs, instead of being a measure in the best interests of children, may in practice contribute to their entry into contact with the criminal justice system;
>
> (c) That most children subject to them are from disadvantaged backgrounds. (2008: 20)

In 2004 the Audit Commission had reported that too many minor offences were being brought to court, taking up time and expense. The current evidence suggests that the formalization of early intervention, particularly through final warnings, has indeed led to a net widening where more children are being prosecuted for trivial offences and with a subsequent related impact on the rate of custodial sentencing. Between 2003 and 2006 there was a 25 per cent increase in the numbers of 10–14-year-olds receiving reprimands, final warnings or conviction: a rise that has been explained with reference to a greater willingness of the police to criminalize minor misdemeanours in order to meet government targets of increasing detections from 1.02 million in 2002 to 1.25 million in 2007–8.

2. Failure to use custody as a last resort

Age reductions in the detention of children coupled with increases in the maximum sentence have always put the UK at odds with the CRC. On signing the CRC in the early 1990s around 1,400 children were being held in the secure estate in England and Wales at any one time. In 2002 it reached a peak of almost 3,200, and has not fallen below 2,600 ever since. Most notable has been the incarceration of younger age groups. In 1992, 100 under 15-year-olds were held in custody – all under 'grave crime' provisions. In 2005–6 there were over 800 but only 6 per cent of these were for 'grave crimes'. Such data place England and Wales as one of the most punitive in western Europe: incarcerating five times more than France and ten times more than Italy (both countries with roughly the same number of under 18-year-olds in the general population; Muncie 2008: 116). As a result:

> The Committee is concerned that:
>
> - The number of children deprived of liberty is high, which indicates that detention is not always applied as a measure of last resort;
>
> - The number of children on remand is high;
>
> - Children in custody do not have a statutory right to education. (UN Committee 2008: 19)

3. Inhumane and degrading treatment

Children in custody are routinely drawn from some of the most disadvantaged families and neighbourhoods. They are already likely to have endured family discord and separation, ill-health and physical and emotional abuse. The vast majority have been excluded from school and over a half have had previous contact with care and social services agencies. With high reconviction rates and increasing evidence of inappropriate and brutalizing regimes characterized by racism, bullying, self-harm and suicide, it is widely acknowledged that child incarceration is an expensive failure (as well as rights violating). One in every 20 children in custody has been reported as inflicting self-injury during their sentence. Between 1990 and 2007, 30 children died while in penal custody.

The excessive use of restraint techniques has been a recurring concern. For example, it has been estimated that 'pain compliant' distraction techniques were used over 10,000 times on children in custody between April 2007 and June 2008, causing over 1,300 injuries. Youth Justice Board targets to reduce the use of custody, and thereby prevent further harm, have never been met:

> The Committee, while welcoming the introduction of statutory child death reviews in England and Wales, is very concerned that six more children have died in custody since the last examination as well as at the high prevalence of self-injurious behaviour among children in custody. (UN Committee 2008: 7)

> The Committee remains concerned at the fact that, in practice, physical restraint on children is still used in places of deprivation of liberty. (UN Committee 2008: 9)

4. Denial of freedom of movement

In 2004 'dispersal zones' were established in over 800 areas of the UK. The legality of one such zone in Richmond was successfully challenged in the High Court by a 15-year-old in 2005 (BBC News 20 July 2005). The increasing use of ultrasonic devices to disperse young people – their sound is only audible to those under the age of 25 – explicitly degrades and discriminates against children rather than treating them with the principles of dignity and respect enshrined in the CRC.

In 2008 new initiatives were announced giving the police greater powers to stop and search without having to state a reason and encouraging the police actively to harass groups of children on the streets. This included 'frame and shame' operations (pioneered by Essex Police in Basildon) to film and repeatedly follow and stop 'persistently badly behaving youths'; and 'voluntary' curfews (pioneered by Devon and Cornwall Police in Redruth) targeted at under 16-year-olds during the school summer holidays but backed up by parenting orders and ASBOs. 'The Committee is concerned at the restriction imposed on the freedom of movement and peaceful assembly of children by the anti-social behaviour orders (ASBOs) as well as by the use of the so-called "mosquito devices" and the introduction of the concept of "dispersal zones"' (UN Committee 2008: 8).

5. Failure to protect privacy

It has been estimated that at least 1.1 million children had their DNA recorded between 1995 (when the database was established) and April 2007, with more than half a million being aged between 10 and 16, and including 100,000 under 18s who had subsequently been found not guilty or had charges dropped. No other country in Europe has adopted such a practice. In December 2008 the European Court of Human Rights ruled that the indefinite holding of DNA and fingerprints contravened the right to a private life (*S and Marper* v. *the United Kingdom*).

In addition the committee noted that the then recently published *Youth Crime Action Plan* (DCSF 2008) included a proposal to remove reporting restrictions for 16- and 17-year-olds facing criminal proceedings – justified by the government as a way of 'improving the transparency of the youth justice system'. As a result:

The Committee is concerned that:

(a)   DNA data regarding children is kept in the National DNA Database irrespective of whether the child is ultimately charged or found guilty;

(b)   the State Party has not taken sufficient measures to protect children, notably those subject to ASBOs, from negative media representation and public 'naming and shaming' (UN Committee 2008: 8).

Protecting children's rights

Some countries, it seems, give lip service to children's rights simply to be granted recognition as a 'modern developed state'. For others it is simply an instrumental observance to gain acceptance into world monetary systems or entry into other supra-national bodies such as the EU. The pressure to ratify is both moral and economic. However, in many countries it is abundantly clear that it is possible to lay claim to upholding rights while simultaneously pursuing policies which exacerbate children's marginalization and criminalization and increase the punitiveness of institutional regimes. The USA case is indicative. Violations of the convention appear built in to aspects of USA law which allow for life imprisonment without parole and prosecution in adult courts and which fail to specify a minimum age of criminal responsibility (Campaign for Youth Justice 2007). Moreover, relying on international statements of due process and procedural safeguards may do little to deliver 'justice' on the ground. Little attention, for example, has been given to the extent to which the notion of universal rights may itself be grounded in western notions of *individualized justice* rather than as facilitating any movement towards global *social justice* (Muncie 2008).

At the core of the contemporary governance of children in many western jurisdictions, including the UK, seems to be the view that they have already been fully (or over-) endowed with rights. Lawbreaking and transgression are used to circumvent argument that the state too has *responsibilities* – as in the UK ethos of *Every Child Matters* (DfES 2004) – for the welfare of *all* its citizens. It is far from clear how a dismantling of many of the distinctions between juvenile and adult justice and how failure to incorporate the CRC into domestic agendas can be construed as acting in a child's 'best interests'.

While it is important to acknowledge some of the limitations of rights discourses (as weak and open to interpretation), it is equally important to appreciate their continuing potential. In this respect, the CRC and related international directives (such as those established by the 142 rules laid out by the European Committee on Crime Problems 2008) provide a strong basis for *rethinking* juvenile justice (Goldson and Muncie 2006). Global inequalities and social injustices may always impede the realization of a universal and fully rights-compliant juvenile justice. But this should not preclude the insistence that nation-states move to comply with their international obligations and to uphold those measures to which they have put their name. Until then, there are so many examples of the rights of children in 'conflict with the law' being ignored that nobody, whether policy-makers, the media, elected politicians, practitioners or citizens, can simply stand by with indifference.

References

Abramson, B. (2000) *Juvenile Justice: The 'Unwanted Child' of State Responsibilities. An Analysis of the Concluding Observations of the UN Committee on the Rights of the Child, in Regard to Juvenile Justice from 1993 to 2000, International Network on Juvenile Justice/Defence for Children International* (available online at www.defence-for-children.org).

Abramson, B. (2006) 'Juvenile justice: the unwanted child', in E. Jensen and J. Jepsen (eds) *Juvenile Law Violators, Human Rights and the Development of New Juvenile Justice Systems*. Oxford: Hart.

Audit Commission (2004) *Youth Justice 2004: A Review of the Reformed Youth Justice System*. London: HMSO.

Campaign for Youth Justice (2007) *Jailing Juveniles: The Dangers of Incarcerating Youth in Adult Jails in America.* (available online at www.campaignforyouthjustice.org).

Children's Rights Alliance for England (2005) *State of Children's Rights in England*. London: CRAE.

Department for Children, Schools and Families (2008) *Youth Crime Action Plan*. London: DCSF.

Department for Education and Skills (2004) *Every Child Matters: Change for Children*. Nottingham: DfES.

European Committee on Crime Problems (2008) *Draft Commentary to the European Rules for Juvenile Offenders Subject to Sanctions and Measures*. Strasbourg: Council for Europe.

Goldson, B. and Muncie, J. (2006) 'Rethinking youth justice: comparative analysis, international human rights and research evidence', *Youth Justice*, 6: 91–106.

Muncie, J. (2008) 'The punitive turn in juvenile justice: cultures of control and rights compliance in western Europe and the USA', *Youth Justice: An International Journal*, 8: 107–21.

Nacro (2008) *Children's Human Rights and the Youth Justice System. Youth Crime Briefing*. London: Nacro.

Pinheiro, P.S. (2006) *World Report on Violence against Children*. Geneva: United Nations.

UK Children's Commissioners (2008) *Report to the UN Committee on the Rights of the Child*. London: 11 Million, NICCY, SCCYP, Children's Commissioner for Wales.

UN Committee on the Rights of the Child (2008) *Consideration of Reports Submitted by States Parties under Article 44 of the Convention: United Kingdom of Great Britain and Northern Ireland* (49th session, CRC/C/GBR/CO/4). Geneva: United Nations.

United Nations (1989) *The United Nations Convention on the Rights of the Child*. New York, NY: United Nations.

United Nations Committee on the Rights of the Child (2007) *Children's Rights in Juvenile Justice* (44th session general comment No 10, CRC/C/GC/10). Geneva: United Nations.

Cases cited

S and Marper v. *the United Kingdom.*
T v. *United Kingdom* (1999) 7 BHRC 659.
V v. *United Kingdom* (1999) 30 EHRR 121.

20

Human rights and youth justice in Europe

Rob Canton

Introduction

This chapter considers how human rights might provide an ethical foundation for youth justice. It draws attention in particular to the work of the Council of Europe in setting standards and in offering guidance about the real implications of human rights for law, policy and practice. Values should guide action, and the Council of Europe has taken a lead in proposing how values may be given expression in the work of youth justice.

Human rights and the value of youth justice

In England and Wales, criminal justice policy has been preoccupied with *what works*, but the question 'what's right?' is just as important a question, though less commonly posed. If we are to take seriously the idea that we work in youth *justice* – not just a system for managing young people's offending but a principled and ethically significant set of policies and practices – then we need to think hard about how justice is to be done.

Penality – the institutions and practices of punishment – expresses and communicates the values of a society (Duff 2001; Rex 2005), as well as striving to achieve instrumental objectives such as crime reduction. Our youth justice practices unavoidably say something about how we regard young people and what we take to be our responsibilities towards those of them who have offended. But are they saying the right thing?

So how should we talk about the ethical character of youth justice practice? The preceding chapter provided an introduction to the issue of rights, while other chapters in this volume consider in detail the role of ethics in youth justice work with children and young people. In this chapter it is suggested that the *language* of human rights is the most promising discourse within which to affirm the wellbeing of children and to defend the rights of young people.

It is plain that the rights of young people in their dealings with the criminal justice system are extremely vulnerable. Some scholars have defined punishment as a restriction on rights (Rawls 1967). From this perspective, it may well be proper to punish people for their wrong-doings, although the efficacy of doing so may be contested, but a just and proportionate punishment should reflect the seriousness of the offence; and the person's rights may not be compromised to any extent beyond the requirements of the (lawfully imposed) sanction itself. We must be no less vigilant when the ostensible purpose of intervention is said to be the young person's own welfare: the claim to be acting in the young person's own interests has sometimes been used to authorize a much greater intrusion and trespass on people's rights than a justly deserved punishment (Thorpe *et al.* 1980). A large part of the 'justice model' critique of the 'treatment model' was that, on the pretext of the young person's interests, intrusion was countenanced beyond what was merited for the offence. Youth justice, then, is unavoidably concerned with human rights.

There are three particular advantages to discussing the ethics of youth justice in the language of human rights. The first advantage is that it casts the debate in recognizable, mainstream ethical terms. One way of trying to articulate the values of youth justice might be in the idiom of *social work values*. Social work has, after all, been a central influence on the development of youth justice, and social work is a profession that is reflexive and self-aware about its values (see, for example, Clark 2000). Whether or not this is an adequate characterization of the *substance* of youth justice values, it may be *politically* insufficient. It is not being suggested that the values of social work should be jettisoned from youth justice but that, as a symbol of what youth justice stands for, they have little or no resonance with other professions or with the general public. As Nellis comments in a related context, probation 'never effectively projected a compelling and persuasive image of what it stood for into the public domain, too easily allowing itself to be caricatured as "a *mere* welfare service for offenders"' (2007: 239). While the professions of (for example) medicine or education can draw on wide support for the principles of their work, the objectives of youth justice are radically contested and an articulation of its values in the discourse of social work risks being simply dismissed. So to the extent that youth justice involves punishment for wrong-doing, as well as meeting welfare needs, the language of social work values will struggle to represent the ethics of youth justice in robust and often harsh penal debate. The language of human rights, by contrast, is increasingly recognized as a shared discourse in which values can be affirmed and debated.

The substantive values of social work can in any case be expressed in this idiom of human rights. Anti-discrimination, for example, and the valuing of diversity are strongly advanced by the discourse of human rights. Moreover, while human rights (no more than any other ethical discourse) cannot *by itself* guarantee a proper regard for diversity and challenge to unfair discrimination, it is a very promising beginning. Not only are the principles of anti-discrimination explicitly identified in most of the conventions and recommendations; more than this, human rights are rights that we have in virtue of our humanity – they do not depend upon the contingencies of our individual identities or abilities. They do not have to be 'earned'. And they are not at the disposal of the state. These are rights that belong to everyone, so that the rights of offenders and victims and of the general public are all affirmed and represented in debate.

A second advantage in framing youth justice values in the language of human rights is that it invokes an international dimension. An international understanding of youth justice is valuable in all kinds of ways. Although there are many limitations in the scholarship of comparative analysis (Goldson and Muncie 2006), an awareness that other countries respond differently to youth crime is in itself enlightening and a stimulus to better practice. Some of our own practices are altogether too close for us to be able to criticize them readily, and a reminder that policy and practice differ in different countries, as well as across time, brings a deeper critical understanding of the shortcomings – and often the strengths – of our own practices.

Some key human rights concepts are intrinsically comparative. The idea that a response to an offence should be *proportionate*, for example, is central to several conventions and recommendations (van Zyl Smit and Ashworth 2004). But how are we to know whether a sanction or measure is proportionate without some kind of comparator? One promising way is *to consider the practices of those countries with whom we may wish to compare ourselves* – specifically, in this case, with other member states of the Council of Europe. Again, it is usual for a convention to urge that custody should be a sanction of 'last resort', but how can it be determined if it is really being used in this way except by comparison with other jurisdictions? Are our levels of punishment comparable with theirs? Do we send more young people into custody than do other countries? Are our sentences longer? Comparison is complex, to be sure (Goldson and Muncie 2006), but it is hard to see how else we can get any purchase on *proportion*.

Again, it is not uncommon for countries to invoke such concepts as 'public protection' or 'national emergency' to seek to justify punishments that are, in other respects, excessive. It is by no means always the case that the safety of the public is advanced by severe punishment (Canton 2009), but there may well be circumstances where the rights of some individuals are (or are said to be) in opposition to those of others. In recent years, for example, anxiety about crime and terrorism has often been the pretext for increased surveillance and intrusion. Where such claims are made, can nation-states be trusted to make principled judgements of their own conduct? Not only tyrant states but also states in crisis or in abnormal times have invoked the public good or some similar abstraction to seek interventions that would in other circumstances be seen as oppressive, and the reaction of the international community is one test of the standing of this claim. Membership of an international community helps us to achieve the ethical standards to which a liberal democracy should aspire and it is disappointing when politicians regard human rights as an obstruction to the achievement of their 'higher' purposes.

The third advantage is closely related to this. Human rights are *justiciable* – capable of being put to test and determined in a court of law. This is not usually true of other ethical claims. It means that politically expedient decisions can be challenged in court – domestically, through the Human Rights Act 1998, and internationally through the European Court of Human Rights. The possibility of invoking human rights to challenge current practice is invaluable and has been employed to good effect in recent years. The Howard League, notably, has used the processes of *judicial review* to clarify and promote recognition of the rights of young people in custody and the duties that are owed to them. Their 'Growing up shut up' campaign insists that duties of care, during and after a custodial sentence, must be respected, that the state is not absolved of its duties to young people because they are designated 'young offenders' (Howard League 2008). The league has represented a significant number of children and young people, often asking the courts to rule on the specific implications of human rights legislation.

It has been argued, then, that the values of youth justice can be articulated in the language of human rights. More, they *should* be so articulated so that they can take their place in the mainstream of ethical debate, can connect practice in the UK with the standards and practices of other jurisdictions in Europe and can make the policies and practices of youth justice more amenable to determination in court.

Limitations?

There are, however, arguably two limitations in a focus on human rights that need to be addressed. First, rights seem to be very *minimal*. The rights of the European convention prohibit (for example) torture, but surely youth justice ethics can do better than that: what is required is a positive action-guiding ethics, not merely a set of proscriptions about what can readily be recognized as gross violations of human rights. Part of the answer to this problem lies in what jurists refer to as *positive obligations* (Mowbray 2004). A *right to life* is minimally a liberty or right of forbearance (the state may not put people to death), but it can be transformed into a potentially much more far-reaching claim (the state should take steps to protect people against death). Article 1 of the convention calls on states to 'secure' the rights of those under their jurisdiction and this calls for positive action, not merely forbearance – claims as well as liberties. Many of the rights affirmed in international conventions are of this character, calling upon the state not merely to refrain from oppression but to create opportunities for people to thrive.

A second misgiving, however, is linked with the consideration that rights are justiciable. It is no doubt valuable that rights are amenable to determination by a court, but is it not also the case that rights are framed so generally that their precise scope and application remain to be decided? We cannot know their detailed implication until the issue has been put to test in court. People have certain rights and this calls, in some circumstances, for positive action (not merely forbearance) from the state. But what kinds of action? What are the precise obligations here? And in particular in the real world, where some people's rights may be in conflict with the rights of others, how are such tensions to be resolved in a principled manner? For example, the rights of an (ex?)-offender to privacy may be in conflict with the rights of others to know about their circumstances and behaviour in the interest of public protection. Over time, case law will give a much more precise meaning to the application of the very general rights, but waiting for the courts to rule could be a slow process.

The work done by the Council of Europe in its active promotion of human rights starts to address this limitation. Before looking in detail at how this is achieved, it is important to appreciate the status and function of the Council of Europe. We then turn to consider its attempts to enhance the ethical standards of youth justice across the continent.

The Council of Europe

The standing and importance of the Council of Europe are not widely recognized in the UK. It is, for example, a quite separate organization from the European Union. Apart from Belarus (whose political arrangements have been found not to meet the required democratic standards), every recognized country in geographical Europe is a member. The council is Europe's oldest political organization. Based in Strasbourg, it was established soon after the Second World War to defend human rights, parliamentary democracy and the rule of law. The council stood for Europe's determination to guard against any recurrence of the atrocities witnessed during the war. The Convention for the Protection of Human Rights and Fundamental Freedoms (adopted in 1950) affirmed fundamental human rights. Some of these are rights that the state may not take away in any circumstances; others may only be denied or compromised in specifically defined circumstances. Over time the convention has been refined and added to in a series of protocols. Individuals who believe that the state has unjustifiably denied them their rights and who have not found satisfaction through national legal processes may have recourse to the European Court of Human Rights.

The Human Rights Act 1998 incorporated the convention into the law of the UK. This gave effect in UK law to the convention's general principles. Parliament was to have explicit regard to the convention in its legislation; public authorities were required to act in a manner compatible with the Human Rights Act; and, rather than needing to seek redress in Strasbourg, people could expect the courts of the UK to make their judgements in accordance with the Act and the convention. It was for this reason – and because the UK had been among the most influential proponents of the convention – that the Home Secretary, Jack Straw, felt able to tell the Labour Party conference: 'we are bringing the British people's rights home' (1997).

The Council of Europe advances its work through the following:

- *Setting standards*: the European Prison Rules, for example, apply the (often necessarily quite general) principles of the convention to the specific circumstances of imprisonment. There are also European rules on community sanctions and measures (CSMs), which include practices of probation and offender management and, as we shall see, rules on youth justice.

- *Inspection*: the council inspects the practices of member states to check their conformity with the convention. The Committee for the Prevention of Torture (CPT), notably, undertakes visits to examine the treatment of those detained to protect them from torture and inhuman treatment.

- *Co-operation*: as well as calling states to account, the council supports them in developing good practice. In penal affairs, this is achieved through the work of committees of experts, twinning projects and advisory groups.

The council's decision-making body is the Committee of Ministers (foreign ministers or their deputies) who adopt recommendations. Although not legally binding, these 'recommendations' have been formally approved by very senior representatives of each nation and consequently bear considerable authority. They have been, therefore, sometimes used in hearings to help the court to establish the scope and significance of the European convention.

In penal affairs, perhaps the best known and most influential of these recommendations are the European Prison Rules (Council of Europe 2006), and their principles have been cited in the judgements of the European Court of Human Rights. In *Dickson* v. *the United Kingdom*, the court was invited to rule on the applicant's claim that his right to respect for private and family life (Article 8) had been violated. The substance of this case is beyond the scope of this chapter, but the *process* followed shows the potential influence of the council's recommendations. In trying to determine which of a prisoner's rights were necessarily forfeit and which should be retained and defended, the court referred explicitly to the European Prison Rules, using them to elucidate the meaning of the convention *as it applies to serving prisoners*. The emphasis in the rules on rehabilitation and resettlement influenced the court to decide in the applicant's favour.

So while these recommendations are not legally binding in a formal sense, they have considerable authority. It is for this reason that the new recommendation for juvenile offenders – which sets out to clarify what the convention should mean *as it applies to young offenders* – will be of especial interest to youth justice practitioners.

European rules for juvenile offenders subject to sanctions or measures

On 5 November 2008, the Committee of Ministers adopted Recommendation CM/Rec. (2008)11 on the *European Rules for Juvenile Offenders Subject to Sanctions or Measures* (Council of Europe 2008a). The rules amount to a code of practice for working with young offenders – a code based on the challenges of trying to give expression in practice to the principles of the European convention. If the claim that 'Human rights are the values we live by – and we must be true to them as a society' (Falconer 2007) is to be taken seriously, we must study carefully the authoritative guidance of a recommendation intended to advance these rights in the ethically complex world of youth justice.

The rules begin with a statement of basic principles. For example, the second principle is: 'The sanctions or measures that may be imposed on juveniles, as well as the manner of their implementation, shall be . . . based on the principles of social integration and education and of the prevention of re-offending.' The idea that social integration and education, no less than crime reduction, should guide the character of sanctions for young people is a powerful affirmation that immediately puts to test some of the sentencing practices of member states. As the accompanying commentary – an indispensable guide to the (relatively formal) rules themselves – explains:

> All juvenile justice and welfare systems are based on the principles of social integration and education. This leaves a much lesser place, and in some countries no place at all, for the principle of general deterrence or other (more punitive) aims that are a feature of the criminal justice system for adults.

Example 1

> Basic Principle 6: 'In order to adapt the implementation of sanctions and measures to the particular circumstances of each case the authorities responsible for the implementation shall have a sufficient degree of discretion without leading to serious inequality of treatment.'
>
> • Can your agency policy accommodate this?
>
> • How does the implementation of national standards fit with this principle?
>
> • What can be done to make sure that the exercise of discretion does not lead to unfairness?

After clarifying their scope and definition, the rules proceed in Part II to cover community sanctions and measures, setting standards for the legal framework, and for the conditions of implementation and consequences of non-compliance. Part III is about deprivation of liberty, and covers institutional structure, placement, admission, accommodation, hygiene and health. It moves on to deal with regime activities ('All interventions shall be designed to promote the development of juveniles, who shall be actively encouraged to participate in them'), contact with the outside world, freedom of thought, conscience and religion. Further sections deal with searching, the use of force, physical restraint and weapons, separation for security and safety reasons, discipline and punishment, transfer between institutions, and preparation for release. There is a specific section on 'Foreign nationals' – whose distinctive circumstances, needs and rights are likely to become ever more of a challenge to the nations of Europe at a time of so much migration and movement on the continent. Other sections cover 'ethnic and linguistic minorities' and juveniles with disabilities. Further sections relate to the variety of institutions to which these rules apply (detention in police stations, for example, 'welfare institutions' and mental health institutions). Legal advice, complaints procedures and monitoring are all considered in Part V, while Part VI covers staff, including their training requirements. The concluding sections are on evaluation, research, work with the media and the public. The scope of the rules, then, is quite comprehensive, although inevitably 'broad brush'. The commentary (Council of Europe 2008b) is more specific and just as valuable a resource to policy-makers, managers and practitioners who want to ground their work with young offenders on an ethical basis.

One way of beginning to give effect to these rules would be for practitioners to consider conducting an audit of the policies and practices of their own agency, team or unit and mapping these against the rules. It seems likely that in many cases practitioners will find that their work measures up well. This in itself would be worth knowing. In some respects, looking to the spirit as well as the letter of the recommendation, youth offending teams may wish to review their practice and to consider how its standards might be enhanced to give fuller expression to respecting human rights. The rules and the commentary will give invaluable guidance about how this might be achieved.

Example 2

> Rule 31.2: 'Juveniles shall be encouraged to discuss matters relating to the implementation of community sanctions and measures and to communicate individually or collectively with the authorities about these matters.'
>
> • How does your agency encourage this at the moment?

> - What opportunities are given to young people to express their views about their dealings with the agency?
> - Are there clear procedures in place?
> - Are any such procedures genuinely accessible to all service users?

Conclusion

In this chapter it has been suggested that the discourse of human rights can and should become the way in which youth justice articulates its ethical values. In this way, the values of youth justice can be made mainstream, international and justiciable. While some limitations of human rights have been recognized, it has been argued that the work of the Council of Europe advances the cause. The new recommendation on the *European Rules for Juvenile Offenders Subject to Sanctions or Measures* has been referred to, and its detailed explanatory commentary recommended to practitioners, together with a suggestion about how it could be used in practice to enhance the ethical standards of youth justice work.

References

Canton, R. (2009) 'Nonsense upon stilts? Human rights, the ethics of punishment and the values of probation', *British Journal of Community Justice*, 7: 5–22.

Clark, C. (2000) *Social Work Ethics: Politics, Principles and Practice*. Basingstoke: Macmillan.

Council of Europe (2006) *Recommendation Rec. (2006)2 of the Committee of Ministers to Member States on the European Prison Rules* (adopted by the Committee of Ministers on 11 January 2006 at the 952nd meeting of the ministers' deputies) (available online at https://wcd.coe.int/ViewDoc.jsp?id=955747).

Council of Europe (2008a) *Recommendation CM/Rec. (2008)11 of the Committee of Ministers to Member States on the European Rules for Juvenile Offenders Subject to Sanctions or Measures* (adopted by the Committee of Ministers on 5 November 2008 at the 1040th meeting of the ministers' deputies) (available online at https://wcd.coe.int/ViewDoc.jsp?id=1367113&Site=CM&BackColorInternet=9999CC&BackColorIntranet=FFBB55&BackColorLogged=FFAC75).

Council of Europe (2008b) *Commentary on the European Rules for Juvenile Offenders Subject to Sanctions or Measures* (available online at https://wcd.coe.int/com.instranet.nstraServlet?Index=no&command=com.instranet.CmdBlobGet&InstranetImage=1017553&SecMode=1&DocId=1299142&Usage=2).

Duff, R.A. (2001) *Punishment, Communication and Community*. Oxford: Oxford University Press.

Falconer, C. (2007) 'Human rights are majority rights.' The Lord Morris of Borth-y-Gest Memorial Lecture, Bangor University, 23rd March (available online at http://www.dca.gov.uk/speeches/2007/sp070323.htm).

Goldson, B. and Muncie, J. (2006) 'Rethinking youth justice: comparative analysis, international human rights and research evidence', *Youth Justice*. 6: 91–106.

Howard League (2008) 'Growing up shut up' (available online at http://www. howardleague.org/index.php?id=641).

Mowbray, A. (2004) *The Development of Positive Obligations Under the European Convention on Human Rights by the European Court of Human Rights*. Oxford: Hart.

Nellis, M. (2007) 'Probation values', in R. Canton and D. Hancock (eds) *Dictionary of Probation and Offender Management*. Cullompton: Willan Publishing.

Rawls, J. (1967) 'Two concepts of rules', in P. Foot (ed.) *Theories of Ethics*. Oxford: Oxford University Press.

Rex, S. (2005) *Reforming Community Penalties*. Cullompton: Willan Publishing.

Straw, J. (1997) Speech to the Labour Party conference (available online at http://www.prnewswire.co.uk/cgi/news/release?id=33162).

Thorpe, D., Smith, D., Green, C. and Paley, J. (1980) *Out of Care: The Community Support of Juvenile Offenders*. London: Allen & Unwin.

van Zyl Smit, D. and Ashworth, A. (2004) 'Disproportionate sentences as human rights violations', *Modern Law Review*, 67: 541–60.

Cases cited

Dickson v. *the United Kingdom* (2007) (Application no. 44362/04) (available online at http://cmiskp.echr.coe.int/tkp197/view.asp?item=2&portal=hbkm&action=html&highlight=Dickson&sessionid=17546405&skin=hudoc-en).

21

Values in youth justice: practice approaches to welfare and justice for young people in UK jurisdictions

Bill Whyte

Introduction

Approaches to dealing with children and young people who break the law vary much more widely in the UK than the equivalent justice systems for adults. In addition to cultural and institutional differences, youth systems vary in their structures and age jurisdiction as well as in the underlying normative and value assumptions underpinning policy and practice.

Systems of youth justice in the UK share a commitment to common goals, including prevention, early intervention, and better integrated and co-ordinated provision for young people involved in crime. However they have pursued them in contrasting and distinctive ways within the different legal jurisdictions. Even so, most analysts of youth justice (Haines and Drakeford 1999; Tonry and Doob 2004) recognize that practice has to be grounded in a comprehensive theoretical and evaluative framework. Currently, the concepts of interdisciplinary, multidisciplinary or transdisciplinary practice are promoted by all UK systems as providing future directions (Whyte 2008). However, while these concepts provide some consistency to the direction of travel at the level of policy, the orientation of practice and practitioners themselves to a consistent, unified or even identifiable practice paradigm, has proved far more elusive.

Social work values

Reference to values and ethics is integral to social work training and features prominently within the regulatory framework for social work. Alongside statements of values, principles and standards for youth justice practice which vary in each UK jurisdiction, the British Association of Social Workers (BASW) promotes a definition of social work issued by the International Federation of Social Workers and the International Association of Schools of Social Work which applies to social work practitioners and educators in every region and country in the world.

The social work profession promotes social change, problem-solving in human relationships and the empowerment and liberation of people to enhance wellbeing. Utilizing theories of human behaviour and social systems, social work intervenes at the points where people interact with their environments. Principles of human rights and social justice are fundamental to social work (see http://www.basw.co.uk).

The BASW's code of ethics consists of five basic values and a set of practice principles associated with each basic value to guide and underpin ethical professional practice. These are summarized as follows: 'social work practice should both promote respect for *human dignity* and pursue *social justice*, through *service to humanity*, *integrity* and *competence*' (1976: para 3. emphasis added (http://www.basw.co.uk/Default.aspx?tabid=64)).

All those working in social care in England and Wales, including youth justice, are required to work to standards set down by the General Social Care Council (GSCC) and the Care Council for Wales (CCW); in Scotland the equivalent body is the Scottish Social Services Council (SSSC) and in Northern Ireland, the Northern Ireland Social Care Council (NISCC). The codes of practice for the NISCC (2002), GSCC (2003) and SSSC (2004) define the standards of professional conduct required of all practitioners. With the expectation that practice is principled, honest and value based, these include to:

- protect the rights and promote the interests of service users and carers;

- strive to establish and maintain trust and confidence of service users and carers;

- promote the independence of service users while protecting them as far as possible from danger or harm;

- respect the rights of service users while seeking to ensure that their behaviour does not harm themselves or other people;

- uphold public trust and confidence in social care services; and

- be accountable for the quality of their work and take responsibility for maintaining and improving their knowledge and skills.

Fine words and sentiments, however, do not in themselves guarantee that even value-directed practice will be given expression in ethical practice, particularly where involuntary involvement is often a distinguishing feature of youth justice practice. Vulnerable young people can be difficult to work with on an involuntary basis, particularly when they are 'defensive and oppositional', yet may be less co-operative and less responsive to overly directive approaches (Trotter 2006). Where a young person's choices are 'restricted', it is essential to build a working alliance based on principles of participation to support the sequencing of day-to-day, face-to-face tasks and activities which are required in most cases to secure compliance, to generate motivation, to achieve cohesion, to integrate planning and to achieve and maintain positive outcomes.

UK systems of youth justice raise many ethical challenges for practitioners locked into the dominant value frame operating within the respective systems. The challenges arise from the combination of two concepts often characterized as reflecting welfare and justice approaches (see below) – special responses to children and young people, and equal rights under the law. Their coexistence in youth justice generates considerable tension in how best to reconcile the competing claims of the law, judicial process, community safety and punishment with the need to consider the best interests and the rights of the child or young person, while effectively reducing offending in politically acceptable ways.

Practice values in UK jurisdictions

The manner in which each country has responded to children's offending cannot be understood in isolation from their historical development (see Tonry and Doob 2004; Muncie and Goldson 2007; Chapter 22 this volume), which makes comparison and contemporary analysis complex, if not problematic. Youth justice systems have tended to be evaluated against the two dominant paradigms of *welfare* or *justice*. As with all ideal types, models are seldom found in a pure form and most jurisdictions combine elements of both approaches.

The 'welfare model' is often associated with child development and change through social and educational intervention rather than punishment. In contrast, the 'justice model' assumes that children and young people (above a certain age which varies between countries) should be held accountable before the law for their criminal actions. In the justice model the degree of culpability should be assessed and punishment apportioned in accordance with the seriousness of the offending behaviour. For this reason the child or young person must be accorded full rights to due process to ensure that state powers are predictable and determinate. Between the two models the value contrast is strongest where there is a separation between systems dealing with the care and protection of children and young people (*child welfare*) and responses to offending by children and young people (*youth justice*). In general, welfare approaches focus on what can be considered to be the underlying causes or needs in addition to those that sustain and support crime directly, while justice approaches tend to concentrate more closely on the offence, risks and immediately associated crime-related ('criminogenic') needs. Questionable assumptions about maturity and capacity for criminal intent are factored into systems' responses.

UK countries show signs of discomfort with too rigid a demarcation or separation between justice and welfare. As a result there are many variations in practice seeking to balance the 'ingredients' of prevention, early intervention, diversion, social intervention, treatments and sanctions or punishments required for effective child welfare, protection and youth justice. The systems in England, Wales and Northern Ireland have the age of criminal responsibility set at 10 but deploy systems of diversion from prosecution and restorative approaches for young people up to the age of 17 (Bateman and Pitts 2005). None the less, all children and young people, aged 10–17 years, when dealt with formally or compulsorily for offending, are likely to be dealt with in youth courts. The formal system is based on a traditional adversarial justice approach with decision-making lying with the court, as in the adult criminal justice system.

In Scotland, while the age of criminal responsibility is currently lower, at 8, few young people under 16 will appear in a criminal court, youth or adult, compared with most other UK countries, and most are dealt with in Scotland's integrated welfare-based children's hearing system. The Scottish system is intended to operate within a social education paradigm (Smith and Whyte 2008).

Converging or diverging values in practice in the UK?

Scotland's system for dealing with young people who offend is based on the philosophy of justice and welfare advocated by the Report of the Kilbrandon Committee (SHHD 1964). This recommended the establishment of an extra-judicial system of children's hearings to provide a unified system for dealing with young people alleged to have committed criminal offences and those deemed to be in need of care and protection. The rationale was that the similarities in the underlying situation of these two groups of children 'far outweigh the differences' (1964: para. 15), in particular, difficulties arising from family upbringing, social environment and schooling.

Kilbrandon, Scotland's senior Law Lord at the time, viewed the criminal justice process as having two fundamental functions: the adjudication of legal facts – whether or not an offence had been established beyond reasonable doubt – and the decision concerning disposal once these facts have been established. The committee concluded that these two functions required 'quite different skills and qualities' and attempting to combine them was a source of 'dissatisfaction' (1964: para. 71). While it was never argued in any simplistic way that social adversity caused or fully explained offending, it drew on developments in the social sciences at the time, which suggested that social and emotional deprivation associated with disorganized neighbourhoods, family disruption, separation and poor parenting would have a major impact on the subsequent behaviour of the young. The importance of positive schooling and the crucial role of parental supervision in preventing delinquency were strongly emphasized. Theories of victimology, though undeveloped at the time, are none the less implicit in the assumptions that young people are often themselves victims of their upbringing and circumstances as well as 'villains' or perpetrators of crime.

Young people who offend were to be viewed not as criminals but as young people whose upbringing had been unsatisfactory and where responsibility for their offending behaviour should be a shared one between the young person, the family, the community and the state. Where possible, resolutions would be sought without recourse to formal proceedings. The resulting welfare-based system has a clear commitment to the 'paramountcy principle' (subsequently outlined as a foundation principle in the UN Convention on the Rights of the Child (UNCRC)) up to the age of 16 and, to a lesser extent, to 18.

Despite the wide-ranging differences in structures across the different UK jurisdictions, some commentators have suggested that there are similar practice issues as a result of converging themes in all UK jurisdictions (Bottoms and Dignan 2004). Each jurisdiction shares, at face value, a commitment to preventive goals in regard to youth crime. All emphasize the importance of multidisciplinary responses, although approaches vary greatly in practice from area to area. The same strong emphasis is apparent on effectiveness and the reduction of reoffending, standardized need–risk assessment and a growing concern with victims and the harm caused by criminal behaviour but they are pursued in contrasting ways.

Commentators suggest that, despite an emphasis on welfare within justice in England and Wales in the 1960s and 1970s, practice and policy, particularly since the Crime and Disorder Act 1998, have reflected a 'new youth justice' philosophy stressing individual criminal responsibility (Goldson 2002; Chapter 19 this volume). This reflects a struggle to secure a 'paramountcy approach' (the principle that the best interests and welfare of children must be a primary consideration in any proceedings involving children) alongside and within judicial and criminal structures. Systems are constantly undergoing political 'doctoring' to managing the 'mix' between social and protective measures, punitive responses and sanctions. The separation of family courts dealing with care and protection from youth courts could be argued to have reinforced criminalizing principles because of the strong emphasis on the individual responsibility of offenders, parental irresponsibility, victim reparation and punishment: 'in England, for children and young persons coming before the courts, there is now a deliberate institutional separation between the "care jurisdiction" (dealt with by the family proceedings courts) and the "criminal jurisdictions" (dealt with by what is now called the Youth Court)' (Bottoms and Dignan 2004: 25).

Children or offenders first?

The near universal ratification of the UNCRC has placed importance on providing 'a level playing-field' of values and principles for all children through universal prevention and early social intervention measures. Most mainland European jurisdictions deal with children who offend within a welfare system up to age of transition to (youth or adult) court systems, which is generally around 14 or 15 years old. European rules for juvenile offenders subject to sanctions or measures, adopted on 5 November 2008 (Council of Europe 2008; see Chapter 20 this volume), require that the age of criminal responsibility is set 'not too low' (2008 para. 4). The recommended age is at least 14–16 years of age, while the age of 18 is set as the ideal.

UK jurisdictions, based on common law, vary much more widely from European countries. In all UK jurisdictions the 'reach' of children's legislation is the age of 18, yet many, if not most, young people involved in crime are 'criminalized' in some way long before that age, despite the evidence suggesting that early criminalization is one of the best predictors of sustained criminality (Kemp *et al.* 2002). These circumstances present day-to-day challenges for practitioners concerned with effectiveness, values and ethical practice. They must contend with variable definitions and statutes across the UK about what constitutes 'a child' and 'a youth' (see Chapter 6 this volume). Alongside this, the demarcations between those who are and are not deemed 'fully criminally responsible', or between those considered best dealt with in criminal proceedings and those not, also varies across the UK jurisdictions.

Despite the modern 'sanitization' or humanizing of criminal proceedings, they remain, symbolically at least, medieval public shaming exercises in which a person considered singly, solely and, to a large extent, fully (subject to mitigating circumstances) responsible for their actions, metaphorically or literally, stands alone 'in the dock' (Braithwaite 1989). The outcome of a criminal 'conviction' is a public stain on their character which, despite rehabilitative legislation, is almost impossible to live down.

In the criminal justice paradigm no one else need accept any share of responsibility for a young person's action intended by children's legislation and expected by UNCRC principles. Indeed, criminalization can be seen to absolve adults and service providers from accountability for 'failure'. While persistent and serious offending cannot be condoned or excused, there is little evidence to suggest that service failure is seriously factored into decision-making. Criminal justice processes have a tendency to 'translate' service failure into individual responsibility – that of the young person or individual family failure. Wider society is 'conveniently' excused.

What values and principles should guide UK practice?

This lack of social consensus on what UK youth justice systems should be or what they are intended to achieve creates major value challenges and ethical dilemmas for practitioners. Practice or prosecution guidance in the UK makes little reference to existing international standards. Yet benchmarks for practice have been set by UNCRC instruments and guidance and the European Convention on Human Rights (ECHR).

Article 3 of the UNCRC requires that 'in all actions concerning children, whether undertaken by public or private social welfare institutions, courts of law, administrative authorities or legislative bodies, the best interests of the child shall be a primary consideration'. The qualification of 'a' primary consideration rather than 'the' primary consideration can find expression in quite different practices which invoke the public interest as over-riding the interests of the child when it comes to criminal matters for relatively minor, even if persistent, offending.

Since the incorporation of the ECHR into law in UK jurisdictions in 1998, a number of practices have changed to comply with European court rulings. In the Bulger case (*Venables* v. *Crown*) the European court recognized that the ECHR had little to say about children and young people involved in crime, and drew on UNCRC guidance for benchmark standards to direct its rulings. In effect the European court confirmed that the fulfilment of the ECHR requires the application of UNCRC principles. The publication of European rules in 2008 is a step further to establishing 'soft' law to guide practice in line with the UNCRC principles outlined below (see Chapter 20 this volume). No UK jurisdiction has fully incorporated the UNCRC within legislation, and practice remains some distance from the 'spirit', if not the obligations and requirements, of being signatories. The preamble to the UNCRC stresses the dynamic nature of the framework and that it expects it to be continually fleshed out and developed on the basis of research and practice-related evidence.

A number of UN promulgations are of particular importance in providing directing values and principles for youth welfare and justice practice. The key UN guidance for youth welfare and justice includes the following:

- The Standard Minimum Rules for the Administration of Juvenile Justice (Beijing Rules), 1985.

- The Directing Principles for the Prevention of Juvenile Delinquency (Riyadh Guidelines), 1990.

- The Rules for the Prevention of Juveniles Deprived of Liberty (Havana Rules), 1990.

- The Standard Minimum Rules for Non-custodial Measures (Tokyo Rules), 1990.

- The Economic and Social Council Guidelines for Action on Children in the Criminal Justice System (Vienna Guidelines), 1997.

The Beijing Rules set standards for the administration of justice, placing particular emphasis on children's rights, and stressing the importance of the wellbeing of the young person. They recommend that the age of criminal responsibility is based on 'emotional, mental and intellectual maturity' and that it should not be fixed too low. These standards stress the adoption of social educational responses to youth crime rather than punitive (criminal) ones. Rule 11 *requires* consideration of diversion from criminal proceedings with the young person's consent. The emphasis in these standards is, where possible, to avoid drawing young people unnecessarily into any formal processes and thus avoiding the amplifying and confirmatory effect (net widening) generally associated with criminalization. At the same time they stress the importance of the young person's right to representation and the avoidance of deprivation of liberty unless the seriousness of the offence merits it and then only as a last resort.

The Directing Principles of Riyadh stress the value of child-centred early intervention, shared responsibility in the socialization of young people and the promotion of non-criminogenic attitudes through multidisciplinary approaches to crime prevention. They focus on 'young persons who may or may not be in conflict with the law' and 'who are abandoned, neglected, abused, exposed to drug abuse, in marginal circumstances and who are at general social risk' (Marshall 2007: 7). They promote a 'progressive universalism', signalling a major overlap between children and young people in adversity and for those in conflict with the law, and that meeting needs and building 'human capital' is a priority to avoid escalating offending trajectories and so reducing risks.

The Havana Rules stress the independence of prosecutors and their role in promoting diversion from criminal proceedings for young people up to the age of 18. From existing practice evidence, this is not something that UK prosecutors seem to have shown much independent concern for. The recently published Council of Europe rules (2008) provide a stronger basis for practice within the context of the ECHR.

The Tokyo Rules are intended to promote greater community involvement and community-based responses to crime. They reflect a growing debate on the need to promote young people's 'social capital'.

The Vienna Guidelines stress the indivisibility and interdependence of the rights of children outlined in the UNCRC. Guideline 11 specifically encourages the development of child-oriented youth justice systems. Guideline 15 explicitly supports prevention and diversion from criminal systems and the importance of dealing with underlying social causes: 'one of the obvious tenets in juvenile delinquency prevention and juvenile justice is that long-term change is brought about ... when root causes are addressed' (Guideline 41). The UNCRC sets out the terms in which children and young people 'by reason of

... physical and mental immaturity, need special safeguards and care, including appropriate legal protection'. It is the most widely ratified human rights treaty in the world.

While the UK has entered reservations to the UNCRC's guiding principles, international law requires that none of these reservations compromises the spirit or principles of the convention. Despite the existence of these important standards and the consistent practice philosophy running through them, it is difficult to argue from evidence on UK criminalization and detention of young people under the age of 18 that the obligations implied by the UNCRC have featured greatly in the priority of youth justice policy-makers, decision-makers or practice agencies to date.

However the signal judgements of the High Court in England following judicial reviews instigated by the Howard League in 2007 and 2002 have confirmed that English, and by extension UK, jurisdictions cannot designate young people under 18 as 'ex-children' simply by their entrance to the criminal justice system (see Chapter 19 this volume). The High Court commented that 'local authorities across the country are failing to provide proper assessments and care plans for vulnerable children' entering and leaving detention, particularly where they are in danger of returning to precisely the same situations that led to their crimes and imprisonment in the first place (Howard League for Penal Reform 26 July 2007). These judgements confirm the need to strengthen policy and practice approaches to this difficult age group by recognizing their status as young people.

Conclusion

Ratification of the UNCRC has created pressure on many western countries to try to find a better balance and to construct a kind of synthesis between two basic sets of value principles subsumed within notions of justice and welfare. Inadequacies in preventive welfare provision can create conflicts of interest when the main service provider, youth justice practitioners, are responsible for ensuring that children's 'best interests' and needs are met as well as the public interest. Too often young people in need seem to 'slip' too readily from 'care' status to 'criminal' status, relabelling and reprocessing them as 'offenders'. It is as if, by entering criminal justice processes, they become 'former' or 'ex'-children, stripped of those protective rights that recognize their less-than-fully adult status.

Practitioners in the UK have to operate within the constraints set by their own jurisdiction. At the same time issues of professional integrity confront practitioners on a day-to-day basis with consequences both for children and young people who offend and for those who suffer as a result of their offences. If practice is to be evidence-led and effective, and if the BASW's definition that 'social work practice should both promote respect for *human dignity* and pursue *social justice*, through *service to humanity, integrity* and *competence*' given earlier in this chapter is to be given meaning, practitioners have a responsibility to operate in a principled and value-based manner even though this may create tensions between them and their organizational system (Hill *et al.* 2006).

References

Bateman, T. and Pitts, J. (2005) *The RHP Companion to Youth Justice.* London: Nacro.

Bottoms, A. and Dignan, J. (2004) 'Youth justice in Great Britain', in M. Tonry and A. Doob (eds) *Youth Crime and Youth Justice.* Chicago, IL: University of Chicago Press.

Braithwaite, J. (1989) *Crime, Shame and Reintegration.* Cambridge: Cambridge University Press.

Council of Europe (2008) *European Rules for Juvenile Offenders Subject to Sanctions or Measures.* Geneva: Council of Europe.

Goldson, B. (2002) 'New punitiveness: the politics of child incarceration', in J. Muncie *et al.* (eds) *Youth Justice: Critical Readings.* London: Sage.

Haines, K. and Drakeford, M. (1999) *Young People and Youth Justice.* London: Macmillan.

Hill, M., Lockyer, A. and Stone, F. (eds) (2006) *Youth Justice and Child Protection.* London: Jessica Kingsley.

Kemp, V., Sorsby, A., Liddle, M. and Merrington, S. (2002) Assessing responses to youth offending in Northamptonshire, *Research Briefing 2.* London: Nacro.

Marshall, K. (2007) 'The present state of youth justice in Scotland', *Scottish Journal of Criminal Justice Studies*, 13: 4–19.

Muncie, J. and Goldson, B. (2007) *Comparative Youth Justice: Critical Issues.* Oxford: Blackwell.

SHHD (1964) *Children and Young Persons, Scotland* (the Kilbrandon Report). Edinburgh: Scottish Education Department.

Smith, M. and Whyte, B. (2008) 'Social education and social pedagogy: reclaiming a Scottish tradition in social work', *European Journal of Social Work*, 11: 15–28.

Tonry, M. and Doob, A. (eds) (2004) *Youth Crime and Youth Justice: Comparative and Cross-national Pespectives.* London: University of Chicago Press.

Trotter, C. (2006) *Working with Involuntary Clients: A Guide to Practice* (2nd edn). London: Sage.

Whyte, B. (2008) *Youth Justice in Practice.* London: Policy Press.

Cases cited

Venables v. *Crown; R* v. *Thompson and Venables*, Preston Crown Court, 1–24 November 1993.

22

The dragonization of youth justice

Kevin Haines

The United Kingdom of Great Britain and Northern Ireland is a complex legislative and constitutional entity. Most non-British people have no idea of the complexities of governance within which we live out our lives. Indeed, many British people are unaware of the subtleties, and some of these subtleties are, in fact, contested. More so, some of this contested territory, both geographical and governmental, includes a growing range of significant issues. Such is the complexity of its structures of governance that it is quite difficult to make wholly accurate statements concerning the polity of the United Kingdom. For example, one could say that the UK is, at the same time, both one country and four countries – although this is not quite accurate.

Northern Ireland, for example, has constitutional roots in the Act of Union 1800 between Ireland and Great Britain. It was legally established under the Government of Ireland Act 1920 after the rest of Ireland secured its independence as a fully self-governing nation-state, leaving six of the nine counties of Ulster as a contested administrative subdivision of the UK. 'Northern Ireland' had its own government and Parliament, based in Stormont near Belfast, until it was suspended by the UK Parliament in 1972 and then abolished in 1973. After 25 years of armed and constitutional conflict with Irish Nationalists and Republicans, 'direct rule' from Westminster was replaced, at the end of the 1990s, by the present Northern Ireland Assembly, established through the signing of the Good Friday Agreement in 1998.

Scotland, by contrast, was an independent kingdom until 1707, when it entered into a political union with the Kingdom of England to form a single united kingdom of Great Britain. This joining together was a genuine but, for some, controversial act brought into effect by the Acts of Union passed by both the Scottish and English Parliaments, although it should be noted that Scotland has always maintained its own distinct legal, educational and religious systems.

Wales was a separate nation until it was subjugated by England in the early 1500s by the Laws in Wales Acts 1535–42, laws which established the legal entity of 'England and Wales'. For much of the last 500 years Wales has been ruled in all matters social and political by England – although notions of Welsh nationhood were never fully extinguished by the English as exemplified, perhaps, by the long struggle to sustain the Welsh language and the proclamation of Cardiff as the national capital in 1955.

Multinational interests

As both one country and four 'countries', therefore, social and political life in the UK and its four constitutive entities is a complex mix of jurisdictional authorities and responsibilities. While some matters are dealt with at a UK level, others are dealt with at national level. Matters such as defence, foreign affairs and the tax system have traditionally been UK based – and remain so, even under 'devolution'. On the other hand, Scotland, as noted, has its own legal system. The 'separate' legal system of Northern Ireland exists by the delegated authority of the Westminster Parliament but England and Wales share the same legal system. The complexity of who governs whom has, of course, deepened with the processes of devolution and the establishment, at the end of the 1990s, of a national Parliament in Scotland and National Assemblies in Wales and Northern Ireland. Wales, for example, now governs its own educational and health systems and, as time passes, the processes of devolution expand and deepen Welsh governance of Welsh affairs.

The jurisdictional differences in the legal systems in the various parts of the UK have meant that both traditionally and in the present, both Scotland (see, for example, Chapter 21 this volume) and Northern Ireland (see, for example, O'Mahony and Deazley 2000; Chapman and O'Mahony 2007) have had their own separate and distinct juvenile justice systems. Wales, on the other hand, shares the same juvenile justice system as England (for an account which traces the development of juvenile justice in England and Wales up to the end of the 1990s, see Haines and Drakeford 1998). In Wales, therefore, as in England, at the present time, juvenile/youth justice is the shared responsibility of the Ministry of Justice and the Department for Children, Schools and Families – a shared responsibility discharged through the Joint Youth Justice Unit. In practical terms, juvenile justice services throughout England and Wales are provided (mainly) by youth offending teams (YOTs), located in the management and organizational structures of local authorities. At a national (England and Wales) level the work of these YOTs is directed by the Youth Justice Board (YJB) for England and Wales – which exercises highly prescriptive control over the work of YOTs and the nature of juvenile justice services (see, generally, Goldson 2000; Goldson and Muncie 2006).

Evolving devolution – current trends

At face value, therefore, in terms of governance, policy, strategy, management and practice, juvenile/youth justice in Wales is/should be the same as that in

England. However, in recent times a distinctively Welsh juvenile justice has begun to emerge – a process which we may refer to as the dragonization of juvenile justice. (The dragon is the national symbol of Wales, featuring on the flag and other national paraphernalia.) Formally speaking, this process of dragonization is not a direct product of devolution, as the Welsh Assembly holds no formal responsibility for youth justice or YOTs. Unquestionably, however, national devolution and the processes surrounding it have created the space in which the dragonization of juvenile justice has taken and is taking place. It is the nature of this space, its changing scope and contours, and the way in which this space is being filled, differently and distinctively, in Wales, which form the basis of dragonization.

The extent to which children who offend are treated as children with particular needs or as young offenders has varied over time nationally and internationally – the classic welfare versus justice debate. At the level of England and Wales, in official policy as espoused by the YJB the extent to which children who offend (and, indeed, those who are just a nuisance and even those who have the potential to become a nuisance or to offend) are marked out as offenders for distinctive treatment/intervention targeted at their offending behaviour has never been higher. While this is a reality of juvenile justice in England and Wales, it must be set against another reality – that of national youth policies (see also Muncie 2006). Here we see some important and significant divergences between England and Wales (and, indeed, between all parts of the UK – see Williamson 2007, 2009 for a broader discussion of the development of youth policies in the UK and beyond).

The UK Social Exclusion Unit published the *Report of Policy Action Team 12: Young People* in March 2000, signalling a shift of discourse away from addressing the problem of youth towards a view of young people as social actors negotiating multiple socioeconomic factors in the path to adulthood. The report and the shift in thinking that accompanied it at government level provided the context for the four countries of the UK to develop strategies designed to promote positive outcomes for children.

In England, *Every Child Matters: Change for Children*, provides a framework 'to build services around children and young people so that we maximize opportunities and minimize risk' (Department for Education and Skills 2004). Thus in England the dominant approach is one based on creating opportunities for children, but opportunity in the English context is not politically neutral and is wedded to the notion of responsibilization (see Goldson 2002). As Tony Blair (2004) said, those 'who play by the rules are not going to see their opportunities blighted by those who don't'. The clear implication in England is that children who fail to take advantage of their opportunities or those who break the rules (children who offend or are anti-social) will have their opportunities taken away from them. In Scotland the executive published *For Scotland's Children: Better Integrated Children's Services* (2001). Building on a long-established welfarist tradition and reflecting the principles of the children's hearing system, *For Scotland's Children* espoused social justice and was focused on the reduction of inequality and the provision of services and support for children. The strategy in Northern Ireland, by contrast, drew firmly from the human rights discourse that formed the basis of the settlement made in the Good Friday Agreement. It was based on a children's rights approach that clearly referenced the UN Convention on the Rights of the Child (UNCRC): 'All children and young people in Northern Ireland, according to their age and maturity, will know their rights and the rights of others; are equally enabled to exercise these rights and that these rights and responsibilities are respected, promoted and protected (Children and Young People's Unit 2004). These rights, however, were not elaborated beyond those contained in the UNCRC, nor were there clear mechanisms to ensure access to these rights by children – who were also now given 'responsibilities'.

The approach taken in Wales was, like Northern Ireland, based on children's rights and also drew heavily on the UNCRC, but the Welsh approach was distinctive in a number of ways. Reflecting a widespread enthusiasm for making things better for children, Wales moved more quickly to publish its strategy than the other parts of the UK, producing *Extending Entitlement: Supporting Young People in Wales* (Policy Unit 2000) in 2000 and the full strategy, *Extending Entitlement: Support for 11 to 25 Year Olds in Wales* (Welsh Assembly Government 2002), two years later. *Extending Entitlement*, as it is known, was also explicitly policy focused rather than being limited to discussing services for children and it raised the age limit for inclusion to 25 years. It is in the nature of this policy focus that *Extending Entitlement* is unique. *Extending Entitlement* set out and established ten universal entitlements for all children in Wales:

Every young person in Wales aged 11–25 has a basic entitlement to:

- education, training and work experience – tailored to their needs

- basic skills which open doors to a full life and promote social inclusion

- a wide and varied range of opportunities to participate in volunteering and active citizenship

- high quality, responsive, and accessible services and facilities

- independent, specialist careers advice and guidance and student support and counselling services

- personal support and advice where and when needed and in appropriate formats – with clear ground rules on confidentiality

- advice on health, housing benefits and other issues provided in accessible and welcoming settings

- recreational and social opportunities in a safe and accessible environment

- sporting, artistic, musical and outdoor experiences to develop talent, broaden horizons and promote rounded perspective including both national and international contexts

- the right to be consulted, to participate in decision-making and to be heard, on all matters which concern them or have an impact on their lives

In an environment where there is:

- a positive focus on achievement overall and what young people have to contribute;

- a focus on building young people's capacity to become independent, make choices, and participate in the democratic process; and

- celebration of young people's successes.

These universal entitlements offer the promise for all children in Wales of participation and access to a wide range of support, provision and opportunities as of right. Thus the distinctive ideological approach in Wales eschews notions of risk, responsibility or containment and is based on a commitment to a rights-based approach with the creation of 'a set of rights, which are, as far as possible: free at point of use; universal and unconditional' (Morgan 2002). Moreover and most significantly, *Extending Entitlement* clearly makes it the responsibility of all those who work with or provide services to children to ensure that all services to all children are provided in a manner which gives full expression to the vision of *Extending Entitlement* and maximizes the extent to which all children access their entitlements.

The counterpoint between, for example, Wales and England is clear. Children in England who fail to take advantage of their opportunities and those who commit offences or who are anti-social will have these opportunities taken away from them and they are likely to be subject to increasingly interventionist measures of containment or control. In Wales, by marked contrast, all children (including those who might offend, etc.) have basic entitlements as of right and these cannot be taken away – indeed, it is the responsibility of those adults who work with children to redouble their efforts to ensure that, whatever services are provided to/for/with all children these maximize every child's access to their entitlements.

Not only are there clear differences and tensions between Wales and England in their respective child/youth strategies but there are also important, significant and different implications of these strategies for the way in which agencies work with children and services are provided to children who commit offences or who are anti-social. These tensions are quite real in both political and everyday life and, in the nine years since devolution, they have been growing. It is not surprising, therefore, to find that structures have been created to manage these tensions.

Welsh presence, Welsh strategies

Shortly after devolution, YOT managers in Wales formed a unified committee – YOT Managers Cymru (Cymru – Welsh for Wales) – to provide a focus for the development of juvenile/youth justice in Wales and to represent YOTs in Wales with a single voice. Most recently, YOT Managers Cymru has produced a series of ten 'position statements' outlining distinctively Welsh aspects of juvenile/youth justice, including; substance use and crime prevention and published a website (see www.yotmanagerscymru.co.uk).

Paralleling this development, a YJB in Wales was established and managed jointly by the YJB for England and Wales and the Welsh Assembly. Standing with a foot in both camps, the YJB in Wales has, for example, agreed performance indicators for YOTs in Wales, some of which are drawn from the YJB performance indicators, while others reflect the particular circumstances in Wales.

Finally, the Wales Youth Justice Committee was created to align policy between England and Wales. Representation on the Wales Youth Justice Committee is made up of:

- the YJB;

- the Welsh Assembly Government, including the Department for Children, Education, Lifelong Learning and Skills; the Department for Health and Social Services; and the Department for Social Justice and Local Government;

- the Home Office;

- the police;

- the National Offender Management Service;

- the third sector in Wales; and

- YOT Managers Cymru.

The Wales Youth Justice Committee thus oversees the implementation in Wales of policies that apply to both England and Wales – for example, identifying or modifying those parts of the YJB *Youth Crime Action Plan* that are relevant to Wales. The committee has also developed policies of its own as well as considering how wider Welsh policies impact on the delivery of juvenile/youth justice services (see Table 22.1).

Perhaps most notable of the policies developed by the Wales Youth Justice Committee is the *All Wales Youth Offending Strategy* (YJB/WAG 2004). The *All Wales Youth Offending Strategy* was signed by Edwina Hart, Minister for Social Justice and Regeneration, and Rod Morgan, Chair of the YJB. In their joint 'Foreword' they stated:

The framework for youth justice services in Wales is significantly different from that in England. As in England there are local, multidisciplinary Youth Offending Teams. But the funding arrangements are different as is the configuration of adjacent services vital to the prevention of youth offending.

I am delighted, therefore, that together with the Welsh Assembly Government, the Youth Justice Board for England and Wales has agreed this Strategy document. It incorporates the aims of both the Youth Justice Board and Welsh Assembly Government policies. It lays a shared foundation which should ensure that Youth Offending Teams and other agencies are able to work more effectively to prevent offending by young people in Wales. (YJB/WAG 2004)

Table 22.1 Scope of policies in England and Wales

Policy initiative	England	Wales
Neighbourhood Policing	✓	✓
Offences Brought to Justice	✓	✓
Youth Crime Action Plan	✓	✓
Youth Taskforce	✓	
Children's Trusts	✓	
Every Child Matters	✓	
Integrated Targeted Youth Support	✓	
Local Area Agreements	✓	
Social Exclusion Action Plan	✓	
Local Service Boards and Agreements		✓
Seven Core Aims for Children in Wales		✓
All Wales Youth Offending Strategy		✓
Children and Young People's Partnerships		✓
Communities First		✓
Extending Entitlement		✓

Source: WAG/YJB (2008).

Although officially a joint document, the *All Wales Youth Offending Strategy* does not present a compromise between the different stances towards children espoused by the Welsh Assembly Government (WAG) and the YJB, nor does it actually attempt to 'align' their different strategies; rather, the strategy contains elements that are clearly derived from the YJB (e.g. YJB-set performance measures) and clear statements about the distinctive approach to be taken towards juvenile/youth justice in Wales. This sometimes leads to confusing and even contradictory statements, such as the following – the first sentence of which is YJB derived, the second contains both YJB and WAG sentiments and the last part is distinctively Welsh:

A balance between the interests of the child or young person and the interests of the wider community and potential victims can be maintained through early intervention, restorative justice measures, appropriate punishment and supported rehabilitation. Promoting the welfare of children and young people reduces the risk of offending and re-offending and in doing so protects the public. The strategy therefore promotes the principle that young people should be treated as children first and offenders second. (YJB/WAG 2004: 3)

The production and publication of the *All Wales Youth Offending Strategy* can be seen as a deliberate and joint commitment to partnership working between the YJB and the WAG. On the other hand, it can also be seen as an attempt to manage the tensions between the WAG and the YJB and as an effort to stave off a constitutional crisis. Whatever view one takes, the strategy does articulate several features (not found in English youth justice) that are distinctively Welsh, notably that:

- the UNCRC is the cornerstone for the strategy;

- the strategy is derived from and should give expression to the principles of *Extending Entitlement*;

- young people should be treated as children first and offenders second;

- the prevention of offending and reoffending should be taken seriously and in line with the first three statements above; and

- custody for children really should be a last resort.

These developments have taken place, of course, in a context where responsibility for youth justice policy is not devolved to Wales from Westminster, but other allied areas are Welsh responsibilities. In addition to education and health, harking back to the complex of UK and Welsh governmental authorities referred to above, the WAG also has direct responsibility for social services, housing, youth services and inclusion, regeneration and community development as well as substance use. Thus although policing, crime prevention and juvenile/youth justice are not currently fully devolved, the WAG does have direct responsibility for a range of policy areas/services which adjoin and sometimes overlap with areas of criminal justice governed from Westminster. While in England this list of policy responsibilities tends to be dealt with separately and, consequently, in a non-joined-up manner, in Wales the agenda of the WAG is to achieve coherence across all areas of devolved and sometimes non-devolved policy. Thus, the overall strategy for Wales highlights nine key themes:

- The development of a safer and more inclusive society where everyone has the chance to fulfil his or her potential;

- The promotion of a culture in which diversity is valued and equality of opportunity is a reality;

- A community-led approach to finding local solutions;

- An integrated approach that makes the link between health, employment, skills, communities and other policy areas;

- Building equality of opportunity into everything we do;

- Championing the rights of children and young people in ways that reflect the Assembly's responsibilities in full;

- Promoting locally determined partnerships in every local authority area to ensure support for children and young people;

- Encouraging constructive play, voluntary sector initiatives and out of school activities through the provision of grant support to local partnerships;

- Creating comprehensive services for young people offering opportunities, advice and support to help them achieve their aims and aspirations. (National Assembly Policy Unit 2002: 2)

In line with these ambitions and in addition to *Extending Entitlement* and the con-joined *All Wales Youth Offending Strategy*, the WAG has produced a range of strategies, has provided direct funding and has co-ordinated services to children through a range of structures – the details of which are beyond the scope of this chapter. However, by way of example, joined-up 'children first' (see also Haines and Drakeford 1998) services to children who offend include such provisions as follows:

- *Education, training and employment*: ensuring that all supervised young offenders are in education, training or employment, that Safer Schools partnerships between schools and the police are in place and that Careers Wales conducts interviews with children and young people newly released from custody.

- *Substance use*: that multi-agency substance misuse action teams in local authority areas plan and fund substance use prevention and treatment for children.

- *Housing*: that accommodation-focused needs assessments are completed for all children and young people newly released from custody.

- *Communities*: that multi-agency community safety partnerships and YOTs jointly plan and target crime prevention programmes and interventions with funding from the WAG Safer Communities Fund.

Conceiving a difference – real or imaginary dragons?

The important question is, of course, what difference do these distinctively Welsh developments make? There are a number of points that need to be made in moving towards an answer to this question. First, devolution is but nine years old. Thus the processes of devolution and the measures described above are still 'works in progress'. The full impact of these measures is yet to be fully realized or felt, and there remains a lack of mature evidence/research designed to assess progress or impact (although see Haines *et al.* 2004 for an evaluation of *Extending Entitlement*). Secondly, despite the above, there are those in Wales who question the commitment to and delivery of Welsh policies by those in government and among those responsible for delivering services, etc. That there is, indeed, an implementation failure and that, while there is much to commend in the distinctive Welsh policy and genuinely innovative child-focused practice taking place (see WAG/YJB 2008), it would be quite wrong to presume that everything in the garden is rosy. Lastly, the uneven deployment of resources and services across Wales means that 'justice by geography' characterizes practice in Wales now, just as in the past and as it does in other parts of the UK.

Notwithstanding the above caveats, there is some tentative evidence emerging concerning the relative impact of, *inter alia*, the *All Wales Youth Offending Strategy*. Data provided by the YJB in Wales, for example, suggest that, between 2002–3 and 2006–7 officially recorded juvenile crime in Wales is showing a declining trend, whereas in England the general trend is upwards – although the actual differences are small. Unpublished YJB data also show that first-time entrants into the formal juvenile/youth justice system, between 2005–6 and 2006–7, decreased in Wales by 14 per cent, whereas in England and Wales combined a 7 per cent increase occurred – although there were regional/area departures from these national trends.

Further unpublished YJB in Wales data suggest that there is a broad similarity in the range of formal disposals imposed on children across the range of juvenile/youth justice intervention between England and Wales. What this data masks, however, is the nature/content of the intervention. In parts of England, slavish adherence to YJB-prescribed models of practice and performance indicators has led to a dogmatic focus on process at the expense of the amount and quality of contact with children and a neglect of preventative work. In contrast, while YOTs in Wales have demonstrated an ability to achieve their YJB-set performance indicators, risk-led practices have been eschewed by many in favour of entitlements-based work with young people, and strong interagency partnerships have led to an increase in the amount and scope of preventative activity.

The dragonization of youth justice has clearly begun. The question now becomes one of how far this approach can/will go. Just as dragonization has progressed in Wales, so too has the YJB progressed its levels of control and penetration of YOT policy and practice in both England and Wales. The tensions arising out of these divergent approaches have, so far, been manageable and managed. However, as the approach taken by the YJB ever deepens and with the forthcoming rollout of the scaled approach, there are those in Wales who see the tensions between England and Wales becoming too great to hold together and the inevitability of a formal split on the horizon.

References

Blair, T. (2004) 'The opportunity society.' Speech delivered at the Labour Party annual conference, Brighton Centre, 28 September.

Chapman, T. and O'Mahony, D. (2007) 'Youth and criminal justice in Northern Ireland', in G. McIvor and P. Raynor (eds) *Developments in Social Work with Offenders*. London: Jessica Kingsley.

Children and Young People's Unit (2004) *Making it r wrld 2: Consultation on a Draft Strategy for Children and Young People in Northern Ireland*. Belfast: Office of the First Minister and Deputy First Minister.

Department for Education and Skills (2004) *Every Child Matters: Change for Children*. Nottingham: DfES.

Goldson, B. (2000) *The New Youth Justice*. Lyme Regis: Russell House Publishing.

Goldson, B. (2002) 'New punitiveness: the politics of child incarceration', in J. Muncie *et al.* (eds) *Youth Justice: Critical Readings*. London: Sage.

Goldson, B. and Muncie, J. (2006) *Youth Crime and Justice*. London: Sage.

Haines, K., Case, S., Isles, E., Rees, I. and Hancock, A. (2004) *Extending Entitlement: Making it Real*. Cardiff: Welsh Assembly Government.

Haines, K. and Drakesford, M. (1998) *Young People and Youth Justice*. London: Macmillan.

Morgan, R. (2002) Annual lecture of the National Centre for Public Policy, Swansea University.

Muncie, J. (2006) 'Governing young people: coherence and contradiction in contemporary youth justice', *Critical Social Policy*, 26: 770–93.

National Assembly Policy Unit (2002) *A Plan for Wales, 2001*. Cardiff: Welsh Assembly Government.

O'Mahony, D. and Deazley, R. (2000) *Juvenile Crime and Justice: Review of the Criminal Justice System in Northern Ireland*. London: HMSO.

Policy Unit (2000) *Extending Entitlement: Supporting Young People in Wales* (a report by the Policy Unit, National Assembly for Wales). Cardiff: Welsh Assembly Government.

Scottish Executive (2001) *For Scotland's Children: Better Integrated Children's Services*. Edinburgh: Scottish Executive.

Social Exclusion Unit (2000) *National Strategy for Neighbourhood Renewal*, Report of Policy Action Team 12: Young People (available online at http//www.cabinet-office.gov.yk/seu/2000/pat12/default.htm).

Welsh Assembly Government (2002) *Extending Entitlement: Support for 11 to 25 Year Olds in Wales*. Cardiff: Welsh Assembly Government.

Welsh Assembly Government/Youth Justice Board (2008) *Youth Crime Prevention in Wales: Strategic Guidance*. London: Youth Justice Board.

Williamson, H. (2007) 'Youth policy in Wales: from vision to vacuum?', *Contemporary Wales*, 19: 198–216.

Williamson, H. (2009) 'European youth policy and the place of the United Kingdom', in J. Wood and J. Hine (eds) *Work with Young People: Theory and Policy for Practice*. London: Sage.

YJB/WAG (2004) *All Wales Youth Offending Strategy*. London: Youth Justice Board.

23

The development of restorative justice in Northern Ireland

Kelvin Doherty

The date 10 April 1998 was a landmark in the history of Northern Ireland. On this day the Belfast Agreement was signed by all the major political parties in the province and the British and Irish governments. This agreement brought an end to over 30 years of civil conflict that disfigured the political and social landscape. The Belfast Agreement or, as it is commonly known, the Good Friday Agreement, enacted a wide-ranging review of the criminal justice system in Northern Ireland. The agreement also set out what the participants in the negotiations believed the aims of the criminal justice system should be. These included the delivery of a fair and impartial system of justice which, importantly, was responsive to the community's concerns, encouraged its involvement where appropriate and had the confidence of all sections of the community.

When the Agreement was signed there was a broad consensus for the need to reform the criminal justice system. The review of justice was carried out between June 1998 and March 2000 by the Criminal Justice Review Group; this included both civil servants and a majority element drawn from academia and the legal profession. The review group commissioned a programme of research into public attitudes in Northern Ireland to criminal justice and also into the experience of other jurisdictions on a range of key issues, including the application of restorative justice principles within the justice system. The initial attitudinal research indicated that a significant minority of the population of Northern Ireland lacked confidence in the fairness of the existing criminal justice system. Although the majority of such concerned respondents were from the Catholic/Nationalist community (39 per cent), this was not exclusive. Indeed, 23 per cent of the Protestant/Unionist community also reported a similar lack of confidence (Criminal Justice Review Group 2000). In respect of the application of restorative justice in Northern Ireland, the research focused on common-law jurisdictions with experience of restorative justice initiatives, such as New Zealand, England and Wales, and Australia. One exception was

South Africa that, although a non-common law jurisdiction, had recent experience of restorative justice. South Africa, like Northern Ireland, had experienced inter-communal conflict.

Understanding restorative justice

Restorative justice has been depicted as an alternative paradigm to retributive justice (Zehr 1990), a critique of the retributive justice system (Crawford and Newburn 2003) and as a set of values and goals (Maxwell 1998). Whatever the particularities of the different definitions of restorative justice, there are a number of core attributes that cut across them (Zehr 1990, 2005). Essentially, restorative justice understands crime as an act that causes harm to victims and communities. The traditional, or retributive, criminal justice system views crime as a transgression of laws and therefore the state, or Crown, is identified as the victim. The focus of the retributive system is on offenders being punished for their offending, resulting in the victim being considered primarily as material evidence, with their recovery from victimization being, at best, a secondary concern.

Conversely, restorative justice understands crime as an act that causes harm which generates needs in victims (and communities) that must be met by a process of 'restoration' focused on repairing the harm done. In this way, restorative justice invokes an obligation in offenders to 'make good' or make amends. However, this cannot happen without the victim(s) and offender(s) engaging in a process that promotes dialogue to understand and repair the harm.

Restorative justice in Northern Ireland: a response to offending or part of a transitional justice strategy?

While the review group's brief was to 'advise on the applicability of restorative justice reforms in northern Ireland' (Dignan 2000), it chose to focus its comparative research on a number of common-law jurisdictions around the world. The final report to the review group also opted to consider specifically the experiences of justice reform in South Africa.

The report identified the key concepts that underpin restorative justice practices in criminal justice around the world and, in particular, the key attributes of these practices. These included the following:

- The principle of inclusivity. For offenders to be reintegrated back into the community and victims to have a sense of restoration, then the process must include all those affected by the crime.

- Balancing the needs of participants. The focus of the retributive justice system is on punishment and deterrence often to the detriment of those affected by the harm, whereas restorative justice attempts to meet the competing needs of individuals.

- Non-coercion, or voluntary participation in the process.

- A problem-solving approach. It is insufficient to deal only with the aftermath of the crime and repair the harm. Restorative justice also has a forward-looking problem-solving focus with prevention as its aim.

In fulfilling these attributes, advocates of restorative justice contend that it overcomes many of the criticisms levelled against the traditional retributive system (Campbell *et al.* 2006). However, and importantly, the report also referred to the applicability of restorative justice as an alternative dispute resolution for problems associated with social exclusion and inter-communal conflict. It is within this context that the South African model could have been more extensively researched. In his report to the Criminal Justice Review Group, Dignan (2000) refers to the potential restorative justice could have in a transitional phase or peace-building process. The inter-communal struggles that manifested under the apartheid policy have an obvious resonance in a Northern Irish context and might have been made more explicit in the report.

The South African model operates under the overarching remit of the Truth and Reconciliation Commission (Huyse 1998) and deals with the following matters: establishing the 'truth' in relation to human rights abuses; determining who should qualify for amnesty; and providing compensation to victims. This model is very much part of a transitional justice strategy, driven by the need for national reconciliation which, although required in the authors' opinion to help the healing of society in Northern Ireland, was understandably not deemed applicable for young offenders in mainstream criminal justice. However, and perhaps in hindsight, a restorative approach to dealing with the past could have been more comprehensively investigated. It could have become part of a multi-modal approach to truth recovery instead of a legalistic approach as exemplified in the Bloody Sunday enquiry (Hamber 2008).

Contextual factors for restorative justice in Northern Ireland

The fact that restorative justice approaches have been shown to be successful in New Zealand, Australia or South Africa does not guarantee transferability from one jurisdiction to another. In each of these countries the nature of restorative practices was influenced by specific historical, cultural and political factors. The social and political context of Northern Ireland has its own cultural, historical and national legacies that require recognition and accommodation. Any attempt to apply restorative justice to Northern Ireland needs to take account of such contextual factors.

One of the research conclusions was that, for any restorative justice scheme to be successful, the operational model and implementation would need to take account of the certain specific factors. It noted the following:

- *Legitimacy deficit*: as indicated above, a substantial minority of Northern Ireland's citizens questioned the legitimacy of judicial institutions which, in their eyes, only offered justice to the Unionist community.

- *Inter-communal conflict*: the troubles in Northern Ireland only served to reinforce violent sectarianism and segregation. For restorative justice to be successful it would need to be viewed as capable of bridging the sectarian divide.

- *Crime prevention vacuum*: a by-product of the legitimacy deficit and inter-communal conflict was that local communities did not develop formal crime prevention and community safety partnerships.

These three factors also contributed to the growth in community-based informal 'justice', or 'vigilantism', in both Loyalist and Republican working-class communities. Paramilitary organizations reinforced local norms by threatening, beating and shooting members of their communities who transgressed them. Critically, therefore, for restorative justice to be effectively implemented, local communities affected by offences or high levels of crime could and should have their voices heard in the process. This would move Northern Ireland society towards a greater emphasis on producing outcomes that are fair and meet better the needs of society. The implicit democratization of the criminal justice process and empowerment of communities would also help remove the need for established forms of informal 'justice'.

Restorative justice in practice

The report referred to restorative justice schemes in a number of other jurisdictions, including South Africa, New Zealand, Canada and the USA. However, what the review group was particularly impressed with in the South African model was the explicit use of 'reintegrative shaming' (Braithwaite 1989). Braithwaite proposes that, 'reintegrative shaming means that expressions of community disapproval, which may range from mild rebuke to degradation ceremonies, are followed by gestures of reacceptance into the community of law abiding citizens' (1989: 55). This suggests that societies which foster effective reintegrative shaming generally witness less crime than those societies which operate a retributive system of justice. In the latter, shaming is stigmatizing and directed at the wrongdoer, whereas reintegrative shaming focuses on the harm caused and not the person who caused the harm. As its name suggests, it prioritizes inclusion over exclusion.

The review group drew particular attention to the New Zealand family group conferencing model which was well established, having originated in 1989. This form of restorative justice was fully integrated into the youth justice system in New Zealand and was based on a model that brought together the young person, victim and family members into conference (Department of Justice, New Zealand 1992). The conference would discuss the harm caused by the young person's behaviour and how that harm could be repaired. Evidence from a number of evaluations suggested that use of the family group conferencing model achieved lower rates of recidivism than the traditional retributive system and therefore offered potential for transfer to Northern Ireland (Maxwell 2005). In addition, among the strengths of the New Zealand model was that it was anchored in Maori cultural practice and emerged from Maori struggles for greater cultural recognition, and against the manifest injustice of the unreconstructed colonial 'Pakeha' system of justice.

The Northern Ireland Office became committed to putting restorative justice at the heart of the criminal justice system for young offenders. The implicit objectives in pursuing this course were to reduce the rate of youth reoffending, to reduce the seriousness of subsequent offending and to improve victim satisfaction with the criminal justice system. However, the system in New Zealand, drawing on Maori patterns of kinship, placed a significant emphasis on the role of the extended family in determining the outcome of the conference and any subsequent supervising of the young person to ensure completion of an action plan. It was envisaged that, to be successful in Northern Ireland, there had to be a rebalancing of the competing needs of the young person, their family, the community and the victim(s).

Any restorative justice model must meet the needs of victims. Nils Christie (1978) has long argued that crime is essentially an output from an interpersonal conflict. According to Christie, the state and its officials – such as solicitors, probation officers and judges – 'hijack' this conflict and 'resolve' it on behalf of the offender and victim. Unfortunately, the adversarial nature of the system rarely results in a satisfactory resolution, leaving the victim feeling dissatisfied and often angry. Again according to Christie, this inability to service the needs of victims is the primary cause of poor victim satisfaction in a retributive criminal justice system. This contrasts with examples such as New Zealand, where 49 per cent of victims expressed satisfaction with the outcome of restorative justice conferences (Maxwell and Morris 1993) or the Australian 'RISE' project, in which 70 per cent of victims who participated expressed satisfaction (Strang 2002). According to Campbell *et al.* (2006), factors which may help a victim achieve a positive experience include the following:

- Actual involvement in the restorative process.

- Being given the opportunity to explain the consequences of the harm caused by the perpetrator.

- Gaining an understanding of why the harm was caused.

- Receiving an apology.

- Receiving reparation (of various forms).

- Gaining an insight into the perpetrator's circumstances.

Reasons for negative experiences included lack of support, lack of remorse from the offender, dissatisfaction with the 'agreed' plan and a sense of being forced to relive the crime. Victims have also consistently criticized poor levels of information on the progression of their cases as a distinct source of dissatisfaction (Hoyle *et al*. 2002).

A recent history of restorative justice in Northern Ireland

In 1994 the Ulster Quaker Public Service Committee hosted a restorative justice conference which was attended by representatives from the statutory and voluntary sector and from representative from both the Loyalist and Republican communities. This was the time of the first IRA ceasefire of the 1990s. Attendees from the conference, which included the future Irish President, Mary McAleese, then a law lecturer in Queen's University Belfast, continued to meet on an *ad hoc* basis to promote restorative justice in Northern Ireland. Meanwhile the community representatives were also developing their own local schemes.

While the steering group was analyzing the suitability of different restorative justice projects as potential comparator models for Northern Ireland, there was a movement in both Republican and Loyalist communities to move away from violent community-based justice to one informed by the principles of restorative justice (Auld *et al*. 1997). Two projects were set up with organic connections to paramilitary organizations: 'Community Restorative Justice' in Republican west Belfast and 'Northern Ireland Alternatives' in the Loyalist Shankill area of west/north Belfast. These schemes sought to bring victims and offenders into contact with each other with the aim of achieving a resolution rather than pursuing criminal sanctions (Mika 2006). Although both schemes are now accredited to government standards, the success of both has not been a straightforward process. They have been criticized on the grounds that they are a front for paramilitary organizations; that they rely on coercion and not consent; and that they effectively deny people access to due process and potentially expose members of their communities to double jeopardy (Criminal Justice Inspection Northern Ireland 2007). In 2008, following recommendations in the 2007 inspection report that both schemes comply with a government protocol, they were fully accredited and received government funding.

New Zealand as a comparator model

The Criminal Justice Steering Group in its summary review identified four options for the implementation of restorative justice reforms (Dignan 2000). The first option advocated the pursuit of reparative outcomes, such as court-ordered compensation for victims. While this provides practical redress for victims, it would not repair any broken relationship between the victim, offender and community or offer anything to address the victim's mental/emotional condition.

The second option was to promote restorative justice programmes outside mainstream criminal justice but in a supplementary capacity. This is similar to Canadian-based restorative justice schemes, in which the courts refer cases to voluntary organizations that are part state funded. These cases are then conferenced and, if the offender complies, are taken out of the system. However, as is the case in Canada, under this proposal restorative justice would be on the margins of the criminal justice system.

The third option was one that would be partially integrated into criminal justice. This is the practice in England and Wales where courts can sentence young offenders to a referral order. A potential meeting will then be arranged between members of a 'panel' (consisting of members of a local community) and the offender and victim after the order is made. The achievements of referral orders and other similar, partially integrated restorative justice programmes are still relatively modest in respect of victim and community participation, with the former being only 13 per cent in referral orders (Campbell *et al.* 2006).

The fourth proposal from the summary review was for restorative justice to be fully integrated into the youth criminal justice system, from police-facilitated restorative cautions to a youth justice system which would offer all young people a restorative justice-based sentence for all offences bar murder and manslaughter. No other jurisdiction had accomplished this, although New Zealand had come closest.

The impact of the Youth Conference Service on youth offending in Northern Ireland

Loosely based on the New Zealand model of youth conferencing, the Youth Conference Service was launched as a pilot in 2003 as part of the new Youth Justice Agency. Young people are referred by the courts or prosecution service after admitting guilt and giving consent to their involvement in a youth conference. The conferencing process involves a meeting with the young person who has offended, the victim and others who have been affected by the crime. The focus is on all parties resolving how the young person can make amends to the victim(s) and what can be done to prevent further offending.

Recent narrative research on the experiences of young people who participated in a youth conference confirmed many of the propositions of theorists such as John Braithwaite (Maruna 2008), especially the effectiveness of shame management/integrative shaming. Both victims and young people indicated high levels of satisfaction with the process, 92 per cent and 93 per cent, respectively (Campbell *et al*. 2006), as did sentencers. Recent research into recidivism has also been promising, with reoffending rates approximately 10 per cent lower than other community sentences in pilot areas (Lyness 2008). When measuring the comparative effectiveness of the youth conferencing model in Northern Ireland with the traditional retributive system, there is a tendency to focus solely on recidivism. However, tentative studies elsewhere have also indicated a reduced cost to the criminal justice system (Gabbay 2005). The success of the Youth Conference Service is to a certain extent due to the time spent preparing young people and victims for the restorative encounter. Indeed, the rate of face-to-face victim participation is 65 per cent, higher than any other restorative sentence in the UK and higher than that of New Zealand.

None the less, the restorative model has not been without criticism. Some local community-based restorative justice schemes view the youth conference as being state mandated and therefore compromised or watered down. For them it is restorative justice that pays only lip service to the needs of communities.

Conclusion

In 1998 the criminal justice system in Northern Ireland was widely perceived to be failing to represent the community as a whole. For civil society to be functional, the criminal justice system must be seen as responsive to the needs of the population. Among those needs are feeling protected and confidence that justice is fair and transparent.

Critically and perhaps paradoxically, for restorative justice to become fully integrated and effective in Northern Ireland it had to be state mandated; otherwise it would have faced the problems of marginalization and subordination to a retributive system. In establishing restorative justice as a mainstream response to youth offending, at the centre of the criminal justice system, the latter has not occurred.

It may not be perfect or without criticism but there is widespread acknowledgement that these restorative justice initiatives, and in particular the work of the Youth Conference Service, are both a break with the past and a signal to the future. Victims and communities are no longer marginalized by the criminal justice system but viewed as key stakeholders who have an active role to play in resolving the harm caused by crime. Justice, in this new participatory format, is now seen to be done.

References

Auld, J., Gormally, B., McEvoy, K. and Ritchie, M. (1997) 'Designing a system of restorative community justice in Northern Ireland.' A discussion document, published by the authors.

Braithwaite, J. (1989) *Crime, Shame and Reintegration*. Cambridge: Cambridge University Press.

Campbell, C., Devlin, R., O'Mahoney, D., Doak, J., Jackson, J., Corrigan, T. and McEvoy, K. (2006) *Evaluation of the Northern Ireland Youth Conference Service*. Belfast: Northern Ireland Office.

Christie, N. (1978) 'Conflicts as property', *British Journal of Criminology*, 17: 1–15.

Crawford, A. and Newburn, T. (2003) *Youth Offending and Restorative Justice: Implementing Reform in Youth Justice*. Cullompton: Willan Publishing.

Criminal Justice Review Group (2000) *Review of the Criminal Justice System in Northern Ireland*. Belfast: HMSO.

Department of Justice, New Zealand (1992) *Adult Pre-trial Diversion in New Zealand*. Wellington: Department of Justice.

Dignan, J. (2000) *Restorative Justice Options for Northern Ireland: A Comparative Review*. Norwich: HMSO.

Gabbay, Z. (2005) 'Justifying restorative justice.' Paper presented at the conference, 'The next step: developing restorative communities', Manchester, 9–11 November.

Hamber, B. (2008) 'Putting the past in perspective.' Paper presented at the 'Putting the past in perspective' seminar, Queen's University Belfast, 17 May.

Hoyle, C., Young, R. and Hill, R. (2002) *Proceed with Caution: An Evaluation of the Thames Valley Police Initiative in Restorative Cautioning*. York: Joseph Rowntree Foundation.

Huyse, L. (1998) *Young Democracies and the Choice between Amnesty, Truth Commissions and Prosecutions*. Leuven: University of Leuven.

Lyness, D. (2008) *Northern Ireland Youth Re-offending: Results from the 2005 Cohort*. Research and Statistical Bulletin 7/2008, Belfast: Northern Ireland Office.

Maruna, S. (2008) *Youth Conferencing as Shame Management: Results of a Long-term Follow-up Study*. Belfast: Youth Justice Agency.

Maxwell, G. (1998) 'Changing hearts and minds.' Paper presented at the conference, 'Restorative justice and outcome: emerging theories of restorative justice', Florida, November.

Maxwell, G. (2005) 'Achieving effective outcomes in youth justice: implications of new research for principles, policy and practice', in E. Elliot and R.M. Gordon (eds) *New Directions in Restorative Justice: Issues, Practice and Evaluation*. Cullompton: Willan Publishing.

Maxwell, G. and Morris, A. (1993) *Family, Victims and Youth Culture: Youth Justice in New Zealand*. Wellington: University of Wellington.

Mika, H. (2006) *Community-based Restorative Justice in Northern Ireland*. Belfast: Queen's University.

Strang, H. (2002) *Repair or Revenge: Victims and Restorative Justice*. Oxford: Clarendon Press.

Zehr, H. (1990) *Changing Lenses: A New Focus for Restorative Justice*. Scottdale, PA: Herald Press.

Zehr, H. (2005) 'Evaluation and restorative justice principles', in E. Elliot and R.M. Gordon (eds) *New Directions in Restorative Justice: Issues, Practice and Evaluation*. Cullompton: Willan Publishing.

Conclusion

Wayne Taylor, Rod Earle and Richard Hester

Cannery Row in Monterey in California is a poem, a stink, a grating noise, a quality of light, a tone, a nostalgia, a dream. Cannery Row is the gathered and the scattered, tin and iron and rust and splinted wood, chipped pavement and weedy lots and junk heaps, sardine canneries of corrugated iron, honky-tonks, restaurants and whore-houses, and little crowded groceries, and laboratories and flop-houses. Its inhabitants are, as the man once said, 'Whores, pimps, gamblers, and sons of bitches', by which he meant Everybody. Had the man looked through another peephole he might have said, 'Saints and angels and martyrs and holy men', and he would have meant the same thing. (Steinbeck 1945: 1)

Behind all the theories of punishment (including those encouraging rehabilitation) are a set of assumptions about the subject of formal sanctions – the 'criminal'. What does this label mean? What does it say, if anything, about the person behind the label? Are people who commit offences of a similar 'type', or are we all opportunists who would become criminals if we felt the benefits outweighed the costs? Reflecting on this, commentators have identified two dominant models of criminal motivation that have vied for supremacy over the last century (Garland 1985; Hughes 1998). These have been described as *Homo economicus* – the rational, calculating criminal of classical criminology – and *Homo criminalis* – the happenstance criminal as product of unfortunate psychological and social circumstances. Historically, the trend has been from *Homo economicus* to *Homo criminalis* and, in the last few decades, back again (Hudson 1996: 139).

The relative strength of each model varies from sector to sector with, for example, the notion of *Homo economicus* central to many primary – or situational – crime prevention initiatives but less integral to tertiary crime prevention. Nor, it seems, is there ever total victory of one model over the other. Hence, most commonly, criminal justice work involves an uneasy alliance or 'pick and mix' approach which uses *both* models. The nature of the mix itself will determine the nature (including the philosophical underpinnings) of the intervention chosen. The changes in this mix reflect the history of youth justice, with its 'liberal' and 'punitive' turns.

Assumptions about the nature of criminal motivation are important because they have ramifications in terms of the societal response to criminal misconduct and the question of 'just' punishment. Models such as *Homo economicus* and *Homo criminalis* provide ready-made (although different) answers to questions around culpability, responsibility and intent. As a consequence, the policies, institutions and intervention strategies within the criminal justice system reflect either the dominance of one of these models or some variant of the two combined. These models of motivation also connect (in often quite surprising ways) with wider discourses or 'understandings' about crime and its control. Consider, for instance, how *Homo economicus* and *Homo criminalis* relate to Garland's discussion of rival criminological understandings of 'offenders' that can result in profoundly different responses:

> There is *a criminology of the self*, that characterizes offenders as rational consumers, just like us, and there is *a criminology of the other*, of the threatening outcast, the fearsome stranger, the excluded and the embittered. One is invoked to routinize crime, to allay disproportionate fears and to promote preventive action. The other is concerned to demonize the criminal, to excite popular fears and hostilities, and to promote support for state punishment. (1996: 461 emphasis in original)

As with *Homo economicus* and *Homo criminalis*, it seems that both *a criminology of the self* and *a criminology of the other* exist in relation to youth offending. The interplay between the two can be seen in media representations of young people – which tend to be disproportionately negative – but also in the general consensus that children should be protected and cared for, a concern reflected in the financial and political support for voluntary and statutory childcare provision.

A key concern of this volume has been society's attitude to children and young people. This can be deeply ambivalent, and the actions and policies directed towards them appear, at times, curiously Janus-faced stressing, alternately, liberal and disciplinarian responses to misdemeanours. This ambivalence exists in relation to the concept of 'childhood' itself, which is both idealized and sentimentalized as a time of innocence and, *at the same time*, widely accepted as a potentially troublesome developmental stage marked by problems that necessitate interventions to manage (and resolve) them. This ambivalence – between care and protection, fear and fascination, and regulation and correction – can be found in Young's (1999) imagary of a culture that is willing to assimilate the 'normal' but also determined to exclude and isolate the 'deviant'.

'Youth' and 'crime' are both concepts that are complicated by the baggage that each of these 'social constructions' brings with it. Nevertheless, the themes outlined above – of rival notions of criminality and distinct criminologies – have guided the development of this collection of writings intended to guide and assist practitioners who work where they meet.

The volume opened with a chapter concerned to delineate the contours of a youth justice system that continues to mirror the social and economic inequalities of wider society, where there is far greater chance of young people from disadvantaged backgrounds being subject to criminal justice sanctions and where 'differences', such as 'race', can have a seriously deleterious impact on life chances. The central concern here was that the dominant focus on individual pathology within 'what works' has shifted the attention of policy-makers and practitioners away from structural factors that play a central role in presenting some young people, rather than others, to the criminal justice system. The downside of such an approach is the inward-looking nature of youth justice – both in terms of its focus on the individual in isolation and in the way it generates self-referential horizons that may obscure the wider concerns of social justice.

The youth justice system is sometimes thought of as the product of the decisions of politicians, policy-makers and key bodies, such as the Youth Justice Board. Equally, however, the way the youth justice system is experienced by children and young people is heavily dependent on the day-to-day actions and decisions of practitioners. This is a crucial theme of the current volume (as well as being a recurrent motif in the courses that make up the Open University's Foundation Degree in Youth Justice). It is for this reason that many of the contributors to this volume have emphasized the practitioner's professional responsibility to think carefully and critically about not only what they do, but also how they do it and, most crucially, why. As the contributors to Part II illustrate, sometimes theory and policy in youth justice can gain a special status of 'truth', which appears to float free of actual practice, disconnected from the realities of both young people and the professionals who work with them. The emphasis on 'effective practice', research evidence, policy and procedures in youth justice has tended to suppress the 'affective' world of youth justice, how it is 'felt', experienced and given meaning by those most intimately involved with it.

This has had at least two negative consequences: first, scant attention is paid to the question of how interventions 'feel' and are experienced by the professionals who implement them; and, secondly, it has tended to neglect (or failed to take sufficiently seriously) the thoughts and feelings – the 'voices' – of young people themselves. For the cultural critic Raymond Williams (1978), the interplay of formal social structures and the social world as it is lived could not be discounted. He wrote extensively on what he described as the 'structures of feeling' that, even when apparently marginalized, continue to shape the social process of change.

This has also been a theme adopted in this volume, with its strong endorsement of a reflective examination of practice and a 'reflexive' attitude towards theory. Of course, there is a difference between criticizing practice and teaching the techniques of critique. In questioning some contemporary 'truths' in youth justice, this volume has been wary about replacing these with another set of orthodoxies – no matter how appealing. Instead, it has sought to show how research, evidence and knowledge in youth justice are constructed and influenced by a variety of 'discourses'. It is up to the readers to take this further – using critical reflection to challenge and resist those aspects of current practice they feel are problematic while supporting the development of those that are ethical, appropriate and effective. Central to this stance is the view that practioners are social agents, not simply the functionaries or automatons of a 'korrectional karaoke' (Pitts 2001). By drawing attention to some of the submerged sociological, cultural and historical dimensions of professional youth justice, as the authors have done in this collection, and by pointing to the ways in which practitioners reflect on personal practice and the contexts of change, we believe that struggles 'for youth justice with integrity' (Goldson and Muncie 2006) can be developed and solidarities constructed, and that practitioners may become agents of change rather than its objects.

So what can practitioners do – constrained as they are by their accountability to their organizations – to create a more humane and progressive youth justice? This is a difficult question to answer, not least because the devil is so often in the detail of how work is undertaken with young people on a day-to-day basis. This volume has sought to encourage the process of reflection largely by airing a set of 'counter' discourses to current practice and in providing a sense of wider *contexts*.

In terms of a more enabling vision, the concluding part – which examines progressive policies in other jurisdictions and considers the way recent international legislation might influence the emergence of a more proactive advocacy of children's rights – was designed to provide readers with 'food for thought' in their critical reflections. To reflect, in the words that opened this volume, 'what has never been, but one day may be.'

Returning to the words of Steinbeck, it is the contention of this volume that a vision of future practice should be an open one. Those who now inhabit the Cannery Rows of Britain are neither 'sons of bitches' or, for that matter, 'angels' but, like all of us, have the potential to be both and neither. Recognizing this in the day-to-day interventions of youth justice interventions is likely to make these both more humane and more effective. It is also one of the most effective means of resisting the punitive and demonizing impulses associated with *a criminology of the other*.

References

Criminal Justice Inspection Northern Ireland (2007) *Inspection of the Youth Conference Service of Northern Ireland*. Belfast: Criminal Justice Inspection, Northern Ireland.

Garland, D. (1985) *Punishment and Welfare: A History of Penal Strategies*. Aldershot: Gower.

Garland, D. (1996) 'The limits of the sovereign state: strategies of crime control in contemporary society', *British Journal of Criminology*, 36: 445–71.

Goldson, B. and Muncie, J. (2006) *Youth Crime and Justice: Critical Issues*. London: Sage.

Hudson, B. (1996) *Understanding Justice: An Introduction to Ideas, Perspectives and Controversies in Modern Penal Theory*. Buckingham: Open University Press.

Hughes, G. (1998) *Understanding Crime Prevention: Social Control, Risk and Late Modernity*. Buckingham: Open University Press.

Pitts, J. (2001) 'Korrectional karaoke: New Labour and the zombification of youth justice', *Youth Justice*, 1: 3–16.

Steinbeck, J. (1945) *Cannery Row*. New York, NY: Penguin Books.

Williams, R. (1978) *Marxism and Literature*. Oxford: Oxford University Press.

Young, J. (1999) *The Exclusive Society*. London: Sage.

Index